This Action
of Our Death

This Action of Our Death

*The Performance of Death
in English Renaissance Drama*

Michael Cameron Andrews

DELAWARE
Newark: University of Delaware Press
London and Toronto: Associated University Presses

Associated University Presses
440 Forsgate Drive
Cranbury, NJ 08512

Associated University Presses
25 Sicilian Avenue
London WC1A 2QH, England

Associated University Presses
P.O. Box 488, Port Credit
Mississauga, Ontario
Canada L5G 4M2

The paper used in this publication meets the requirements of the American National Standard for Permanence of Paper for Printed Library Materials Z39.48–1984.

Library of Congress Cataloging-in-Publication Data

Andrews, Michael Cameron, 1938–
This action of our death.

Bibliography: p.
Includes index.
1. English drama—Early modern and Elizabethan, 1500–1600—History and criticism.   2. English drama—17th century—History and criticism.   3. Death in literature.
I. Title.
PR658.D4A54   1989   822'.3'09   88-45743
ISBN 0-87413-354-8 (alk. paper)

In memory of
Eleanor Lattimore Andrews
Richmond Lattimore
Wayne Andrews

This action of our death especially
Shewes all a man. Here only is he found.

—Samuel Daniel

Contents

Preface

This is a book about what dramatists of the English Renaissance do with the last moments of the dying. In some instances, for reasons that will become evident, I consider the words and actions of characters who are about to die, but whose actual deaths occur offstage. But my main concern is how playwrights from Marlowe to Ford dramatize death, making what characters say and do as they confront and perform the "act" of dying an integral aspect of their plays. The death speech, then, with the actions that accompany it, is the real subject of this study.

For a period in which death has undone so many, the approach is necessarily selective. Chapter 1 emphasizes Marlowe's role as the first Renaissance playwright to capitalize on the dramatic potential of death. The next chapter examines horrific and exemplary presentations of death from the early 1590s to about 1610. Chapter 3, on Chapman and Webster, discusses the plays of the first two dramatists after Marlowe (with the exception of Shakespeare) to make much of the last moments of the dying. Chapter 4 considers the markedly different drama of Beaumont and Fletcher, and of Fletcher's various collaborators. Chapter 5, on Middleton and Massinger, contrasts the treatment of death in the two major playwrights of the 1620s. Chapter 6, on Ford and Shirley, takes this study to its chronological limits. Chapter 7, however, returns to the early 1590s (or late 1580s) and the setting forth of Marlowe's greatest contemporary, who of all Renaissance dramatists makes the most of the "action" of death. Shakespeare is also the subject of chapter 8.

An Appendix, "The Rhetoric of Death," examines speeches that describe, in physiological detail, what is happening within the bodies of the dying.

I wish to thank Hilda Kenner, Liliane McCarthy, and Deb Plummer, for reading and commenting on the manuscript; Gwen McAlpine, for help in verifying references; and Donald Lyons, my copy editor. A semester's research leave from Old Dominion University greatly aided my work. I am also grateful to Stephen Greenblatt for permission to quote from his *Sir Walter Ralegh: The*

9

Renaissance Man and His Roles (Chicago and London: University of Chicago Press, 1980). My greatest debt is to my wife, Louise Efird Andrews, who helped at every stage.

To write a book such as this enforces one's sense of mortal bonds and immortal longings. *Hamlet*'s graveyard is our own. While I was working on the manuscript my mother and my uncles, Richmond Lattimore and Wayne Andrews, died. This book is dedicated to them.

This Action
of Our Death

Introduction

"I have observed," remarks Lisideius in Dryden's *An Essay of Dramatic Poesy,* "that in all our tragedies, the audience cannot forbear laughing when the actors are to die; it is the most comic part of the whole play." That death scenes are so irresistibly comic is not, he explains, the fault of the actors. It is rather the playwrights who are to blame—not for writing such scenes poorly but for writing them at all:

> All *passions* may be lively represented on the stage if to the well-writing of them the actor supplies a good commanded voice, and limbs that move easily, and without stiffness; but there are many *actions* which can never be imitated to a just height: dying especially is a thing which none but a Roman gladiator could naturally perform on the stage, when he did not imitate or represent, but do it; and therefore it is better to omit the representation of it.[1]

What Lisideius says reflects his own neoclassical bias; yet his words are a striking reminder of the great gap in time (and taste) between the first decade of the Restoration and the Renaissance, when scenes representing death could be—and clearly often were—invested with enormous emotional force. In a work published in 1592, Thomas Nashe testifies to the power of Talbot's death (the passage is usually regarded as an allusion to *1 Henry VI*):

> How would it haue ioyed braue *Talbot* (the terror of the French) to thinke that after he had lyne two hundred yeares in his Tombe, hee should triumphe againe on the Stage, and haue his bones newe embalmed with the teares of ten thousand spectators at least (at seuerall times), who, in the Tragedian that represents his person, imagine they behold him fresh bleeding.[2]

Nashe's perfervid rhetoric is more memorable than Talbot's death is likely to seem to us. (See chapter 7.) One wishes for contemporary accounts of the climactic moments of some of the great tragedies of the period. How tantalizing are these lines from an anonymous elegy on Burbage, who is praised not only for making dramatic characters come alive, but for performing death to the life:

> Hee's gone & with him what a world are dead,
> Which he reuiud, to be reuiued soe.
> No more young Hamlett, ould Heironymoe.
> Kind Leer, the greued Moore, and more beside,
> That liued in him, haue now for euer dy'de.
>
> . . . .
>
> Oft haue I seene him play this part [dying] in ieast,
> Soe liuely, that spectators, and the rest
> Of his sad crew, whilst he but seem'd to bleed,
> Amazed, thought euen then hee dyed in deed.[3]

Though one cannot doubt Burbage's ability to "imitate" the "action" of dying "to a just height," the poem makes hungry more than it satisfies. What might the poet have told us, had he cared to, of the deaths of those to whom he refers—"and more beside"? But we are at least fortunate to have a letter in which Henry Jackson, a student at Oxford, describes a visit by the King's Men in 1610:

> —In the last few days the King's players have been here. . . . They had tragedies (too) which they acted with skill and decorum and in which some things, both speech and action, brought forth tears.—

What, precisely, "brought forth tears"? Jackson mentions only one instance, but it is from *Othello*. One might have expected something pertaining to the protagonist, presumably played by Burbage. But what seems to have most impressed Jackson was the boy-actor who played Desdemona:

> —Moreover, that famous Desdemona killed before us by her husband, although she always acted her whole part supremely well, yet when she was killed she was even more moving, for when she fell back upon the bed she implored the pity of the spectators by her very face.[4]

The passage attests to the triumph of the kind of "action" deplored by Dryden's fastidious interlocutor.

One characteristic of the English Renaissance, of course, is an intensely histrionic sensibility. As Stephen Greenblatt has observed, the age is marked by "an increased self-consciousness about the fashioning of human identity as a manipulable, artful process."[5] Nowhere is this concern for "self-fashioning" more pronounced than in the confrontation with death. "The truly memorable death scenes of the age," Greenblatt elsewhere notes, "on the scaffold, at home, or even on the battlefield—Sir Thomas More, Mary Queen of Scots, Sir Philip Sidney, John Donne, Ralegh, Charles I—were precisely that: *scenes,* presided over by actor-playwrights who had brilliantly conceived and thoroughly mastered their roles."[6]

The deaths of Mary and Ralegh may serve to illustrate how one's death might be performed "to a just height." Mary's death at Fotheringay Castle has been eloquently described by J.E. Neale. "Tuesday, February 7th, 1587," Neale writes, "Mary received warning that she was to die the next morning. She showed no terror. She denied complicity in the Babington Plot, inferred that her death was for her religion, and forgave her enemies, in the full confidence that God would take vengeance on them." The next morning, "dressed all in black, . . . a crucifix in her hand, her beads hanging from her girdle," she was brought from her lodgings in the castle to the hall, which had been readied for her execution:

> She wept much at parting from her servants, but was unappalled at the sight of the scaffold, draped in black. "My good servant," she said to one, "thou hast cause rather to joy than to mourn, for now shalt thou see Mary Stuart's troubles receive their long-expected end." With well-meant zeal the Dean of Peterborough exhorted her to change her faith and win salvation: "The hand of death is over your head, and the axe is put to the root of the tree, the throne of the great Judge of Heaven is laid open, and the books of all your life are spread wide, and the particular sentence of Judgment is at hand." "Master Dean," she said, as soon as he began, "trouble me not; I will not hear you; I am resolved in the Roman Catholic faith." He strove to proceed, but she cried out again vehemently, "Peace, Master Dean; you have nothing to do with me, nor I with you." While he prayed, she read her own Catholic prayers in a loud voice, tears flowing from her eyes. The two executioners helped her to disrobe: with a smile she remarked, "I was not wont to have my clothes plucked off by such grooms." Quite quietly she laid her head on the block, repeated *"In manus tuas, Domine,"* and with perfect fortitude met her death.[7]

No less conspicuous than Mary's fortitude is the magnificent theatricality with which she embraced and enacted the role of royal martyr. One detail not mentioned by Neale is perhaps the most brilliantly histrionic of all. When her black gown was plucked from her, those in whose presence she was about to die saw "the Queen, clad from head to foot in crimson silk, the colour of her Church's martyrs."[8]

Greenblatt's account of Ralegh's last hours provides an equally striking example of an execution transformed into a final triumphant "performance":

> It appears that from the moment when he perceived that there was no further hope, he became almost totally self-possessed and seemed even to savor what lay before him. Encountering an old acquaintance during the brief transit from the Hall [Westminster] to the gatehouse, Ralegh asked him to come the next morning, adding, "I know not what shift you will make, but I am sure to have a place." The friends who came to the prison that evening to bid him farewell were struck by his calmness, even mirth. A kinsman . . . was disturbed and advised him, "Sir, take heed, you goe not too muche upon the brave hande; for your enemies will take Exceptions at that." Ralegh replied with a consciousness of the role he had determined to play: "Give me leave to be mery for this is the last merriment that Ever I shall have in this worlde: but when I come to the sad parte, thou shalte see, I will looke on it like a man."[9]

When the time came to play the "sad parte," Ralegh "ascended the scaffold with a smiling face and greeted his acquaintances and the important personages in the crowd." Addressing this select audience, he expressed his gratitude that "God, of his Infinite Goodness, . . . hath sent me to Die in the sight of so Honourable an Assembly, and not in Darkness." In order that they might hear him without making him strain his voice, the lords joined him on the scaffold. He then proceeded with his oration—a speech that one of those present described as being delivered with such "unmoved courage and placid temper that, while it changed the affection of the enemies who had come to witness it, and turned their joy to sorrow, it filled all men else with emotion and admiration."[10] Ralegh's final moments were now at hand. "[T]he sheriffs ordered the scaffold cleared of spectators, and Ralegh gave some clothes and money away to those near him and said farewell to his friends, remarking, 'I have a long Journey to go, and therefore will take my leave.'" He also spoke to the executioner, asking to see his axe: "When the man held back, he repeated, 'I pray thee let me see it. Dost thou think that I am afraid of it?' He ran his finger along the edge and then, smiling, said to the sheriff, 'This is a sharp Medicine, but it is a Physitian for all Diseases.'" All this seems so carefully rehearsed in the theater of Ralegh's imagination that one almost suspects Ralegh of having assigned a part to one of his friends. For when he placed his head on the block, "Someone suggested that he ought to face the east, and Ralegh replied, 'What matter how the head lie, so the heart be right.'" His final words, addressed to the executioner, turned suffering into a kind of action:

The role was practically played out. Refusing the executioner's offer of a blindfold, Ralegh told the man to strike when he lifted his hand. After a brief pause, he gave the signal. The executioner did not move. In a last magnificent assertion of courage and the will to control his own destiny, Ralegh shouted, "What dost thou fear? Strike, man!" In two blows the head was severed, and the performance was over.[11]

It is a death worthy of the man Ralegh had sought to be, of Ralegh's Ralegh. "Each death," Montaigne observes, "should be such as the life hath been. By dying we become no other than we were."[12]

1

Making Death Matter: Marlowe and His Predecessors

Mary and Ralegh may be too extraordinary to be entirely representative, but their attitudes toward death spring from habits of mind deeply rooted in the age. Men and women in the Renaissance were good at dying; they made the most of it. Yet for years theatrical representation lagged behind what may be called the art of life. If one asks what dramatists starting out in the 1580s might have learned from language spoken by the dying in the works of their immediate predecessors, the answer must be "Almost nothing."[1] In Thomas Preston's *Cambyses* (1561),[2] for example, Cambyses enters wounded, informing us that he has stabbed himself in the side while leaping on his horse:

> I feele myself a-dying now, of life bereft am I,
> And Death hath caught me with his dart, for want of blood, I spy.
> Thus gasping heer on ground I lye, for nothing I doo care.
> A just reward for my misdeeds my death dooth plain declare.
> [*Heer let him quake and stir.*]
>
> (1167–70)[3]

The rocking-horse gait of Preston's fourteeners and his intrusive moralizing do less to vitiate these lines than does the air of relentless *demonstration*. It is no wonder that Shakespeare, in *A Midsummer Night's Dream,* has Bottom take "thus" one step further, giving his Pyramus a kind of posthumous eloquence:

> Come tears, confound,
> Out, sword, and wound
> The pap of Pyramus;
> Ay, that left pap,
> Where heart doth hop. [*Stabs himself.*]
> Thus die I, thus, thus, thus.
> Now am I dead,

18

> Now am I fled;
> My soul is in the sky.

>   (5.1.295–303)[4]

Preston, of course, has his own dramatic forebears. But if one compares the death of Cambyses to those of characters in medieval drama, one finds that there has been little or no progress. Consider, for example, the death of Herod in the Chester *The Slaughter of the Innocents*:

> I wott I must dye soone.
> Booteles is me to make mone,
> for dampned I must bee.
> My legges roten and my armes;
>
> . . . .
> I have donne so much woo
> and never good syth I might goo;
> therefore I se nowe comminge my foe
> to fetch me to hell.
> I bequeath here in this place
> my soule to be with Sathanas.
> I dye now; alas, alas!
> I may no longer dwell.

>   (419–22; 426–33)[5]

Here too is the demonstrated death, but the language is at least free of Preston's turgidity. In some medieval plays, moreover, such as *The Castle of Perseverance* (1405–1425), the terse, stabbing phrases convey the suddenness with which death seizes Humanum Genus:

> I deye, certeynly!
> Min[e] hert brekith. I syhe sore.
> A word may I speke no more.
> I putte me in Goddys mercy! [*Dies.*]

>   (3003–6)[6]

Yet again, of course, death is demonstrated rather than enacted.

Between *Cambyses* and the time of Marlowe, there is no English drama that need concern us. There is, however, John Studley's translation of *Hercules Oetaeus* (publ. 1581), in which the agony of the dying Hercules is recounted in relentless physical detail:

> . . . hoat within my boyling bones the seathing Marowe burnes.
> My River whilom ranke of bloude my rotting Lunges it tawes,

> And teareth them in shattred gubs, and filthy withered flawes.
> And now my Gall is dryed up, my burning Lyver glowes. . . .

Moments later Hercules will announce that his "Lyver quite is rent," and that the "corpulent Carkas is consumde of Hercules every lim."[7]

After such rhetoric, what we hear of his offstage death by fire must seem almost anticlimactic. (He is, we are given to understand, a model of Stoic deportment.)

In the late eighties and early nineties, if one excludes Marlowe and Shakespeare, there are no memorable speeches accorded to the dying. Kyd, whom one might have expected to attempt such speeches, altogether eschews them in *The Spanish Tragedy* (1587); indeed Hieronimo, the protagonist, bites out his tongue before taking his own life.[8] But in many plays the dying employ their last moments in speech. Often one is reminded of the physiological catalogue in *Hercules Oetaeus*—though there are other ways of writing badly. In the anonymous *Soliman and Perseda* (1591), a play sometimes attributed to Kyd, the death of Soliman is rendered in crudely workmanlike fashion. As Soliman explains,

> The poison is disperst through euerie vaine,
> And boyles, like *Etna,* in my frying guts
>
> . . . .
>
> And now pale Death sits on my panting soule,
> And with reuenging ire dooth tyrannise,
> And sayes: for *Solimans* too much amisse,
> This day shall be the peryod of my blisse.
>
> (5.4.145–46; 152–55)[9]

In the anonymous *Locrine* (1591), the death of Brutus is comparably devoid of dramatic force:

> Mine eies wax dimme, ouercast with clouds of age,
> The pangs of death compasse my crazed bones;
> Thus to you all my blessings I bequeath,
> And with my blessings, this my fleeting soule.
> My glasse is runne, and all my miseries
> Do end with life; death closeth vp mine eies,
> My soule in haste flies to the Elisian fields.
>
> (1.1.220–26)[10]

And, having given this grave and detached account of his plight, bestowing his blessings, and in effect providing himself with his own cue, he dies.

The same technique is employed by George Peele in *The Battle of Alcazar* (1589) and *The Old Wives Tale* (1590). In the former Abdelmelec takes a brief farewell:

> My sight doth faile, my soule, my feeble soule
> Shall be releaste from prison on this earth:
> Farwell vaine world for I have playd my parte. [*He dyeth.*]
>
>   (1221–23)[11]

The death speech of Stukley, which is remarkable for its length (1324–72), is a direct address to the audience: "Harke freindes, and with the story of my life / Let me beguile the torment of my death" (1326–27). The long account proceeds with no apparent discomfort to the speaker. He then readies himself for death:

> Stukley, the story of thy life is tolde,
> Here breath thy last and bid thy freindes farwell.
> And if thy Countries kindnes be so much,
> Then let thy Countrie kindely ring thy knell.
> Now goe, and in that bed of honour dye
> Where brave Sebastians breathles Course doth lye.
> Here endeth Fortune, rule, and bitter rage:
> Heere ends Tom Stukleys pilgrimage. [*He dyeth.*]
>
>   (1365–72)

The death of Sacrapant, in *The Old Wives Tale,* differs from those just considered in presenting a catalog of some of death's (conventional) harbingers:

> Alas, my veins are numbed, my sinews shrink,
> My blood is pierced, my breath fleeting away;
> And now my timeless date is come to end.
> He in whose life his actions hath been so foul,
> Now in his death to hell descends his soul.
>
>   (849–53)[12]

Such, then, is the early history of the representation of death in Elizabethan drama. Characters (if they speak at all) inform us that they are dying; death itself remains curiously remote, demonstrated rather than enacted. The drama has come little closer to effective presentation of death than in *Cambyses.*

Until characterization becomes sufficiently convincing, only a kind of reportage is possible; for a character to die, he must first be made to live. "It was Marlowe," as Theodore Spencer along ago remarked, "who first discovered how to use death dramatically, for he realized that the manner in which a character acts at the moment of death throws an emotional light on his personality which can be obtained in no other way."[13] According to Spencer, the first such death occurs in *2 Tamburlaine* (1588); the character, predictably, is Tamburlaine himself, whom Marlowe has infused with abundant life over the course of two plays. Yet as early as *1 Tamburlaine* (1587), with the death of Zabina, Marlowe goes far beyond his contemporaries. In *Dido* (1587) and *The Massacre at Paris* (1593), Marlowe makes little of death; *The Jew of Malta* (1589), though theatrically effective, treats death as a matter for harsh derision. But it is, ironically, in two plays which deprive the dying of a chance to speak, *Doctor Faustus* (1592)[14] and *Edward II* (1592), that Marlowe gives death a new and shocking intensity.

The suicide of Dido is closely patterned on the *Aeneid,* from which she quotes before casting herself into the flames. The suicides of Iarbus and Anna (not in Virgil) swiftly follow; the deaths themselves are wordless. In *The Massacre at Paris,* scenes of death abound, but are for the most part crudely rendered. When the Duke of Guise sends poisoned gloves to Navarre's mother, she describes their effect in language that seems strikingly inept for a play from the early 1590s.[15]

> The fatal poison
> Works within my head. My brain-pan breaks.
> My heart doth faint. I die. [*She dies.*]
>
> (sc. 4, 18–20)[16]

The celebrated Ramus dies a wordless death, but King Charles is given a more verbose version of the lines just quoted:

> A griping pain hath seized upon my heart,
> A sudden pang, the messenger of death.
> . . . .
> My sight begins to fail!
> My sinews shrink; my brain turns upside down;
> My heart doth break. I faint and die. [*He dies.*]
>
> (sc. 12, 2–3; 13–15)

Nor does Navarre's death rise above the tepidly conventional. Stabbed by a friar with a poisoned knife, he merely remarks:

> Salute the queen of England in my name,
> And tell her Henry dies her faithful friend. [*He dies.*]
>
> (sc. 23, 102–3)

Only the death of Guise is imbued with character and histrionic power:

> O, that I have not power to stay my life,
> Nor immortality to be revenged!
> To die by peasants, what a grief is this!
>
> . . . .
>
> *Vive la messe!* Perish Huguenots!
> Thus Caesar did go forth, and thus he died. [*He dies.*]
>
> (sc. 20, 79–81; 86–87)

Here is language written to be spoken by a particular character. In the moment of his death, the image of Guise is fixed.

In *1 Tamburlaine,* characters either die wordlessly or express themselves in the dialect of the tribe already encountered. But although this is true of those actually in the process of dying, Marlowe does create one death scene of remarkable force: the double suicide of Bajazeth and Zabina. Here Marlowe surprises us by humanizing these hitherto unsympathetic figures, and emphasizing the love each has for the other. Seeking a way to kill himself without his wife being present, Bajazeth asks her to bring him some water; alone, he dashes his head against the bars of their cage. When she returns and finds him dead, she lapses into madness, and takes her own life:

> Down with him [Tamburlaine]! Down with him! Go to, my child. Away, away, away! Ah, save that infant! Save him, save him! . . . The sun was down—streamers white, red, black. Here, here, here! Fling the meat in his face! Tamburlaine, Tamburlaine! Let the soldiers be buried. . . . Make ready my coach, my chair, my jewels. I come, I come, I come! [*She runs against the cage and brains herself.*]
>
> (5.2.249–55)

Like other characters in the play, Zabina is used to heighten our awareness of aspects of Tamburlaine's nature. Yet her words do more. As Wolfgang Clemen has noted, "The random succession of confused thoughts and impressions that rush through Zabina's mind . . . ; the way in which her thoughts turn again to the red and white [and black] flags, and her recollection of the child . . . ; the grand, monumental quality of the command with which the outburst ends . . . ; all this has a striking dramatic immediacy of a kind that had not been achieved before." [17]

Cosroe, in marked contrast, does not die in a way that makes him live in the imagination. He begins by describing the effect Tamburlaine's sword has produced:

> An uncouth pain torments my grieved soul,
> And death arrests the organ of my voice,
> Who, entering at the breach thy sword hath made,
> Sacks every vein and artier of my heart.

(2.7.7–10)

Whatever virtue these lines may possess, they are not dramatic ones. Substance and mode of expression do not so much embrace as collide; Cosroe says he is in his mortal throes, but speaks with such imperturbable copiousness that we cannot believe him.[18] Nor should we. Death is notably dilatory in arresting the organ of his voice; finally, however, Marlowe draws toward an end with him:

> My bloodless body waxeth chill and cold,
> And with my blood my life slides through my wound;
> My soul begins to take her flight to hell
> And summons all my senses to depart.
> The heat and moisture which did feed each other,
> For want to nourishment to feed them both,
> Is dry and cold; and now doth ghastly death
> With greedy talents gripe my bleeding heart
> And like a harpy tires on my life.
> Theridamus and Tamburlaine, I die—
> And fearful vengeance light upon you both!

(42–52)

The convention by which the dying refer to physical symptoms of their approaching ends, apparently originating in *Hercules Oetaeus,* is one that we have already encountered in the drama of Marlowe's contemporaries. Yet the present passage, according to Douglas Cole, has the historical interest of antedating anything of its kind written for the English theater:

Marlowe's attempt at the dramatization of physical suffering by such means is a completely original phenomenon; as far as I have been able to find, no English play before *Tamburlaine* relies on these physiological details to express the process of death, pain, or hunger. . . . The closest parallel to which one can point is Seneca's rendering of the suffering of Hercules.[19]

Certainly Marlowe out-Senecas "Seneca," out-Studley's Studley. But as Cole notes, Marlowe's language "calls attention to [Corsoe's] suffering and yet does not attract very much sympathy or pity. . . ."[20] With the exception of *slides,* which gives a vivid sense of Cosroe's fugitive lifeblood, we are brought no nearer to experiencing the reality of Cosroe's death.

The other character permitted a death speech, Arabia, dies very differently. His last words show that his thoughts are of another person, Zenocrate. He would converse with her if he could:

> Ah, that the deadly pangs I suffer now
> Would lend an hour's licence to my tongue,
>
> . . . .
>
> But, making now a virtue of thy sight,
> To drive all sorrow from my fainting soul,
> Since death denies me further cause of joy,
> Deprived of care, my heart with comfort dies,
> Since thy desired hand shall close mine eyes.
>
> (5.2.359–60; 365–69)

He does not attempt to describe either the physical cause of death or (apart from "fainting soul") how it feels to die. Indeed, there is nothing in the diction or movement of the speech that gives any sense that it is spoken at point of death. Arabia takes his courtly farewell, then expires. The death that touches him spares his language.

In 2 *Tamburlaine,* there are three speeches to consider: those of the Captain of Balsera, Zenocrate, and Tamburlaine himself.[21]

The Captain speaks in accordance with the usual formula. Fatally wounded by a bullet, he describes with clinical detachment his wound and its effect:

> A deadly bullet gliding through my side
> Lies heavy on my heart; I cannot live.
> I feel my liver pierced, and all my veins,
> That there begin and nourish every part,
> Mangled and torn, and all my entrails bathed
> In blood that straineth from their orifex.
> Farewell, sweet wife! Sweet son, farewell! I die.
>
> (3.4.4–10)

One feels Marlowe wrote these lines hastily with almost mechanical ease. Though life may be said to slide from a wound (as in the death of Cosroe), a bullet breaches the body violently, with impact. This one, however, stealthy as it is deadly, "glides" to its fatal destination, piercing his liver and coming to rest on his heart. Only the sudden sense of human immediacy created by the last line gives this speech dramatic force.[22]

Zenocrate, like Arabia, dies thinking of another. Knowing that death is near, she addresses Tamburlaine:

> . . . let me die, my love; yet let me die;
> With love and patience let your true love die.
>
> (2.4.66–67)

After kissing Tamburlaine and saying farewell to her sons and to Theridamus, Techelles, and Usumcasane, she calls for music: "Some music, and my fit will cease, my lord" (77). Dying to music, she never speaks again.

In the case of Tamburlaine, death also comes by the sudden onset of a mysterious malady. To Techelles's assurance that his illness will not last, he replies:

> Not last, Techelles? No, for I shall die.
> See where my slave, the ugly monster Death,
> Shaking and quivering, pale and wan for fear,
> Stands aiming at me with his murdering dart,
> Who flies away at every glance I give,
> And when I look away, comes stealing on.
>
> (5.3.66–71)

Physicians supply medical commentary reminiscent of the familiar physiological death speech:

> this day is critical,
> Dangerous to those whose crisis is as yours.
> Your artiers, which alongst the veins convey
> The lively spirits which the heart engenders,
> Are parched and void of spirit. . . .
>
> (91–95)

When death comes, Tamburlaine, who has spent his life compelling others to submit to his will, experiences compulsion:

> Farewell, my boys! My dearest friends, farewell!
> My body feels, my soul doth weep to see
> Your sweet desires deprived my company,
> For Tamburlaine, the scourge of God, must die.
>
> (245–248)

Theodore Spencer, in support of his contention that this is the first instance in which death is "treated dramatically," calls attention to several aspects of Marlowe's achievement:

To begin with, through his use of language Marlowe personifies death more vividly than any dramatist had done before, so that we see the eyeless monster, as Tamburlaine sees him, standing before us. In the second place, he describes a hero's reaction to death as an indication of character. And in the third place, he seems to be aware that death can be employed in the drama to give wider implications to the action than would otherwise be possible. Tamburlaine's death is not the violent kind he is familiar with; it is an extinction of life by the more subtle and common enemy of disease; a material ambition meets a material defeat.[23]

Spencer's first point (the vivid personification of death) has, I think, little weight: we do not see what Tamburlaine sees; the image is more properly to be regarded as part of the second (the protagonist's *characteristic* attitude toward death). For Tamburlaine is as singular in confronting death as in shaping his life: Death, long his "servant," shrinks back in fear, only daring to approach when his master looks away. Nor does Tamburlaine envision death as the painfulness of personal extinction; his soul weeps because others will have to do without him, not because he will never see them again. Indeed, he perceives death as a rite of initiation to a new life, the prelude to apotheosis:

> In vain I strive and rail against those powers
> That mean t'invest me in a higher throne,
> As much too high for this disdainful earth.
>
> (5.3.120–22)

The experience of dying does not appear to disclose a different—and more tragic—perspective.[24] Hence the unchanging quality of Tamburlaine's language, which never reflects weakness or uncertainty, is in keeping with Marlowe's conception of his character. What in other plays of the period is a defect is here in keeping with decorum.

The Jew of Malta, unlike *Tamburlaine,* makes death an occasion for laughter. Only the deaths of Abigail and Barabas require comment.

Abigail, poisoned by Barabas, dies with commendable piety:

> Death seizeth on my heart. Ah, gentle friar,
> Convert my father that he may be saved,
> And witness that I die a Christian.
>
> (3.6.37–39)

But any potential pathos is immediately undercut by the friar's response: "Ay, and a virgin, too—that grieves me most" (40).

Marlowe gives Barabas a full-scale death speech, but not of the sort appropriate for a tragic protagonist. Speaking from the caldron into which he has fallen, he proudly recounts his villainous deeds. Then the end is upon him:

> But now begins the extremity of heat
> To pinch me with intolerable pangs.
> Die, life! Fly, soul! Tongue, curse thy fill, and die!
>
> (5.5.87–89)

As J. B. Steane has observed, the last line "cannot have passed, even around 1590, as tragic utterance intended to impress a straight-faced audience. True it does not read as a parody. . . . But situation, character and diction all combine to produce farce."[25] Barabas's final words are, however, thoroughly in keeping with the tone of the play, with its derisive humor and puppet-show violence. The contrast with the death of Tamburlaine could scarcely be greater. But in one respect Marlowe's dramaturgy has not changed. Both plays insist that we keep our distance. Neither the lives nor the deaths of the characters are in any sense ours. They might be called *noli me tangere* plays.[26]

Neither *Edward II* nor *Doctor Faustus* has what would usually be considered a death speech, yet both make death terrifying. *Tamburlaine* and *The Jew of Malta* do not threaten us; part of us reels backward during the last moments of Edward and Faustus.

Like *Tamburlaine* and *The Jew of Malta*, *Edward II* generally eschews human warmth and intimacy; one can understand why its dispassionate, distancing manner attracted Brecht. Yet Edward's death, too ghastly to be distanced,[27] has almost the elemental power of the blinding of Gloucester. He speaks no words. What words could he speak? His pain when the red-hot spit penetrates his body is such that language is reduced to mere outcry. His agonized scream ("I fear me that this cry will raise the town," says Matrevis [5.5.113]) resounds in the mind long after the play has ended.

In *Doctor Faustus,* though Faustus's actual death is not dramatized, Marlowe gives us something vastly different from the shocking and dehumanized death of Edward II. Faustus, with "but one bare hour to live" (5.2.131), makes us participate in the terrified dartings of his spirit:

The stars move still; time runs; the clock will strike;
The devil will come, and Faustus must be damned.
O, I'll leap up to my God! Who pulls me down?
See, see, where Christ's blood streams in the firmament!
One drop would save my soul, half a drop! Ah, my Christ!
Rend not my heart for naming of my Christ!
Yet will I call on him. O, spare me, Lucifer!
Where is it now? 'Tis gone. And see where God
Stretcheth out his arm and bends his ireful brows.
Mountains and hills, come, come, and fall on me,
And hide me from the heavy wrath of God.

(140–50)

Faustus's hysterical outcries when midnight strikes draw us toward him, forcing us to experience infinite terror in a little room:

O, it strikes, it strikes! Now, body, turn to air,
Or Lucifer will bear thee quick to hell.
O soul, be changed to little water-drops,
And fall into the ocean, ne'er be found.
      [*Thunder, and enter the Devils.*]
My God, my God, look not so fierce on me!
Adders and serpents, let me breathe a while!
Ugly hell, gape not! Come not, Lucifer!
I'll burn my books! Ah, Mephistophilis!

(180–87)

At the very last, as the devils bear him from the stage, he too has no language but a cry.

Marlowe, then, was the first to seize upon the dramatic possibilities of the last moments of the dying. But he did so in his supremely individualistic way. The deaths of Tamburlaine, Edward, and Faustus are all special cases. Tamburlaine, who remains fully self-possessed in the face of death, and learns nothing, dies in a way appropriate for a character of his extraordinary nature. Edward and Faustus are even more exceptional. Edward is slain in a manner that deprives him of anything but a scream; his death, perhaps too ghastly to achieve a tragic effect, does not derive its power from either his stature or eloquence, but from being the shockingly sadistic murder of a *king*.[28] Faustus, whose eloquence makes his last moments unforgettable, is a man about to be damned.

Yet it is surely in the deaths of Edward and Faustus that Marlowe made his greatest contribution with respect to the representation of death. Compared to them, death scenes in the works of other dramatists of the day seem stilted, lacking in psychological or dramatic force. The conventional speech detailing the failure of the vital parts, whether it entered Elizabethan drama by way of Marlowe or crept out from under Hercules' robe, proved a dramatic dead end, however long it lingered on the stage.[29] Such matters are the province not of the dramatist, but of the coroner.

2
Deaths Horrific and Exemplary

If one excepts Shakespeare and Chapman, surprisingly little is done with the dying moments of characters between the early 1590s and about 1610. Dramatists tend to focus on the brutality or fiendish artistry of those who kill, not the significance of life and death for those who perish.[1] The anonymous *Arden of Feversham* (1591), unusual both in being a domestic tragedy and in having an English setting, is representative in its treatment of death. Thus Arden, pulled from his stool while playing at tables, is permitted only a single line—"Mosby! Michael! Alice! What will you do?"—before his murderers strike:

> *Will.* Nothing but take you up, sir, nothing else.
> *Mosby.* There's for the pressing iron you told me of. [*He stabs Arden.*]
> *Shakebag.* And there's for the ten pound in my sleeve. [*He stabs him.*]
> *Alice.* What, groans thou?—Nay, then give me the weapon!—
> Take this for hind'ring Mosby's love and mine. [*She stabs him.*]
> (sc. 14, 233–38)[2]

What complexity there is lies with the motives of Arden's killers. As Alexander Leggatt notes, "Each of the three characters who stabs him gives a reason. . . . Mosby remembers a social insult . . . ; Shakebag is thinking of his fee; and Alice announces the motive to which the play has given the greatest prominence, striking the last blow as she does so."[3]

Turning from this crime-and-punishment play to the anonymous *Alphonsus, Emperor of Germany* (1594), one finds the same emphasis. Instead of making the most of Alphonsus's death, the author has him die at the hands of his tool villain, Alexander, whose father he has murdered, in a way that deprives him of speech. Alexander promises Alphonsus that he will spare his life if he will bequeath his soul to the devil. Alphonsus does so—and Alexander takes his Cutwulfian vengeance:

> Thus will I make delivery of the deed,
> Die and be damn'd! Now I am satisfied! [*Kills him.*]
> (5.1.323–24)[4]

31

So villain destroys villain. The dramatic emphasis is on the witty propriety by which the guiler is beguiled, and on his horrific end. What is lacking is any serious concern with making Alphonsus's death, in Theodore Spencer's phrase, cast "an emotional light on his personality." But of course a character like Alphonsus has no hidden depths, no interiority; he is too much a villain to be a man.

The anonymous *Lust's Dominion, or the Lascivious Queen* (1600) similarly emphasizes the villain's role. King Philip, dying as few do in these bloody plays, of natural causation, speaks with exemplary piety:

> Let none with a distracted voice
> Shreik out, and trouble me in my departure:
> Heavens hands I see are beckning for my soul;
> I come, I come; thus do the proudest die,
> Death hath no mercy, life no certainty.
>
> (1.2.73–77)[5]

As dying speeches go, this is not more than perfunctory; and the same is true of the last words of Maria, wife of the villainous Eleazar (3.2.113–16). The play's climactic moments are in the tradition of *The Spanish Tragedy, The Jew of Malta,* and *Alphonsus,* for Eleazar unwittingly puts himself in his foes' power and suffers the ironic fate of being stabbed to death while fettered in manacles he had intended for one of his enemies. His last speech, clearly influenced by that of Barabas, is in keeping with his role as an incarnation of evil:

> And am I thus dispatch'd;
> Had I but breath'd the space of one hour longer,
> I would have fully acted my revenge.
>
> (5.3.148–50)

After making good on his declaration that he will "curse you all," he comes to his final lines:

> oh! I faint;
> Devills com claim your right, and when I am
> Confin'd within your kingdom then shall I
> Out-act you all in perfect villany. [*Dyes.*]
>
> (163–66)

He dies, in short, every inch a villain.

Marston's *Antonio's Revenge* (1600) provides a more complex and disturbing representation of death. For many playwrights this would have been a play about a successful revenger finally undone by his own villainy; Marston's protagonist, however, is a Herculean purger of the state.

Three deaths are dramatized: that of Strotzo, accomplice of the villainous Duke Piero; that of Piero's son Julio; and that of Piero himself. As in *The Spanish Tragedy,* the emphasis is on silent death. Strotzo, like Kyd's Pedringano, is deceived into believing that he will receive a last-moment pardon, but is strangled by his master and Castilio:

> *Strotzo.* Now change your—
> *Piero.*   Ay, pluck, Castilio!
>   I change my humour! Pluck, Castilio!
>
> (4.3.65–66)[6]

Antonio plans to murder Julio as part of his vengeance on Piero. Julio, however, is Mellida's brother as well as Piero's son, and Antonio decides to spare him. But the ghost of Andrugio, Antonio's father, is adamant—"Revenge!" (3.3.30)—and Antonio proceeds:

> I love thy soul, and were thy heart lapped up
> In any flesh but in Piero's blood
> I would thus kiss it; but being his, thus, thus,
> And thus I'll punch it.
>
> (37–40)

To which Julio mildly replies, "So you will love me, do even what you will" (42). He does not speak again. But it is the death of Piero which reveals Marston at his most Marstonian. Bound by Antonio and his fellow conspirators, Piero has his tongue plucked out:

> *Antonio.* Murder and torture; no prayers, no entreats.
> *Pandulpho.* We'll spoil your oratory. Out with his tongue! [*They pluck out his tongue and triumph over him.*]
> *Antonio.* I have't, Pandulpho; the veins panting bleed,
>   Trickling fresh gore about my fist.
>
> (5.5.32–35)

And this is only the beginning of the sadistic torments inflicted on him. "Behold, black dog!" says Antonio, holding up his tongue (40); others join in taunting him. "He weeps!" exults Pandulpho; "Now do I glorify my hands. / I had no vengeance if I had no tears" (44–45). Antonio now reveals Julio's fate:

> Here lies a dish to feast thy father's gorge.
> Here's flesh and blood which I am sure thou lovest.
>
> (48–49)[7]

Though mute, *"Piero seems to condole his son."* Finally, after more mockery and insults, the conspirators rush at him as if to kill him— but suddenly stop. It is the last sadistic touch before Antonio and the others stab him.

Antonio escapes the death that customarily is meted out to the revenger. Indeed, he is regarded as "another Hercules" for "ridding huge pollution from our state" (5.6.12–13); he and his fellow conspirators are offered rewards befitting such an accomplishment: "What satisfaction outward pomp can yield, / Or chiefest fortunes of the Venice state, / Claim freely" (23–25). That this is an astonishing departure from the conventional revenge pattern is emphasized by Antonio's response: "We are amazed at your benignity; / But other vows constrain another course" (28–29). As Pandulpho explains,

> We know the world, and did we know no more
> We would not live to know; but since constraint
> Of holy bands forceth us keep this lodge
> Of dirt's corruption till dread power calls
> Our souls' appearance, we will live enclosed
> In holy verge of some religious order,
> Most constant votaries.
>
> (30–36)

However one construes these lines,[8] in this strange and disturbing play Marston seems more engaged by those who kill than by those who die.[9]

Chettle's *Hoffman, or A Revenge for a Father* (1602), another play featuring lurid and sensationalistic revenge, differs from *Antonio's Revenge* in taking the more conventional course of presenting the revenger as a murderous villain who himself perishes in appropriately horrific circumstances. Hoffman's first victim, Otho, is made to wear the same "burning Crowne" that was used to execute Hoffman's father; he expires in fiery torment, describing the effect of the onset of death on his brains, body, sinews, nerves and tendons:

> Each part's disioynted, and my breath expires:
> Mount soule to heauen, my body burnes in fire.
>
> (233–34)[10]

The most notable death, predictably, is that of Hoffman himself, by means of the same crown. Having fallen in love (or lust) with Otho's mother, he is credulously led to believe she will yield to him ("I am crown'd the King of pleasure" [2554]), and is surprised by his enemies. The burning crown descends:

> 'tis well, 'tis fit,
> I that had sworne vnto my fathers soule
> To be reueng'd on *Austria, Saxony,*
> *Prussia, Luningberg,* and all there heires:
> Had prosper'd in the downefall of some fiue;
> Had onely three to offer to the fiends,
> And then must fall in loue; oh wretched eyes
> That haue betray'd my heart; bee you accurst;
> And as the melting drops run from my brows,
> Soe fall they on the strings that guide your heart. . . .
>
> (2586–95)

What a failure he has been as a revenger! He dies cursing his enemies and his own folly. Though his enemies say they pardon him and pray for his soul, he remains implacable:

> Soe doe not I for yours, nor pardon you;
> You kild my father, my most warlike father,
> Thus as you deale by me, you did by him;
> But I deserue it that haue slackt reuenge
> Through fickle beauty, and a womans fraud. . . .
>
> (1608–12)

May hell reward them.

The Revenger's Tragedy (1606)[11] resembles *Antonio's Revenge* in according greater emphasis to a revenger's bloody deeds than to the manner in which the dying confront death. As in *Hoffman,* however, the protagonist, Vindice, lapses into self-betrayal; instead of being regarded as a benefactor to the state after the fashion of Marston's Antonio, he is summarily sentenced to death.

Vindice's murder of the Duke is a masterpiece of poetic justice. Before the action of the play begins, the Duke poisoned Gloriana, Vindice's betrothed, because she would not yield to his lust; her skull, "a quaint piece of beauty" (3.5.53),[12] is made the means of poisoning him. Vindice decks out the skull, puts poison where the lips were, and adds a mask; then he and his brother Hippolito present what was once Gloriana to the Duke as "a country lady" who "has somewhat a grave look with her" (137). In the perfumed darkness the Duke (having been told that country ladies lose much of their bashfulness after the first kiss) sets to with alacrity:

> *Vindice.* Back with the torch; brother, raise the perfumes.
> *Duke.* How sweet can a duke breathe? Age has no fault.
>   Pleasure should meet in a perfumed mist.
>   Lady, sweetly encounter'd; I came from court.
>   I must be bold with you. [*Kisses the skull.*] O, what's this? O!
>   (142–46)

Torchlight provides part of the answer, Vindice another: "View it well; 'tis the skull of Gloriana, whom thou poisonedst last" (150–51). "What are you two?" asks the Duke, who now feels the poison work. "Villains all three!" answers Vindice; "The very ragged bone / Has been sufficiently reveng'd" (153–55).

As in *Antonio's Revenge,* when Piero was at the mercy of Antonio and the other conspirators, the revengers inflict the worst torments they can imagine upon their dying enemy. When the Duke calls on Hippolito to cry treason, Hippolito responds: "Yes, my good lord; treason, treason, treason!" (157). The action that accompanies these words is indicated by the stage direction "*Stamping on him.*" The poison eats out his teeth, occasioning mockery—"those that did eat are eaten" (163)—and begins to attack his tongue. Now Vindice casts off his disguise: " 'Tis I, 'tis Vindice, 'tis I"—each stress like a stab—and Hippolito offers mocking words of "comfort": "Our lord and father / Fell sick upon the infection of thy frowns, / And died in sadness; be that thy hope of life" (169–71). But all the vituperation and mockery are inconsequential compared to the final torment of being forced to witness an assignation between his wife and his bastard son. Music is heard, and the Duke begs to be spared the sight; finding the brothers implacable, he cries out. Nowhere is the play more brutal than in Vindice's response:

> Nay, faith, we'll have you hush'd; now with thy dagger
> Nail down his tongue, and mine shall keep possession
> About his heart. If he but gasp, he dies
> . . . .
> If he but wink, not brooking the foul object,
> Let our two other hands tear up his lids,
> And make his eyes, like comets, shine through blood. . . .
>   (197–99; 202–4)

Spurio and the Duchess enter and kiss, make plain their adulterous relationship, and depart to feast. It is too much for the Duke: "I cannot brook—" (222). He dies in midsentence, leaving Vindice to complete the line with a bitter jest: "The brook is turn'd to blood."

The death of the Duke, then, is designed to emphasize the bloody virtuosity of Vindice. The Duke, one may say, is cast in a certain role; but the play is less concerned with his responses than with what is done to him. Vindice dominates. The assassination of Lussurioso, the successor of the Duke, is differently handled. As in *Antonio's Revenge,* this revenge action takes place through the device of a masque.[13] Vindice's scheme is to have a masque of revengers precede the actual masquers; along with Hippolito and two others, he dances before Lussurioso and the three lords who sit with him. The dance being over, the revengers take out their swords and kill their victims—to the accompaniment of thunder. What Vindice does not know is that Spurio, the two sons of the Duchess, and an unnamed fourth man have plotted to murder Lussurioso in the same fashion. When they enter Lussurioso utters his first words since he was stabbed, calling out treason. Supervacuo, the younger son, proclaims himself duke, only to be slain by his brother Ambitioso; Spurio kills Ambitioso, only to be stabbed by the fourth masquer. These deaths are like those of Tamora, Titus, and Saturninus in *Titus Andronicus* (see chapter 7), in that their suddenness and the absence of even perfunctory death speeches both dehumanize the characters and lessen the dramatic impact.[14]

Lussurioso survives the others, and seals the fate of the noble whose sole crime was killing Spurio by testifying: "Those in the masque did murder us" (5.3.68). "How fares my lord the Duke?" asks Vindice, for whom only one more death is requisite for his revenge to be complete. "Farewell to all," Lussurioso replies; "He that climbs highest has the greatest fall." The sententious commonplace is followed by a line that, ironically, reminds us of the fate of his father: "My tongue is out of office" (75–77). It is time for the perfection of Vindice's vengeance:

> Air, gentlemen, air! [*Whispering in his ear.*]
> Now thou'lt not prate on't, 'twas Vindice murder'd thee,—
> *Lussurioso.* O!
> *Vindice.* —murder'd thy father,—
> *Lussurioso.* O! [*Dies.*]
> *Vindice.* —and I am he.
> Tell nobody.
>
> (77–80)

The play to this point has been the triumphant progress of Vindice. He has not only eradicated his enemies, but purged the state.

The new regime is headed by Antonio, whose wife the Duchess's youngest son had ravished. One thing puzzles Antonio—"How the old duke came murder'd" (93). Vindice volunteers that he and Hippolito were responsible. Antonio's response is to order them taken to immediate execution. "Heart, was't not for your good, my lord?" asks Vindice. "My good?" comes the answer; "away with 'em! Such an old man as he; / You that would murder him would murder me" (103–5).

From one point of view this is merely the conventional pattern of action in which a witty villain undoes himself. Yet Vindice's downfall is in most respects highly unconventional. It is ironic, surely, that Antonio judges Vindice worthy of death for killing "such an old man" as the Duke—with whom he identifies by reason of age. Murder in itself seems to be acceptable, provided the victim is not of venerable years.[15] But it is not merely the questionable moral status of the man who speaks for the new regime. Vindice's response shows that life itself is of little consequence to him. As he says to Hippolito:

> May not we set as well as the duke's son?
> Thou hast no conscience; are we not reveng'd?
> Is there one enemy left alive amongst those?
>
> (107–10)

Though orthodox in believing murder will out (111–12), he displays satisfaction rather than remorse.

> And now, my lord, since we are in for ever,
> This work was ours, which else might have been slipp'd,
> And, if we list, we could have nobles clipp'd,
> And go for less than beggars;[16] but we hate
> To bleed so cowardly. We have enough, i'faith;
> We're well, our mother turn'd, our sister true;
> We die after a nest of dukes. Adieu.
>
> (119–25)

Vindice is, indeed, an instance of one consumed by that which he was nourished by. He lives for vengeance; all his enemies lie dead. Since no character in the play, including Vindice, is "invested with much humanity either for good or evil,"[17] we cannot be deeply moved by what happens to either Vindice's victims or Vindice himself. The dramatic interest lies elsewhere. Yet *of course* we know that Vindice is guilty and—barring an ending as extraordinary as that of *Antonio's Revenge*—must perish at the end of the play.

What *The Revenger's Tragedy* does is superbly duplicitous. Indubitably, the play satisfies the dictates of morality; like Hoffman, Vindice must die. But the effect of judgment is undercut. The death of Hoffman is the climactic event in the play to which he gives his name. That of Vindice is not even dramatized; when last seen, he is departing in excellent spirits, well pleased with himself.[18] This ending has, I suggest, less in common with the conventions of revenge tragedy than with Jonson's ironic use of deferred punishment in *Volpone*.[19] In his epistle "To the Most Noble and Most Equal Sisters," Oxford and Cambridge, Jonson explains that he has sought in *Volpone* "to put the snaffle in their mouths that cry out: We never punish vice in our interludes" (109–10);[20] like Jonson, the author (or authors) of *The Revenger's Tragedy* could declare that the play metes out appropriate punishment; like Volpone, Vindice is punished and not punished. And as he leaves the stage one can almost imagine him returning to speak the epilogue—to the great applause of the audience he has horrified and delighted.

Two other villain plays deserve mention here in connection with their representation of death, the anonymous *Claudius Tiberius Nero* and Barnabe Barnes's *The Devil's Charter, or Pope Alexander VI* (both 1607). The former, in which the crafty Tiberius ironically promises Sejanus that he will resign his crown to him, is reminiscent of *Hoffman*: "*He sets the burning Crowne vpon his head,*" saying "All haile Sejanus, Romes great Emperour" (2791–92).[21] And Sejanus, like so many other villains in the period, dies furiously venting maledictions:

> Al haile: Hell, Death, Destruction plague you al
> Let all the tortures, torments, punishments.
> In earth, in heauen, in hell, reuenge my death,
> Whose burning paine torments me not so much
> [A]s that there comes not from my scalded braines,
> Sufficient smoake to smother all of you. [*He dyes.*]
>
> (2793–98)

Among other deaths in the play, one may briefly note that of Tiberius himself, who is not given the opportunity for any final words, being smothered and stabbed by Caligula (3341–46).

The Devil's Charter, though offering as much in the way of lurid criminality as one might expect, is chiefly memorable for what it does not do—make Borgias a character with deeper affinities to Marlowe's Faustus than to the dehumanized villains in the plays we have lately considered. The damnation of Borgias is a potentially tragic subject, though in Protestant England one would hardly expect to find anything other than the melodrama Barnes hashes together. Nonetheless, there are moments when Barnes gives Borgias language that reminds us of Faustus's final moments before the circling clock:

> Arise, arise, aduance, heart clogg'd with sinne,
> Oppressed with damnation: vp, aduance yet.
> Wilt thou not stirre stiffe heart? what am I damn'd?
> Yet a little, yet a little, oh yet: not yet? alas.
> High God of heauens and earth if thou beare loue,
> Vnto the soule of sinfull man shew mercy,
> Mercy good Lord, oh mercy, mercy, mercy.
> Oh saue my soule out of the Lyons pawes. . . .
>
> (M^v)[22]

But Barnes draws back from this. Moments later Borgias is no more than a negative example, a learn-thou-by-me moralist: "Learne wicked worldlings, learne, learne, learne by me / To saue your soules, though I condemned be" (M2). And when the devils surround him his last words have more in common with the astonishing outburst of Beckett's Lucky than with those of any Renaissance protagonist:

> Holla, holla, holla, come, come, come, what, when, where, when, why, deaf, strike, dead, aliue, oh alas, oh alas, alwaies burning, always freezing, always liuing, tormented, neuer ending, neuer, neuer, neuer mending, out, out, out, out, why, why, whether, whether, thether.

"Thether, thether, thether," reply the devils:

> *Thunder and lightning with fearefull noise the diuells thrust him downe and goe Triumphing.* (M2^v)

Sensationalism and grotesquerie dominate.

Tragedies in which the dying are provided with heroic or otherwise edifying sentiments are rarer during this period. Most are eminently forgettable. In the anonymous *Caesar and Pompey, or Caesar's Revenge* (1595), for example, the death of Pompey is a good example of what happens when the author does not strain his meagre endowments:

> O Villaine [says Pompey to Sempronius] thou hast
>   slayne thy Generall,
> And with thy base hand gor'd my royall heart.
> Well I haue liued till to that height I came,

That all the world did tremble at my name,
My greatnesse then by fortune being enuied,
Stabd by a murtherous villaynes hand I died.

(743–48)[23]

Though sufficiently pedestrian, such a passage has at least the virtue of treading on the ground; it is in touch with human reality. The suicide of Brutus, however, is written in what is doubtless meant to be a "tragically" heightened style:

Enter Brutus the Ghost [of Caesar] following him.
Brutus. What doest thou still persue me vgly fend,
  Is this it thou hast thirsted for so much?

  . . . .

  Boyle me or burne, teare my hatefull flesh,
  Deuoure, consume, pull, pinch, plague, paine this hart,
  Hell craues her right, and heere the furyes stand,
  And all the hell-hounds compasse me a round

  . . . .

  O tis the soule that they stand gaping for,
  And endlesse matter for to prey vpon.
  Renewed still as Titius pricked heart.
  Then clap your hands, let Hell with Ioy resound?
  Here it comes flying through this aery round.

(2503–4; 2514–17; 2521–25)

This is sad stuff (the second line after the stage direction is, almost literally, unspeakable; the rest is bombast). Yet the Ghost, no aesthetician, pronounces itself well satisfied.

Chettle and Munday's *The Death of Robert, Earl of Huntington* (1598) does not pinch, pull, or plague us in its representation of death. Huntington (Robin Hood), dying of poison, takes his farewell of his beloved and then makes his will. His end is as courteous as it is undramatic:

My liege, farewell, farewell, my love, farewell!
Farewell, fair Queen, Prince John, and noble lords!
Father Fitzwater, heartily adieu!
Adieu, my yeomen tall. Matilda, close mine eyes.
Friar, farewell! Farewell to all!

(1.3; 8:248)[24]

Matilda, who takes poison rather than yield to John's lust, evinces on her deathbed the same tranquil volubility which distinguishes Robin:

> Oxford, for God's sake, to my father write
> The latest commendations of his child;
> And say Matilda keeps his honour's charge,
> Dying a spotless maiden undefil'd.
>
> . . . .
>
> The king and he will quickly now grow friends,
> And by their friendship much content will grow.
> Sink, earth to earth; fade, flower ordain'd to fade,
> But pass forth, soul, unto the shrine of peace;
> Beg there atonement may be quickly made.
> Fair queen, kind Oxford, all good you attend.
> Fly forth, my soul, heaven's King be there thy friend. [*Dies.*]
>
> (5.1; p. 313)

Her last moments, like Robin's, are exemplary; but neither character, in Hardy's phrase, is "alive enough to have strength to die."

Heywood's *A Woman Killed With Kindness* (1603) makes Anne Frankford's suicide by starvation the means for a deathbed reconciliation with her husband. Knowing she is about to die, he forgives her infidelity and recognizes her as once more his wife:

> My wife, the mother to my pretty babes,
> Both those lost names I do restore thee back,
> And with this kiss I wed thee once again.
> Though thou art wounded in thy honour'd name,
> And with that grief upon thy deathbed liest,
> Honest in heart, upon my soul, thou diest.
>
> (sc. 17, 115–20)[25]

And Anne replies:

> Pardon'd on earth, soul, thou in Heaven art free;
> Once more thy wife, dies thus embracing thee. [*Dies.*]
>
> (121–22)

No ending could more clearly illustrate the chasm that sometimes opens between Elizabethan and "modern" taste.[26]

Marston's *Sophonisba* (1605) is similarly edifying, but offers instead an image of heroic female virtue. Massinissa has promised Sophonisba, his wife, that she will "live free"; but he then yields to the Roman offer to spare Carthage if she is delivered to them. How can Sophonisba keep her husband from being forsworn? Unflinchingly, she follows the dictates of love and honor, drinking poison so that both promises can be kept:

> Deere doe not weepe
> And now with undismaid resolve behold,
> To save *You, you* (for honor and just faith
> Are most true Gods, which we should much adore)
> With even disdainefull vigour I give up,
> An abhord life. [*She drinks.*] You have beene good to me,
> And I doe thank thee heaven, O my stars,
> I blesse your goodnes, that with breast unstaind,
> Faith pure: a Virgin wife, try'de to my glory,
> I die of female faith, the long liv'de story,
> Secure from bondage, and all servile harmes,
> But more, most happy in my husbands armes. [*She sinks.*]
>
> (5.3; 2:61)[27]

Massinissa, who will have her body borne to Scipio, emphasizes the magnitude of her deed:

> Covetous
> Fame-greedy Lady, could no scope of glory,
> No reasonable proportion of goodnes
> Fill thy great breast, but thou must prove immense
> Incomprehense in vertue, what, wouldst thou
> Not onely be admirde, but even adored?
> O glory ripe for heaven?
>
> (5.3; 2:61)

Such is the end of Marston's "wonder of women."

Marston's remaining tragedy, *The Insatiate Countess* (with William Barkstead, 1610),[28] requires little comment. Of the deaths in the play only that of Isabella, the protagonist, is worth noting. About to be executed for her evil deeds, she makes a good end:

> Give me your blessing my Lord Cardinal:
> Lord, I am well prepared:
> Murder and Lust, down with my ashes sink,
> But like ingrateful seed perish in earth,
> That you may never spring against my soul,
> Like weeds to choke it in the heavenly harvest;
> I fall to rise, mount to thy Maker, spirit,
> Leave here thy body, death has her demerit.
> Strike. [*Executioner strikes.*]
>
> (5.1.218–25)

As the Duke of Medina emphasizes, Isabella is Sophonisba's antithesis, a woman whose excesses are monstrous rather than "Incomprehense in vertue":

> She died deservedly, and may like fate
> Attend all women so insatiate.
>
> (230–31)

Like the repentant Anne Frankford, she serves to point a moral.

With Tourneur's *The Atheist's Tragedy* (1609) I end this survey of what dramatists are doing with the words of the dying from the early 1590s to about 1610. In this play, as in others just considered, the highly moralized death speech is given great emphasis. Levidulcia, seeing her husband slain by her lover, expresses her remorse and takes her own life:

> Dear husband, let
> Not thy departed spirit be displeas'd
> If with adult'rate lips I kiss thy cheek.
> Here I behold the hatefulness of lust,
>
> . . . .
>
> Shall I outlive my honour? Must my life
> Be made the world's example? Since it must,
> Then thus in detestation of my deed,
> To make th' example move more forcibly
> To virtue, thus I seal it with a death
> As full of horror as my life of sin. [*Stabs herself.*]
>
> (4.5.65–68; 81–86)[29]

Equally didactic, though far more ghastly, is the death of D'Amville, who kills himself while attempting to execute Charlemont: *"As he raises up the axe [he] strikes out his own brains, [and then] staggers off the scaffold"* (5.2.241 s.d.). Finally, the aptly named villain is brought to acknowledge the power of Providence, which

> hath overthrown the pride
> Of all my projects and posterity,
> For whose surviving blood I had erected
> A proud monument and struck 'em dead
> Before me, for whose deaths I call'd to thee
> For judgment. Thou didst want discretion for
> The sentence, but 'yond powers that struck me knew
> The judgment I deserv'd, and gave it. O,
> The lust of death commits a rape upon me,
> As I would ha' done on Castabella. [*Dies.*]
>
> (5.2.259–68)

Of these and the preceding lines it may be said that few with their brains struck out prove comparably voluble. D'Amville's death takes us, in a sense, full circle; for it is, in Roger Stilling's words, "a retreat . . . to the intellectual and artistic level of *Cambyses*."[30]

3

Chapman and Webster

Chapman seems to tower over the dramatists represented in the previous chapter. He is not interested in the pullulating world of villain-tragedy nor in conventional moralizing, but in titanic and astonishing protagonists. As Edwin Muir has observed, "We can feel his impatience to arrive at those places where the souls of his heroes can expand to their full range, places on the frontier between life and death, time and eternity, where all terms become absolute. Consequently a situation which to other tragic figures would bring despair or resignation, merely evokes new potentialities in his heroes, as if it were the opportunity for which they were waiting."[1] Given Chapman's essential preoccupations, it is scarcely surprising that his characters so often speak out loud and bold, as if making Death proud to take them.

In *Bussy D'Ambois* (1604) only one onstage death precedes that of Bussy. It is, one must acknowledge, ludicrously ineffectual: the expiration of the Friar when he sees Montsurrey torturing Tamyra:

> What rape of honour and religion?
> O wrack of nature. [*Falls and dies.*]
>
> (5.1.147–48)[2]

Nor is it less regrettable that, as if in recompense for this sudden snuffing out, the Friar's *umbra* is granted an unusual degree of participation in the play. But the death of Bussy, for which the whole work is planned, shows both the hero and Chapman at their most impressive.

Bussy goes to his death despite the warnings of the Friar's ghost and the more detailed warning of Behemoth, who informs Bussy that he will die "if thou obey / The summons that thy mistress next will send thee" (5.2.54–55). The admonition is repeated, to the accompaniment of thunder: "If thou yield / To her next summons; Y' are fair warn'd: farewell" (66–67). Bussy responds in a spirit of heroic acceptance:

> I must fare well, how ever: though I die,
> My death consenting with his augury;

45

> Should not my powers obey when she commands,
> My motion must be rebel to my will:
> My will to life. . . .

(68–72)

Moments later, Montsurrey, masquerading as the Friar, brings the letter Tamyra has written with her blood. Though Bussy credulously concludes that Behemoth has lied to him, we know that he would have undertaken in knowledge what he is about to undergo in ignorance.

But before dramatizing the murder of Bussy, Chapman has Monsieur and Guise engage in a curious colloquy—as Eugene M. Waith remarks, these men, "involved as they are in the plot on Bussy's life, discuss him with a detachment which is quite out of character and which tends, therefore, to give their words even more weight."[3] Monsieur has asserted "that Nature hath no end / In her great works, responsive to their worths" (5.3.1–2). When Guise rejects this view, Monsieur insists that Bussy is a case in point:

> Why you shall see it here, here will be one
> Young, learned, valiant, virtuous, and full mann'd;
>
> . . . .
> Yet, as the winds sing through a hollow tree,
> And (since it lets them pass through) let it stand;
> But a tree solid, since it gives no way
> To their wild rages, they rend up by th' root:
> So this full creature now shall reel and fall,
> Before the frantic puffs of purblind Chance
> That pipes through empty men, and makes them dance. . . .

(37–38; 42–48)

His fall, in short, will illustrate the plight "of virtue, now thrown into all men's hate" (56).

After this massive preparation, the scene proceeds. When Bussy enters, Tamyra warns him that he will be murdered. We have reached one of the "places" of which Muir speaks. Instead of fleeing, Bussy responds with words that make one feel his soul stands on tiptoe:

> Let in my politic visitants, let them in,
> Though ent'ring like so many moving armours;
> Fate is more strong than arms, and sly than treason,
> And I at all parts buckled in my Fate:
> Dare they not come?

(85–89)

When the murderers do come, Bussy drives out all but one, whom he kills. Moments later they return, this time with Montsurrey, who attacks Bussy but is soon at his mercy. Tamyra begs his life, and Bussy grants it. Then, shot from behind, Bussy falls.

Chapman protracts Bussy's death to an extent unusual in Renaissance drama. Bussy dies as he lived, "like himself."[4] Indeed, as Waith remarks, "The manner of his death makes it the most impressive act of self-assertion in the play."[5] Refusing Tamyra's aid, he insists on raising himself so he can die upright:

> Prop me, true sword, as thou hast ever done:
> The equal thought I bear of life and death,
> Shall make me faint on no side; I am up
> Here like a Roman statue; I will stand
> Till death hath made me marble: O my fame
> Live in despite of murder: take thy wings
> And haste thee where the gray-ey'd Morn perfines
> Her rosy chariot with Sabaean spices;
> Fly, where the Evening from th' Iberian vales
> Takes on her swarthy shoulders Hecate
> Crown'd with a grove of oaks; fly where men feel
> The burning axletree, and those that suffer
> Beneath the chariot of the Snowy Bear:
> And tell them all that D'Ambois now is hasting
> To the eternal dwellers.
>
>   (142–55)

Chapman too has risen, to the height of his style, joining the voice of his protagonist to that of the "Senecan" Hercules.[6] It is a speech that captures the essence of Bussy's heroic nature.

If these were Bussy's last words his death, while undeniably impressive, would be merely heroic. Like Tamburlaine, he would lack anything resembling a tragic sense of life. But in his final moments, Bussy—to adapt a line later spoken by Montsurrey—"sees and dies."

Continuing to exhibit magnanimity, Bussy forgives his murderers and Montsurrey, to whom he gives his sword. He then asks Montsurrey to forgive Tamyra. It is at this moment that Tamyra, silent since saving Montsurrey's life, begs Bussy to pardon her for writing the letter that has brought him to his death. Showing her wounds, she reveals that she has been tortured. For Bussy, it is the instant of tragic perception:

> O, my heart is broken.
> Fate, nor these murderers, Monsieur, nor the Guise,
> Have any glory in my death, but this:
> This killing spectacle: this prodigy:
> . . . .
> O frail condition of strength, valour, virtue,
> In me like warning fire upon the top
> Of some steep beacon, on a steeper hill;
> Made to express it like a falling star
> Silently glanc'd—that like a thunderbolt
> Look'd to have stuck, and shook the firmament. [*He dies.*]
>
> (178–81; 188–93)

Bussy's accomplishments, as he here acknowledges, are vastly disproportionate to his heroic aspirations. Indeed, as Lee Bliss observes, Bussy "accepts responsibility" for Tamyra's suffering, and recognizes "his failure to live up to his own values and intentions."[7]

Yet Chapman, in effect, has it both ways: Bussy has failed and not failed. For as Waith emphasizes, Bussy

> looks forward to an eternity in the company of the immortals. As a mortal, however, he regrets that his "strength, valour, virtue," have not been adequate to achieve the goals he set for himself. He is Herculean in both his recognition of mortal limitation and his confident assertion of the immortality of his spirit; his death, like Tamburlaine's, is both defeat and transcendence.[8]

Though his death seems to confirm Monsieur's thesis regarding the fate of greatness in the world, it also validates Bussy as a tragic hero. In any event, the play is, in MacLure's phrase, "not a demonstration but an experience";[9] and the heart of that experience is—or should be—a sense of astonishment, of tragic wonder. As the Friar's voluble shade reminds us, in what is almost surely a choral valediction,[10] Bussy is an incarnation of heroic energy:

> Farewell brave relicts of a complete man:
> Look up and see thy spirit made a star,
> Join flames with Hercules.
>
> (268–70)

Such a protagonist is not for all seasons or all tastes. Muir aptly compares the lines in which Bussy "calls up a gigantic vision of his memory being taken into the keeping of universal nature" to Hamlet's last words to Horatio: "The difference is great, the difference between an imagination which penetrates deep into human life, and one which is concentrated upon a great idea."[11] To compare the valedictions of the Friar and Horatio is to reach the same conclusion.

The Revenge of Bussy D'Ambois (1610) could scarcely be more unlike its remarkable predecessor. "It seems safe to say," MacLure observes, "that Chapman's wonder at the Herculean hero . . . diminished as he read more Epictetus 'the good Greek moralist' and began to meditate on Homer's 'fashion of an absolute man' in the *Odyssey*."[12] It also seems safe to say that *The Revenge* is not impressive as either demonstration or experience.

The chief problem, of course, is Chapman's "Senecal" protagonist, Clermont D'Ambois, that most reluctant of revengers. For almost the entire play, Chapman seems intent on using Clermont to exemplify what a man should be. Though deficient in dramatic interest, the play has at least presented a coherent thesis. But when Clermont commits suicide on learning that the Guise is dead, it becomes impossible to say precisely what Chapman has even managed to demonstrate.

The Guise's death is the first of the three deaths dramatized in the play. Struck down by the King's guardsmen, his last thoughts are of Clermont:

> Clermont, farewell, O didst thou see but this!
> But it is better; see by this the ice
> Broke to thine own blood, which thou wilt despise,
> When thou hear'st mine shed. Is there no friend here
> Will bear my love to him?
>
> (5.4.66–70)[13]

Before Aumale informs Clermont of the Guise's death, Clermont finally proceeds against Montsurrey. Forcing him to fight by threatening to let Tamyra torture him, Clermont achieves a most unvengeful vengeance:

> *Montsurrey*. . . . Farewell, I heartily forgive thee; wife, and thee. . . .
>   [*He gives his hand to Clermont and his wife.*]
> *Clermont*. Noble and Christian!
> *Tamyra*.   O, it breaks my heart!
> *Clermont*. And should; for all faults found in him before,
>   These words, this end, makes full amends and more.
>   Rest, worthy soul.
>
> (5.5.111–16)

Clermont's death follows almost at once. He watches in wonder as the ghosts of Bussy and the Guise (and others) dance around Montsurrey's body; then Aumale enters and delivers his message. For Clermont, there is nothing left but to take his own life: "Shall I live, and he / Dead, that alone gave means of life to me?" (149–50). Revenge is out of the question: "There's no disputing with the acts of kings, / Revenge is impious on their sacred persons" (151–52). And, in lines surely intended to contrast with Bussy's Herculean "Prop me, true sword" speech, Clermont prepares to launch himself toward death:

> Now, then, as a ship,
> Touching at strange and far-removed shores,
> Her men ashore go, for their several ends,
> Fresh water, victuals, precious stones, and pearl,
> All yet intentive (when the master calls,
> The ship to put off ready) to leave all
> Their greediest labours, lest they there be left
> To thieves or beasts, or be the country's slaves:
> So, now my master calls, my ship, my venture,
> All in one bottom put, all quite put off,
> Gone under sail, and I left negligent,
> To all the horrors of the vicious time,
> . . . .
> I come, my lord! Clermont, thy creature, comes.
> [*He kills himself.*]
>
> (175–86; 193)

It is an extraordinary speech—and nothing if not un-Stoical. "As for the Senecal man," MacLure remarks, "it is not always observed that *his* dying speech [unlike Bussy's] is almost entirely an act of devotion to his patron. . . . Hardly the last gesture of the self-sufficient man who is one with the All, but the passionate rejection of a world empty without his love."[14] But though Clermont is drawn toward death by his desire for union with Guise, he is also thrust from life by "all the horrors of the vicious time"; better to die than to be "ready every hour / To feed thieves, beasts, and be the slave of power" (191–92). Of this double deviation from the Stoic ideal Chapman makes almost nothing.[15]

Death in *The Tragedy of Caesar and Pompey* (1605)[16] is almost as bizarre, and certainly far more painful to witness. From the first onstage death, that of Crassinius, Chapman is intent on dramatizing what is brutally shocking: ". . . *enter Crassinius, a sword as thrust through his face*" (4.2.12 s.d.).[17] But the deaths that the play emphasizes are those of Pompey and Cato, the human frailty of the former being used as a foil for the perfected self-rule of the Stoic sage.

Pompey, unlike Cato, is a character whose nature is not fixed. The play shows him, in MacLure's words, "moving from Fortune to Virtue, from greatness to goodness. . . . Defeated by Caesar, he wins another kind of victory, because in losing an empire he can become purely a disciple of Cato, not only in justice but in righteousness."[18] By the time that his death is near, Pompey can speak like one for whom inwardness is all. But then the murderers come. At first, Pompey responds with composure, saying that he will kiss his children; he does so, and gives them his blessing. He is now ready to follow the murderers. Almost as soon as we lose sight of him he is attacked; but instead of dying offstage. *"Enter Pompey bleeding"* (259 s.d.). In the presence of his wife and their two children, he takes his anguished leave of the world:

> See, heavens, your sufferings! Is my country's love,
> The justice of an empire, piety,
> Worth this end in their leader? Last yet, life,
> And bring the gods off fairer: after this
> Who will adore or serve the deities?
> [*He hides his face with his robe.*]
>
> (259–63)

At this moment the murderers reappear; their leader issues a terse command: "Help hale him off, and take his head for Caesar" (264). And, to the horrified cries of his little boy ("Mother, O save us! Pompey, O my father!" [265]), Pompey is taken from the stage.

This is, one need hardly say, a scene of exceptional dramatic intensity. Indeed, the closest parallel that comes to mind is the slaughter of Macduff's wife and son. But what gives it the extraordinary *painfulness* of which I have spoken is the utter silence in which Pompey, his face covered, passes to his death. Not for him the splendid flare of courage that might mitigate the horror of his end. A broken as well as a bleeding man, he seems already dead.

The death of Cato, though even more shocking in terms of stage sensationalism, has far less emotional impact. One cannot be greatly moved by the death of someone who looks on life and death as Cato does:

> What have I now to think on in this world?
> Not one thought of the world: I go each minute
> Discharg'd of all cares that may fit my freedom.
> The next world and my soul, then, let me serve
> With her last utterance.
>
> (5.4.128–32)

Confident of immortality, he readies himself for death; his sword, brought by his page, will take him where he wants to go:

> Unsheathe! Is't sharp? T'is sweet! Now I am safe;
> Come Caesar, quickly now, or lose your vassal.
> Now wing thee, dear soul, and receive her, heaven.
> The earth, the air, and seas I know, and all
> The joys and horrors of their peace and wars,
> And now will see the gods' state, and the stars.
>
> (156–61)

He then falls on his sword. But as with the death of Pompey, Chapman insists on making us witness what is shocking and appalling. For Cato, despite his unflinching decisiveness, does his work ill. To finish what the sword began he pulls out his own entrails. Portius, his son, cannot bring himself to look upon him: "Look, look in to my father! O I fear / He is no sight for me to bear and live" (170–71). But Cato's physician, on examining him, discovers that his entrails may be sewed up, "Being yet unperish'd" (175). "Stand off; now they are not," replies Cato:

> [*He thrusts him back and plucks out his entrails.*]
> Have he my curse that my life's least part saves;
> Just men are only free, the rest are slaves. [*Dies.*]
>
> (175–77)

Caesar, entering, learns that he has been left, as Chapman wrote in the play's "Argument," "without his victory victor." Such is the death of Cato, a death no less ghastly than exemplary.[19] "Caesar survives, a slave of policy, ruling slaves."[20]

The death of Byron in *The Tragedy of Charles Duke of Byron* (1608) differs markedly from those just considered. A traitor to his king, he is justly executed. But more important is the fact of his extraordinary eloquence. As is not the case with Pompey or Cato, to think of Byron is to think of what he *says.*

When Byron mounts the scaffold he is still a choleric, intimidating figure. He has much of Bussy about him. One could imagine Bussy greeting the arrival of the executioner as he does: "Death, slave, down, or by the blood that moves me / I'll pluck thy throat out! Go, I'll call you straight" (5.4.164–65).[21]

He insists on blindfolding himself, then rebukes a bishop for admonishing him to look heavenward. Calling the executioner back, Byron has the man guide him to the place he is to kneel. But he is not ready to die yet, and again threatens the executioner. "My lord, you make too much of this your body, / Which is no more your own," says Vitry, Captain of the Guard (190–91). "Nor is it yours," Byron replies:

> I'll take my death with all the horrid rites
> And representments of the dread it merits;
> Let tame nobility and numbed fools
> That apprehend not what they undergo,
> Be such exemplary and formal sheep.
> I will not have him touch me till I will.
>
> (191–97)

In all this he almost seems a tragic version of Shakespeare's Barnardine, who refuses to die on any man's persuasion. The readiness must be *his*. But the lines that follow sound another—and deeper—note. Addressing the soldiers of the guard, he says he would be "much bound" to the man who would shoot him and thus spare him so shameful a death:

> Is it not pity I should lose my life
> By such a bloody and infamous stroke?
>
> (211–12)

And a soldier answers:

> Now by thy spirit, and thy better Angel,
> If thou wert clear, the continent of France
> Would shrink beneath the burthen of thy death
> Ere it would bear it.
>
> (213–16)

Indeed, the soldier goes yet further: even if guilty, Byron has more merit than "the King's chief minion" (220).

Byron now ceases to rage. Instead, he commends his love to those closest to him, then takes his farewell of the world:

> And so farewell for ever! Never more
> Shall any hope of my revival see me;
> Such is the endless exile of dead men.
> Summer succeeds the Spring; Autumn the Summer;
> The frosts of Winter the fall'n leaves of Autumn:
> All these and all fruits in them yearly fade,
> And every year return: but cursed man
> Shall never more renew his vanish'd face.
>
> (245–52)

The tone of these spacious and eloquent lines is unlike anything
else in Chapman. But in his next words Byron discards the elegiac,
exhibiting something of his characteristic aggressiveness:

> Fall on your knees then, statists, ere ye fall,
> That you may rise again: knees bent too late,
> Stick you in earth like statues: see in me
> How you are pour'd down from your clearest heavens;
> Fall lower yet, mix'd with th' unmoved centre,
> That your own shadows may no longer mock ye.
>
> (253–58)

Finally, speaking as if from a position of dominance rather than that
of a condemned man, he orders the executioner to strike:

> Strike, strike, O strike; fly, fly, commanding soul,
> And on thy wings for this thy body's breath,
> Bear the eternal victory of Death!
>
> (259–61)

Whether the victory referred to is the soul's or Death's,[22] Byron has
turned his own death into a triumphant demonstration of greatness.[23]

The Tragedy of Chabot Admiral of France (1622)[24] also dramatizes only the death of its protagonist. Chabot, as Waith observes,
"is what Byron pretends to be—an innocent benefactor of his
country, falsely accused of treason by those who are jealous of
him."[25] Yet Chabot's death, one regrets to say, does not show
Chapman at the height of his powers. The play's theme, according to
Peter Ure, is "a wrong done to the soul," "a tragic assault upon and
invasion of a man's inward authority, created by the envy and
innovating spirit of power."[26] This potentially moving idea is feebly
dramatized. Chabot's death neither rises above nor sinks below the
rest of the play. Kneeling before the King, he takes his "blest
hand":

> live happy.
> May all you trust have no less faith than Chabot!
> Oh! [Dies.]
>
> (5.3.200–2)[27]

"His heart is broken," says his wife; and the King comments that
Chabot "has a victory in's death; this world / Deserv'd him not.

How soon he was translated / To glorious eternity!" (202; 206–8). All in all, as MacLure remarks, "This unhappily anticipates a purple death bed scene from some uplifting Victorian novel."[28] It is dispiriting to find the creator of Bussy end on so edifying a note.

No less than Chapman, Webster stands out among his Jacobean contemporaries for his exceptional emphasis on the dying moments of his characters. In *The White Devil* (1612) Webster dramatizes seven deaths (two in dumb shows), a number less remarkable than the wide range of effects he manages to encompass. The deaths of Isabella and Camillo are distanced by being performed in dumb shows, courtesy of the magic of a conjuror (2.2.23 s.d. 1–12; 2.2.37 s.d. 1–14).[29] Bracciano watches Isabella, his wife, kiss his poisoned portrait "thrice" and die; then Camillo, Vittoria's inconvenient husband, has his neck broken by Flamineo. Both deaths are grotesque, perhaps even the stuff of "horrid laughter."[30] The death of Marcello, Flamineo's virtuous brother, is more shocking, but is presented with the suddenness that one associates with certain forms of comic violence. One expects bloodshed between the brothers—they agree to fight a duel—and Marcello sends his sword so Flamineo can match its length. Then Flamineo enters while Marcello is conversing with their mother: "I have brought your weapon back," he says (5.2.14), running his brother through. "You have brought it home indeed" (15), is the dying Marcello's equally laconic rejoinder.

These deaths are in the tradition of witty villainy, in which greater emphasis is given to the ingenuity of the murderer than to the way those at point of death see the world and themselves. The death of Bracciano, though compassed with the guilefulness proper to this tradition, is unusual in that Webster is equally concerned with what Bracciano experiences during his last moments.

Death comes to Bracciano from Lodovico, who poisons the beaver of his helmet. "O my brain's on fire," he cries out, "the helmet is poison'd" (5.3.4). But he does not die at once; dying is not easy for him:

> O thou strong heart!
> There's such a covenant 'tween the world and it,
> They're loth to break.
>
> (13–15)

His son cries out to him: "O my most loved father!" (15); but Bracciano's thoughts are of Vittoria:

Remove the boy away,—
Where's this good woman? had I infinite worlds
They were too little for thee. Must I leave thee?

. . . .

[*To Vittoria.*] Do not kiss me, for I shall poison thee.

(16–18; 26)

His concern here is both moving and ironic, since we are reminded
of how Isabella came by her death. But Bracciano does not sustain
the note of tenderness, moralizing instead on how "soft natural
death" is not the lot of the great: "horror waits on princes" (29; 34).
And when Vittoria, obviously in tears, calls attention to her
plight—"I am lost for ever" (35)—his only response is to remark:
"How miserable a thing it is to die / 'Mongst women howling!" (36–
37). Informed that Franciscans are ready to give him extreme unc-
tion, he again reveals how hard he clings to life:

On pain of death, let no man name death to me,
It is a word infinitely terrible,—
Withdraw into our cabinet.

(39–41)

When we next see him he is borne in on his bed, mad. He no longer
recognizes Vittoria when she speaks to him (82), but later imagines
"Flamineo that kill'd his brother / Is dancing on the ropes there:
and he carries / A money-bag in each hand, to keep him even" (109–
11). Looking at Vittoria, he asks who she is, and remarks that the
arras powder in her hair "makes her look as if she had sinn'd in the
pastry" (118). He does not speak to her, let alone comprehend what
she suffers.

The death of Bracciano, protracted far beyond the usual limits of
death-by-poison, is now at hand. Last rites are administered to him
by the "Franciscans," who are then left alone with him; as soon as
they have him to themselves they strip off their habits, revealing
themselves as Lodovico and Gasparo, agents of Isabella's brother
Francisco de Medici. What happens next is reminiscent of *Alphonsus, Antonio's Revenge,* and *The Revenger's Tragedy.* Lodovico and
Gasparo subject Bracciano to a barrage of mockery and vituperation. He is, they tell him, deluded, damned; they continue to hurl
insults at him as he lies speechless, seemingly near death:

Gasparo. This is Count Lodovico.
Lodovico.   This Gasparo.

And thou shalt die like a poor rogue.
Gasparo. And stink
Like a dead fly-blown dog.
Lodovico. And be forgotten
Before thy funeral sermon.

(164–67)

Suddenly, with what is obviously shocking vehemence, Bracciano cries out twice for Vittoria. But when Vittoria and her attendants enter, Gasparo sends them away: "For Charity, / For Christian charity, avoid the chamber" (172–73). Lodovico takes no further chances:

> You would prate, sir. This is a true-love knot
> Sent from the Duke of Florence. [*Bracciano is strangled.*]

(174–75)

Finally, this all-but-unkillable man is given his death.

In the death of Bracciano, Webster combines interest in how a dramatic character confronts death and the "quaintness" with which the art of murder is practised. Despite the emphasis on Bracciano in the first stages of his agony, however, his death is dramatized primarily from the latter point of view. Certainly the savage wit of the hovering "Franciscans" dominates his final moments.[31]

The deaths of Vittoria and Flamineo, at the hands of the same limners of night-pieces, reverse the dramaturgical emphasis: here Webster is more concerned with exhibiting how these two extraordinary figures respond to the challenge of death. Indeed, their deaths are such that they almost triumph over their murderers.

Surprised by Lodovico, Gasparo, and two other conspirators, Flaminio is bound to a pillar and forced to undergo ritual abuse before he is killed. But unlike Bracciano (and many another victim in Renaissance plays) he is able to wrest from his murderers much of the pleasure they anticipate. Ironic, cynical, iconoclastic, he refuses to play the role in which they have cast him. To Lodovico's threat that he will "strike [him] / Into the centre" (5.6.190–91), he responds not with fear, but derision and laughter:

> Thou'lt do it like a hangman; a base hangman;
> Not like a noble fellow, for thou seest
> I cannot strike again.

(192–94)

The laughter—so thoroughly in character for Flamineo—leaves Lodovico temporarily at a loss: "Dost laugh?" he asks (194). Instead of dominating the scene he has become, at least for the moment, an inadvertent straight man in Flamineo's "performance." Flamineo's reply—"Wouldst have me die, as I was born, in whining?" (195)—is followed by Gasparo's effort to intervene; he fares no better. By now Lodovico is reduced to ridiculous bluster:

> O I could kill you forty times a day
> And use't four year together; 'twere too little:
> Naught grieves but that you are too few to feed
> The famine of our vengeance.
>
> (198–201)

But Flamineo, it seems, looks as if his mind were altogether elsewhere; for Lodovico asks, "What dost think on?" (201). Flamineo's answer emphasizes the futility of Lodovico's efforts to break his spirit:

> Nothing; of nothing: leave thy idle questions,—
> I am i'th'way to study a long silence,
> To prate were idle,—I remember nothing.
> There's nothing of so infinite vexation
> As man's own thoughts.
>
> (202–6)

As if acknowledging that Flamineo may be killed but not made to exhibit baseness or cowardice, Lodovico now turns his attentions to Vittoria:

> O thou glorious strumpet,
> Could I divide thy breath from this pure air
> When't leaves thy body, I would suck it up
> And breathe't upon some dunghill.
>
> (206–9)

Though Vittoria had earlier sought pity (183–85), the speech fails utterly of its object; Vittoria merely answers that he has too good a face for a hangman, but if he is going to be one he should "do [his] office in right form"—that is, kneel and ask her forgiveness. Lodovico reacts with characteristic violence:

> O thou hast been a most prodigious comet,
> But I'll cut off your train:—kill the Moor first.
>
> (214–15)

Now death is almost upon her. Yet instead of becoming the terrified woman that Lodovico would make her, Vittoria utters an imperious comand: "You shall not kill her [Zanche] first. Behold my breast,— / I will be waited on in death; my servant / Shall never go before me" (216–18). For the last time Lodovico addresses her: "Thou dost tremble,— / Methinks fear should dissolve thee into air" (221– 22). "O thou art deceiv'd," she replies. "I am too true a woman: / Conceit can never kill me" (223–24).[32] When death comes it will find her unintimidated:

> I will not in my death shed one base tear,
> Or if look pale, for want of blood, not fear.
>
> (225–26)

Zanche, showing similar courage, wittily notes that not even death can make her "look pale."

Rarely has a revenger had to put up with such frustration in the very moments of his triumph. A Renaissance revenger denied the customary opportunity to revel and gloat is a diminished thing.

Yet if Lodovico cannot make his victims follow his own imagined scenario, he can at least kill them. "Strike, strike, / With a joint motion," he commands (231–32).[33] Even now Vittoria and Flamineo mock their murderers, dominating the stage with their words,[34] while Lodovico and his followers remain strangely silent:

> *Vittoria.*   'Twas a manly blow—
>   The next thous giv'st, murder some sucking infant,
>   And then thou wilt be famous.
> *Flamineo.*   O what blade is't?
>   A Toledo, or an English fox?
>   I ever thought a cutler should distinguish
>   The cause of my death, rather than a doctor.
>   Search my wound deeper.
>
> (232–38)

Then the tone changes. Speaking with sudden sententiousness, Vittoria reflects that "my greatest sin lay in my blood. / Now my blood pays for't" (240–41). Whether or not she is addressing Flamineo, it is he who answers. Though he was ready to kill her himself earlier in this scene, he now perceives that she is worth his love. He offers not only that, but a kind of apologia for her life:[35]

>   Th'art a noble sister—
>   I love thee now; if woman do breed man
>   She ought to teach him manhood: fare thee well.

> Know many glorious women that are fam'd
> For masculine virtue, have been vicious
> Only a happier silence did betide them—
> She hath no faults, who hath the art to hide them.
>
> (241–47)

But Vittoria is too near death to speak of her affection for him—if indeed she has any:

> My soul, like to a ship in a black storm,
> Is driven I know not whither.
>
> (248–49)

It has recently been said that Flamineo and Vittoria "die apart, with neither interest in nor compassion for each other."[36] This seems true enough of Vittoria, but Flamineo continues to exhibit interest in Vittoria, if not compassion for her, until he believes her to be dead. Instead of passively letting her soul be driven, he advises her, she should "cast anchor" (249):

> We cease to grieve, cease to be Fortune's slaves,
> Nay cease to die by dying. Art thou gone
> And thou so near the bottom?—false report
> Which says that women vie with the nine Muses
> For nine tough durable lives.
>
> (252–56)

By reversing Vittoria's emphasis from "whither" to whence, Flamineo is able to treat death as finality. To "cast anchor," in his terms, is merely to die. In a sense, his speech stands in the same relation to Vittoria's as Hamlet's graveyard ruminations to "To be, or not to be." Yet once one begins to talk of souls, eschatological questions become inescapable: the ship of the soul must finally come to port. Turning from Vittoria, Flamineo now becomes wholly self-absorbed. He has his own dying to do: "I do not look / Who went before, nor who shall follow me; / No, at myself I will begin and end" (256–58). He is himself alone. Suddenly, however, scruples of the sort he rarely admits to[37] force themselves into his consciousness; like Vittoria, he thinks beyond the grave:

> While we look up to heaven we confound
> Knowledge with knowledge. O I am in a mist.
>
> (259–60)

The professed certitude of the cynical naturalist is, for the moment at least, confounded.

Vittoria, if she hears these lines (the counterpart of her earlier reference to her soul), does not look up to heaven at her death. Nor are her final words addressed to Flamineo:

> O happy they that never saw the court,
> Nor ever knew great man but by report. [*Vittoria dies.*]
>
> (261–62)

This couplet has been said to contain "the only words that fall from her which she could never have uttered."[38] Yet as Bliss observes, "Vittoria's final knowledge may indeed be to discover by experience the truth of such maxims"—even though "the trite, simplistic formula inadequately expresses our own response to her life or her death."[39] In any event, Vittoria dies voicing highly conventional sentiments, not aflame with subversive individualism. Of Bracciano and her love for him she makes no mention. But the meaning seems to be: would she had never known him.

Flamineo takes no notice of Vittoria's death. Instead, he gathers himself for a final speech ("I recover like a spent taper, for a flash / And instantly go out" [263–64]). What does Flamineo think of the life he must leave? After such experience, what knowledge?

Like Vittoria, Flamineo comments on the perilous plight of those whose lives come in contact with the great. His, however, is a pander's-eye view; service, not love, has been the element in which he has lived. Hence he addresses those who serve the great:

> Let all that belong to great men remember th' old wives' tradition, to be like the lions i' th' Tower on Candlemas day, to mourn if the sun shine, for fear of the pitiful remainder of winter to come.
>
> (265–68)

He does not renounce serving the great—but one must be more prudent than he has been. Then, shifting from prose to verse, he speaks more directly of his life and death:

> 'Tis well yet there's some goodness in my death,
> My life was a black charnel: I have caught
> An everlasting cold. I have lost my voice
> Most irrecoverably.
>
> (269–72)

In these terse, ironic phrases, Flamineo speaks like one at the point of death. Each phrase seems a separate effort; he does not need to tell us—like Edmund in *King Lear*—that he is gasping for breath.[40]

Lodovico and the other murderers have been silent since the

command to kill. The scene has belonged to Vittoria and Flamineo, who (except for their responses when struck) speak only to each other or to us. Now, as if he had happened to notice them while in the midst of matters of greater consequence, Flamineo turns to Lodovico and his henchmen: "Farewell / glorious villains!" (272)— a mocking tribute, surely. Without further reference to them, he returns to his discourse as if they had never intruded on his consciousness:

> This busy trade of life appears most vain,
> Since rest breeds rest, where all seek pain by pain.
> Let no harsh flattering bells resound my knell,
> Strike thunder, and strike loud to my farewell. [*Dies.*]
>
> (273–76)

Freer, who calls attention to the artful contrast between Vittoria's brevity and Flamineo's extraordinary volubility, approaches these lines as another instance of Flamineo's mockery of his murderers: "the dragging pace of the whole performance," he observes "constitutes Flamineo's last taunting of his impatient and uncomprehending assassins"; even the concluding couplet is "enormously ironic," since it alludes to "the English ambassador knocking down the door."[41]

Critics of Webster should be aware of the danger of confounding knowledge with knowledge. Yet it does not seem to me that these lines, Flamineo's final "performance," are addressed to the onstage audience at all. Certainly it is a bravura performance; Flamineo is so much caught up in it that one is inclined to believe his one acknowledgment of the "glorious villains" accurately reflects the degree to which they now concern him. His terminal couplet, which in fact precedes the ambassador's order to "break ope the doors" (277), should be considered in context. Flamineo has just renounced "This busy trade of life" as "most vain." What of the life to come—if any? Earlier he had asked Bracciano "what religion's best / For a man to die in?" (5.2.129–30). Now he rejects the customary clangor of bells. Others besides Flamineo might describe their sound as "harsh"—but why "flattering"? Perhaps because they speak of a life beyond the grave. In this line, it would seem, Flamineo wittily reverses the conventional expectation that truth should be harsh, flattery sweet. Thunder, equally unconventionally, stands not for the voice of God but for something more akin to the violent energies by which Flamineo has lived and which should flash forth at his death.

Yet even if this is what Flamineo is saying, is it what he actually believes? The final couplet, Ralph Berry observes, "is a superb final curtain, and Flamineo [not to speak of Webster] knows it." For Berry, "Flamineo at the last *is* an actor; or, if one prefers, a *poseur*, a man for whom striking attitudes is existence."[42] Or is one to agree with Freer that "although Webster set limits upon Flamineo's knowledge and voice, the character was still permitted to explore these as fully as possible and finally to understand them for himself"?[43] What one makes of Flamineo will be shaped by the conception of him brought to the final scene. And what Webster has made of him throughout is sufficiently ambiguous to elicit a variety of readings. Flamineo would seem one of those characters created more to raise questions than to answer them.[44]

In *The Duchess of Malfi* (1614), Webster gives even greater emphasis to the dying moments of his characters. Again he dramatizes seven deaths; but in only one instance—and it is a special case— does he deprive the dying of *characteristic* speeches and actions.

Of all the deaths in the play, that of the Duchess is of course the most memorable. Her suffering is far more protracted and psychologically intense than anything in *The White Devil*. One need only mention the scene during her imprisonment when Ferdinand visits her in the darkness, saying he has "come to seal [his] peace with [her]":

> Here's a hand [*Gives her a dead man's hand.*]
> To which you have vow'd much love; the ring upon't
> You gave.
>
> (4.1.43–45)[45]

She kisses the hand, believing it to be that of her husband, Antonio:

> You are very cold.
> I fear you are not well after your travel:—
> Hah! lights!—O, horrible!
>
> (51–53)

What she sees is, in its way, more horrible still:

> *Here is discovered, behind a traverse, the artificial figures of Antonio and his children, appearing as if they were dead.* (55 s.d.)

The Duchess must live on, believing she has lost all those who are most precious to her.[46] Her torments continue, for Ferdinand means "to bring her to despair" (116). Finally, after a visitation by madmen,[47] Bosola enters: "I am come to make thy tomb" (4.2.116). The Duchess shows no fear. But Bosola's purpose is to induce in her a *contemptus mundi* attitude rather than the passionate involvement with life and love that has characterized her throughout. As Roger Stilling has noted, Ferdinand's "final weapon [is] the denigration of the body"—hence Bosola's insistence that the Duchess is "a box of worm-seed" (124). Yet she is what she has always been: "I am Duchess of Malfi still" (142). "The statement is itself," Stilling observes, "an act of romantic self-assertion. She disowns nothing in her past actions or her love and marriage, for to do so would be to disown a part of herself."[48] The Duchess, though Ferdinand's prisoner, is in this essential respect beyond his reach.

Executioners enter, with coffin, cords, and bell. "Here is a present from your princely brothers," says Bosola (166), who continues to strive to "bring [her] / . . . to mortification" (176–77). There is no evidence that he succeeds. He cannot subvert what has given her life meaning. All he can do is kill her.

The Duchess takes her farewell of Cariola, whom she expects to be allowed to live. Then follow some perplexing lines:

> I pray thee, look thou giv'st my little boy
> Some syrup for his cold, and let the girl
> Say her prayers, ere she sleep.
>
> (203–5)

One understands that Webster is seeking to emphasize the tenderly maternal aspect of the Duchess. But, as M. C. Bradbrook observes, "The suggestion that the Duchess knows her children to be alive removes the whole emotional prop and scaffolding of the scene. She had been in a peace 'beyond hope and beyond despair': this touch of 'humanity' is as out of place as it is offensive in itself."[49]

The only possible justification for these lines is one that Webster does not provide—that the Duchess has finally severed contact with a reality too painful to confront. But with the exception of this reference to her children, everything she says suggests self-mastery. Moving closer to death, she forgives her executioners. Bosola, slow learner that he is, tries once again: "Doth not death fright you?" "Who would be afraid on't?" she replies, "Knowing to meet such excellent company / In th' other world" (210–12). "Yet," Bosola persists, "methinks, / The manner of your death should much afflict you, / This cord should terrify you?" (213–15). The Duchess, who has had enough of his hovering ministrations, his importunities, lashes out in exasperation:

Not a whit:
What would it pleasure me to have my throat cut
With diamonds? or to be smothered
With cassia? or to be shot to death with pearls?
. . . .
anyway, for heaven-sake,
So I were out of your whispering:—tell my brothers
That I perceive death, now I am well awake,
Best gift is they can give, or I can take.

(215–18; 222–25)

The executioners are now "ready"; she addresses them with complete composure: "Dispose my breath how please you, but my body / Bestow upon my women, will you?" (228–29). Having been satisfied on this last point,[50] the Duchess orders her executioners to proceed:

Pull, and pull strongly, for your able strength
Must pull down heaven upon me:—
Yet stay; heaven-gates are not so highly arch'd
As princes' palaces, they that enter there
Must go upon their knees.—[*Kneels.*] Come violent death,
Serve for mandragora to make me sleep!
Go tell my brothers, when I am laid out,
They then may feed in quiet. [*They strangle her.*]

(230–37)[51]

The Duchess, as Bliss has remarked, "dies in a way that fuse[s] in one final paradoxical heroism the 'spirit of greatness' with the apparently incompatible, willful, and earthbound 'spirit of woman.'"[52] Duchess of Malfi still, she dies like herself.

Or so it must seem—though in fact Webster, perhaps influenced by *Othello* (see chapter 8), has what is in effect a second death in store for her. Bosola sends someone to kill the two captive children, and has Cariola brought back and strangled; in marked contrast to her mistress, she fights desperately for life, biting and scratching her executioners. Then Ferdinand enters, is shown the children and the Duchess, and offers Bosola only his "pardon" for doing what he had been ordered to do. Left alone with the Duchess, Bosola suddenly detects signs of life:

—she stirs; here's life:
Return, fair soul, from darkness, and lead mine
Out of this sensible hell:—she's warm, she breathes:—
Upon thy pale lips I will melt my heart

To store them with fresh colour:—who's there?
Some cordial drink!—Alas! I dare not call:
So pity would destroy pity:—her eye opes,
And heaven in it seems to ope, that late was shut,
To take me up to mercy.

(341–49)

"Antonio!" the Duchess exclaims (350). Perhaps she is merely expressing her sense of loss. Yet why should the composure with which she met death change to this? Does she imagine that she is waking from death's sleep in Antonio's arms? Fortunately, the idea is as unpersuasive as it is "offensive." Yet it does seem that the Duchess mistakes Bosola for Antonio. Who but her husband would kiss and embrace her? For a far clearer reason than was the case in her earlier reference to her children, she behaves like one in a state of shock. Understandably, she thinks Antonio is holding her. But Bosola, who misses the full significance of what is happening, realizes only that she thinks Antonio is alive. On this he builds: .

> Yes, madam, he is living—
> The dead bodies you saw were but feign'd statues;
> He's reconcil'd to your brothers; the Pope hath wrought
> The atonement.

(350–53)

"Mercy!" (353)—her only other word before she dies—can also mean more than one thing. It may be she believes what Bosola says. Yet she has, after all, no reason to trust him. What if she thinks that he has, in effect, played Antonio in order to plague her, and is now tormenting her with lies? As she said to Bosola earlier, *"It is some mercy, when men kill with speed"* (4.1.110).

Act 5, as Bliss has remarked, "could . . . with some justice be called 'Bosola's Revenge.' "[53] Yet Bosola proves, of course, little more adroit as a revenger than he was as an intelligencer. Inadvertently, he brings about the death of Julia, the Cardinal's mistress, who dotes upon him enough to conceal him while she asks the Cardinal the reason for his melancholy. When he answers that "by my appointment, the great Duchess of Malfi, / And two of her young children, four nights since, / Were strangled" (5.2.267–70), Julia blurts out that he has "undone" himself: "It lies not in me to conceal it" (273,274). Misconstruing her words, the Cardinal immediately acts to silence her, saying he will swear her to secrecy "upon this book" (275). "Kiss it," he continues (276); no sooner has she done so than he reveals it was poisoned. Too late, Bosola attempts to intervene: "For pity-sake, hold!" (281). The well-intentioned line is striking in its irrelevance. In only moments Julia will be dead. Ironically, like the Duchess, she forgives her murderer—though for an entirely different reason:

> I forgive you—
> This equal piece of justice you have done,
> For I betray'd your counsel to that fellow.
>
> (281–83)

"O foolish woman," says Bosola, shirking responsibility for her death, "Couldst not thou have poison'd him?" Her answer, before her final, characteristically Websterian phrase, resonates when spoken to one so given to the optative as Bosola:

> 'Tis weakness,
> Too much to think what should have been done—I go,
> I know not whither. [*Dies.*]
>
> (286–89)[54]

If Bosola intervenes too tardily to save Julia, his precipitancy is directly responsible for the death of Antonio, whom he mistakes for the Cardinal. Arriving at the Cardinal's lodgings at midnight in order to bear away the body of Julia, Bosola overhears the Cardinal plotting his death. Moments later, Antonio, who has come under the preposterous delusion that he can achieve a reconciliation with the Cardinal, crosses his path. "Fall right my sword!" says Bosola, stabbing him; "I'll not give thee so much leisure as to pray" (5.4.45–46). Antonio, who aptly describes himself as "a most wretched thing, / That only have thy benefit in death, / To appear myself" (48–50), has blundered his way to death; his behavior is characteristically ineffectual. And Bosola, with Antonio's blood on his sword, manifests his customary refusal to accept responsibility for his own actions:

> —Antonio!
> The man I would have sav'd 'bove mine own life!
> We are merely the stars' tennis-balls, struck and banded
> Which way please them—
>
> (52–55)

What we have seen, surely, is a rash act by Bosola, insufficient in itself to serve as evidence that human volition is meaningless. The stars, one may say, shine still; but any connection between them and the lives of Webster's *dramatis personae* remains highly questionable. One need seek no further than the fury and the mire of human veins.

Presiding over the death of Antonio as he did over that of the Duchess, Bosola now seeks to speak killing words of truth rather than to preserve life with lies. The Duchess and two of their children, he whispers, are murdered. This revelation not only hastens Antonio's death, but occasions a speech in which he expresses an attitude toward life strikingly reminiscent of that which Bosola futilely sought to instill in the Duchess:

> I would not now
> Wish my wounds balm'd, nor heal'd, for I have no use
> To put my life to. In all our quest of greatness,
> Like wanton boys whose pastime is their care,
> We follow after bubbles, blown in th'air.
> Pleasure of life, what is't? only the good hours
> Of an ague.
>
> (62–68)

How much smaller—and weaker—Antonio is than the Duchess, who could never be brought to espouse such a view of life. He does not expatiate on what the Duchess has meant to him; indeed, her role in his life seems subsumed in the phrase "quest of greatness"— which leads to his final admonition regarding his surviving son: "And let my son fly the courts of princes" (72). The world is fraught with perils—especially the court. The safest life is the best. Prudential, sententious, timorous Antonio: never are we more aware of how much the Duchess married beneath herself.

Having dispatched the wrong man, Bosola confronts the Cardinal, whose cries for help prove futile. (In a variation of the familiar motif of the witty villain who ironically places himself at the mercy of his enemy, the Cardinal has made his guests promise not to heed his cries should he call for help.) But before killing the Cardinal, Bosola stabs Antonio's innocent servant, lest he "unbarricade the door / To let in rescue" (5.5.35–36). The act is not near his conscience; asked to explain why he seeks the Cardinal's death, he reveals the body of Antonio:

> Slain by my hand unwittingly:—
> Pray, and be sudden; when thou kill'd'st thy sister,
> Thou took'st from Justice her most equal balance,
> And left her naught but her sword.
>
> (38–41)

The speech is pure Bosola. No matter that he himself killed Antonio—and the Duchess; the Cardinal is made to absorb total responsibility for both deaths.

The deaths of Ferdinand, the Cardinal, and Bosola occur in the welter of violence that follows.[55] As Bosola discovers when the Cardinal begs for mercy,

> Now it seems thy greatness was only outward;
> For thou fall'st faster of thyself, than calamity
> Can drive thee. I'll not waste longer time: there! [*Stabs him.*]
>
> (42–44)

Yet for all his skill at shedding blood, the Cardinal is "hurt," not slain; Bosola strikes again, this time to better effect: "Shall I die like a leveret / Without any resistance? help, help, help! / I am slain!" (45–47). Instead of summoning aid, these words provide a cue for the entry of Ferdinand, who in his madness stabs the Cardinal and mortally wounds Bosola. Nearing death, the Cardinal turns sententious: "O Justice! / I suffer now, for what hath former been: / *Sorrow is held the eldest child of sin*" (53–55). Cold to the heart, he seems incapable of a more fervent or imaginative response. Bosola next strikes down Ferdinand, "thou main cause / Of my undoing" (63–64). Lucid at the last, Ferdinand expresses a sense of recognition far more compelling than his brother's trite and generalized moral formula:

> My sister! O! my sister! there's the cause on't:
> *Whether we fall by ambition, blood, or lust,*
> *Like diamonds, we are cut with our own dust.* [*Dies.*]
>
> (71–73)

How different this acceptance of one's own self-destructiveness is from the creed of Bosola.

The deaths of the Cardinal and Bosola are further protracted, with greater emphasis, of course, being given to the latter. Bosola's grim satisfaction as he contemplates the Cardinal is devoid, one may note, of moral animus:

> I do glory
> That thou, which stood'st like a huge pyramid
> Begun upon a large and ample base,
> Shalt end in a little point, a kind of nothing.
>
> (76–79)

Here we have what might be called the revenge of Nobody on
Somebody; that the Cardinal is a villain seems less significant than
that he has been one of the great—and that the unthought-on
Bosola has brought him down. Finally, Pescara (who had noticed
that the Cardinal's cries sounded too convincing to be feigned) and
the others break down the doors and enter. "How comes this?"
asks one of them (80). In a single extraordinary sentence, Bosola
answers:

> Revenge, for the Duchess of Malfi, murdered
> By th' Arragonian brethren; for Antonio,
> Slain by this hand; for lustful Julia,
> Poison'd by this man; and lastly, for myself,
> That was an actor in the main of all
> Much 'gainst mine own good nature, yet i'th'end
> Neglected.
>
> (81–87)

How much Bosola has to take vengeance for—and how inextricably
involved he is in the guilt he punishes! Even as he insists that he has
acted contrary to his "good nature," the bitterness of being denied
his reward for services rendered still rankles; his jaws snap shut on
"neglected."

Before Bosola's final speech the Cardinal dies, his last words
unusual in a period so intensely concerned with the perpetuation of
one's name in the world: "And now, I pray, let me / Be laid by, and
never thought of" (89–90). It is as if he acquiesces in the propriety
of his own nothingness. Bosola, whose version of his role in the
events of the play we have just heard, is called a "wretched thing of
blood" by Malateste (92), who asks for more information regarding
how Antonio was slain. "In a mist," he answers:

> I know not how—
> Such a mistake as I have often seen
> In a play:—O, I am gone!—
> We are only like dead walls, or vaulted graves,
> That ruin'd, yields no echo:—Fare you well—
> It may be pain, but no harm to me to die
> In so good a quarrel. O, this gloomy world!
> In what a shadow, or deep pit of darkness,
> Doth womanish and fearful mankind live!
> Let worthy minds ne'er stagger in distrust
> To suffer death, or shame for what is just—
> Mine is another voyage. [Dies.]
>
> (94–105)

Bosola, who wishes he had followed what he believes to have been his essential nature, prefers not to speak of Antonio's death; both "mist" and the allusion to plays are designed, of course, to serve as extenuation, if not exculpation; yet the basic fact is that Bosola cannot provide an adequate explanation: "I know not how." (On the basis of extant Renaissance plays, it is hard to give credence to his assertion that comparable blunders "often" occurred in pre-Websterian drama.) But Bosola—after one of the Websterian "breaks" of the sort noted by M. C. Bradbrook[56]—moves to the more comfortable terrain of generalized moral commentary. His last line, however, tantalizes by its ambiguity. Does he merely mean that his life's voyage is over, and that he is embarking toward death? Or is this an implicit acknowledgment that even his death "[i]n so good a quarrel" does not place him among "worthy minds" who suffer shame or die "for what is just"? Perhaps at the last Bosola is able to see himself without illusions. His life, in any event, has been sordid, mercenary, fraught with self-deception. The "lords of truth," to whom Delio refers in the play's closing lines, are men of another stamp.[57]

4

Beaumont and Fletcher

Shortly before the end of the first decade of the seventeenth century, Beaumont and Fletcher began their brief but momentous collaboration. "The two dramatists," as Clifford Leech has remarked, "worked together for only four or five years, and Fletcher went on writing, alone or in collaboration with others, for twelve years more." Nevertheless, Leech continues, the plays collected in the "Beaumont and Fletcher" Folios (1647, 1679) exhibit "a certain uniformity of style"—attributable "to the almost continuous presence of Fletcher's hand, now dominant, now merely contributory, yet always bestowing a recognisable touch."[1]

What is true of the plays in general is also true of their representation of death. The "Beaumont and Fletcher" plays give considerable emphasis to the exemplary death, already a notable feature of the drama. But their special province is pathos. Unlike both villain-plays and tragedies with a strong heroic element, these plays characteristically invite audiences to weep profusely at what may be called (in the words of the Prologue to *Romeo and Juliet*) "the misadventured piteous overthrows" of the virtuous and innocent.

Though it is easy to deride their sentimentality, these plays appealed deeply to seventeenth century audiences. It is worth asking why. The influence of women in the audience may, one suspects, help to explain the prevalence of characters like Aspatia in *The Maid's Tragedy*. But the appeal of such figures, as these lines from Thomas Stanley's "On the Edition" indicate, extended to men as well:

> He [Fletcher] *to a Sympathie those soules betrai'd*
> *Whom Love or Beauty never could perswade;*
> *And in each mov'd spectatour could beget*
> *A reall passion by a Counterfeit:*
> *When first* Bellario *bled, what Lady there*
> *Did not for every drop let fall a teare?*
> *And when* Aspatia *wept, not any eye*
> *But seem'd to weare the same sad livery;*

By him inspir'd the feign'd Lucina *drew*
More streams of melting sorrow then the true.[2]

It therefore seems evident that these plays provided a means for men to indulge the "tender" or "womanlike" emotions that they were conditioned to suppress in their daily lives.[3] Here the otherwise unacceptable was made not merely licit, but virtually obligatory.[4] "If you have tears," these plays announce in unmistakable accents, "prepare to shed them now." In terms of what they do with death, they seem designed to bring men and women to a similar degree of emotional abandon—a sexual leveling likely to have provided the intimacy of shared experience.

Cupid's Revenge (1608),[5] which "marked the true start of collaboration between Beaumont and Fletcher,"[6] adumbrates the dramaturgy of many of the plays to be considered in this chapter. Pathos, to Beaumont and Fletcher, is what heroic self-assertion is to Chapman; and one can sense their eagerness to reach a scene like the one in which Urania, who has disguised herself as a boy in order to serve Prince Leucippus, saves him from an assassin by interposing her own body. Clearly, here is a death worth protracting. For some twenty lines the two converse, Leucippus continuing to address her as his "boy"; with her last words she reveals her identity, explaining that she has served him

> for love,
> I would not let you know till I was dying;
> For you could not love mee, my Mother was
> So naught.
>
> (5.4.136–39)[7]

It is a remarkable feature of the play that the death of this minor character is emphasized at least as much as that of Leucippus, the protagonist, who is stabbed by Urania's monstrous mother. Neither his death—his final words echo some of Hamlet's—nor her suicide merits comment.

The Maid's Tragedy (1610)[8] makes much more of the potentialities of the death scene. These deaths provide a variety of emotional effects; but again pathos is dominant. Evadne's murder of the King, her lover, resembles many killings in villain-tragedy, in that her motives and her artful contrivance are given greater prominence than the reaction of her victim. The scene, in short, is about Evadne killing the King, not how the King meets death. One remarkable feature of this scene is the psychologically justifiable

inconsistency in the way Evadne thinks and acts. Finding the King
asleep in bed, she decides to wake him:

> Yet I must not
> Thus tamely do it as he sleeps: that were
> To rock him to another world; my vengeance
> Shall take him waking, and then lay before him
> The number of his wrongs and punishments.
> I'll shape his sins like furies till I waken
> His evil angel, his sick conscience,
> And then I'll strike him dead.
>
> (5.1.29–36)[9]

Saying "Your grace and I / Must grapple upon even terms no more"
(37–38), she ties his arms to the bed. The King, sensualist that he is,
takes this for a form of erotic bondage when he comes to his senses,
and he suggests that they reenact the tale of Venus and Mars. But
Evadne, with an irony yet undetected by the King, informs him she
has "brought [him] physic / To temper [his] high veins" (53–54). The
physic she alludes to is a knife; holding it poised, she describes the
transformation wrought in her by the spirit of revenge. No longer is
she Evadne:

> I am not she, nor bear I in this breast
> So much cold spirit to be call'd a woman;
> I am a tiger; I am anything
> That knows not pity.
>
> (64–67)

Like Lady Macbeth, she disclaims woman, and speaks as if her
transformation were more radical than is actually the case. But in
her next lines she reveals that she does know pity; for with a lenity
notably absent in many revengers, she wishes to spare his soul:

> Stir not; if thou dost,
> I'll take thee unprepar'd, thy fears upon thee,
> That make thy sins look double, and so send thee
> (By my revenge I will) to look those torments
> Prepar'd for such black souls.
>
> (67–71)

Since, as Leech has observed, the earlier speech in which Evadne
spoke of the desirability of taking the King waking revealed that she
"wishe[d] him to die in torment, not be rocked to another world,"[10]
these words reveal an alteration in her intent.

Still the King (no swifter of apprehension than Leucippus) fails to realize that Evadne means to kill him. She, who had earlier declared that she would forsake him if he should cease to be king—"I love with my ambition, / Not with my eyes" (3.1.182–83)—assumes the guise of injured innocence. It seems a clear instance of self-deception: this is the way reality must be rewritten if she is to do what must be done:

> I was once fair,
> Once I was lovely, not a blowing rose
> More chastely sweet, till thou, thou, thou foul canker,
> (Stir not!) didst poison me. I was a world of virtue
> Till your curs'd court and you (hell bless you for't!)
> With your temptations on temptations
> Made me give up mine honor, for which, king,
> I am come to kill thee.
>
> (75–82)

His continued refusal to believe she means what she says angers her so much that the oscillation between the desire to damn his soul and the desire to save it is manifested within a single speech:

> Stir nothing but your tongue, and that for mercy
> To those above us, by whose lights I vow,
> Those blessed fires that shot to see our sin,
> If thy hot soul had substance with thy blood,
> I would kill that too.
>
> (85–89)

The King attempts to awe Evadne by reminding her who he is: "I am thy king" (96). This tactic proved efficacious with Amintor, for whom kingship confers mystical authority: "There is / Divinity about you that strikes dead / My rising passions," he had earlier declared (3.1.245–47). But to Evadne the word "king" is merely titular, designating a position in the power structure.[11] Desacralizing his status, she replies:

> Thou art my shame. Lie still; there's none about you
> Within your cries; all promises of safety
> Are but deluding dreams. Thus, thus, thou foul man,
> Thus I begin my vengeance. [*Stabs him.*]
>
> (97–100)

The King, who regards himself, at the least, as a "foul *king*," commands her not to strike again. She is, of course, not to be commanded: "We must change / More of these love-tricks yet" (102–3). Finally, the King realizes he cannot escape death. He merely asks, "What bloody villain / Provok'd thee to this murder?" "Thou, thou monster!" she replies, striking a second time (103–4):

> Thou kept'st me brave at court, and whor'd me, king;
> Then married me to a young noble gentleman,
> And whor'd me still.
>
> (105–8)

Now the King, unable to command, asks pity. Three ritual blows accompany her answer:

> Hell take me then! This, for my lord Amintor!
> This, for my noble brother, and this stroke
> For the most wrong'd of women! [*Kills him.*]
>
> (109–11)

With him dies the spirit of vengeance: "Die all our faults together! I forgive thee" (112).

As the foregoing discussion indicates, Evadne dominates this scene to an extraordinary degree. The King is there to make the appropriate verbal gestures, and to be killed. It is no wonder that Evadne has been called "the most awesome figure in the play."[12]

The deaths of Evadne, Aspatia, and Amintor, which emphasize the way death is sought and embraced, are calculated to evoke a contrastive emotional effect—tears rather than wonder. Aspatia, the woman Amintor has rejected in order to marry in accordance with the King's wishes, chooses a means of death that befits her thwarted love.[13] Dressed in man's apparel, she presents herself to Amintor as "the brother to the wrong'd Aspatia" (5.3.42).[14] Goading him into a duel, she astonishes him by making no effort to defend herself:

> What dost thou mean?
> Thou canst not fight; the blows thou mak'st at me
> Are quite besides, and those I offer at thee,
> Thou spread'st thine arms and tak'st upon thy breast,
> Alas, defenseless!
>
> (101–5)

(How many times, one must wonder, does he strike before noticing this?) But Aspatia has procured what she came for: "I have got enough, / And my desire. There is no place so fit / For me to die as here" (105–7).

Aspatia does not die yet, though she remains speechless until line 151 ("Oh, oh, oh!"); instead the focus shifts to Evadne, who now enters, *"her hands bloody, with a knife."* Here one cannot but feel consistency in character is sacrificed for theatrical effect, for Evadne not only informs Amintor that she killed the King for love of him, but asks that he "take [her] to [his] bed" (153).[15] As she kneels and continues to adjure him to take her home, Amintor begins to feel traces of his former love return:

> I dare not stay thy language;
> In midst of all my anger and my grief,
> Thou dost awake something that troubles me,
> And says I lov'd thee once. I dare not stay;
> There is no end of woman's reasoning. [*Leaves her.*]
>
> (164–68)

Perhaps only Amintor could utter the parting non sequitur—which presumably means that there is no end to his susceptibility. Left alone, Evadne takes her own life:[16]

> Amintor, thou shalt love me now again.
> Go, I am calm. Farewell, and peace forever.
> Evadne, whom thou hat'st, will die for thee. [*Kills herself.*]
>
> (169–71)

Amintor, hearing her resolve, returns: "I have a little human nature yet / That's left for thee, that bids me stay thy hand" (172–73). But her hand has already struck. There he stands, between the two dying women:

> *Evadne.* Thy hand was welcome, but it came too late.
>   Oh, I am lost! The heavy sleep makes haste. [*She dies.*]
> *Aspatia.* Oh, oh, oh!
>
> (174–76)

Aspatia's outcry, like her earlier one, is apparently not noticed by Amintor. Yet he, as he ponders suicide, speaks of the wrong he has done to her:

> my soul will part less troubled
> When I have paid to her in tears my sorrow.
> I will not leave this act unsatisfied,
> If all that's left in me can answer it.
>
> (193–96)

These words usher in another phase of the action, for with them Aspatia wakes: "Was it a dream? There stands Amintor still, / Or I dream still" (197–98). She has heard what he has said, and tells him he is already in Aspatia's presence:

> Thou art there already, and these wounds are hers.
> Those threats I brought with me sought not revenge,
> But came to fetch this blessing from thy hand.
> I am Aspatia yet.
>
> (206–9)

Though in some ways reminiscent of the death of Urania in *Cupid's Revenge,* Aspatia's final moments make the emotional appeal of her predecessor seem almost perfunctory. Struck down by the man she loves, the man who should have been her husband, she lingers long enough to learn that she is now the "greatest blessing of the world" (224) to him. Everything she says is designed to draw tears:

> I shall sure live, Amintor, I am well;
> A kind of healthful joy wanders within me.
>
> (211–12)

From these lines it is an easy transition to the pathos of the might-have-been. Amintor wishes to "bear [her] to some place of help." "Amintor, thou must stay," she answers; "I must rest here":

> My strength begins to disobey my will.
> How dost thou, my best soul? I would fain live
> Now, if I could. Wouldst thou have loved me then?
>
> (214–18)

The final stage, death itself, surprises in its suddenness:

> Give me thine hand: mine hands grope up and down,
> And cannot find thee; I am wondrous sick.
> Have I thy hand, Amintor?
>
> (221–23)

He assures her that she does.

> I do believe thee better than my sense.
> Oh, I must go; farewell. [*Dies.*]
>
> (225–26)

It is a death devoid of agony—a kind of gentle waftage.

Aspatia's death is not only pathetic in itself, but the direct cause of Amintor's lachrymatory suicide. At first he thinks she has merely fainted. He chafes her temples, bows her body; no signs of life appear. He then beseeches the gods to restore her soul for "some few years / . . . to this fair seat again":

> No comfort comes; the gods deny me too.
> I'll bow the body once again.—Aspatia!—
> The soul is fled forever, and I wrong
> Myself, so long to lose her company.
> Must I talk now? Here's to be with thee, love. [*Kills himself.*]
>
> (238–44)

In an atmosphere replete with echoes of *King Lear, Antony and Cleopatra,* and *Romeo and Juliet,* Amintor embraces death.

As was the case with Aspatia, Amintor's death is protracted so as to obtain the greatest possible impact. We have seen him with the two women who have been most important in his life. Now we see him with his friend, Melantius, to whom he is "sister, father, brother, son, / All that I had" (268–69). Melantius asks the identity of the slain youth. "'Tis Aspatia," the answer comes. "My last is said; let me give up my soul / Into thy bosom" (270–72). With these words he expires.

One remarkable feature of *The Maid's Tragedy* is that all its deaths (with the exception of the King's) are caused by love. Evadne dies because of her feelings for Amintor, not because she believes she must punish herself for killing the King; Aspatia is given the death she seeks by the man she loves; and Amintor dies "to be with" her. This emphasis upon love (rather than honor, justice, morality, or some quasi-religious consideration) is also to be found in what remains of the play. Melantius, who says nothing to indicate remorse for inciting his sister to the act of regicide, attempts to take his life because of the loss of his friend. Though thwarted, he swears that, even if barred the use of his hands, he "will never eat, / Or drink, or sleep, or have to do with that / That may preserve life" (290–92). What, then, is one to make of the words of the new ruler, Lysippus, who thus refers to the circumstances through which his brother met his death?

> May this a fair example be to me
> To rule with temper, for on lustful kings
> Unlook'd-for sudden deaths from God are sent;
> But curs'd is he that is their instrument.
>
> (294–97)

About all that one may affirm without qualification is that Lysippus acknowledges his brother's death should remind him of the dangers inherent in intemperate rule. The references to God and his "instrument," however, make Lysippus sound more orthodox than the play itself has been. As John F. Danby observes, "The King . . . is portrayed throughout as merely a person. He has absolute power, but the absolutism is diminished to the political only. Nothing naturally regal or supernaturally sanctioned invests him in fact."[17] And if attributing the King's death to the agency of God seems more than a little odd, what is said of the "instrument" is even odder. Fredson Bowers explains these lines in terms of what he calls "dramatic ethics":

> Legally, of course, Melantius is equally guilty as accessory, but sentimentally he escaped the stain of blood in awakening his sister to vengeance for her moral ruin. He must not stain his hands, because he must survive to justify the vengeance, but Evadne—a woman already smirched with adultery and therefore by dramatic ethics doomed—makes the ideal revenger. . . . Evadne, cursed already by a mortal sin, was the only fit instrument for the vengeance on her sovereign.[18]

Yet Evadne sacrifices herself for love, not from any sense of remorse for regicide. And what ("curs'd is he" encourages such speculation) if Lysippus is speaking of Melantius? Melantius undoubtedly feels acute anguish at the loss of his friend. Yet if this is the curse to which Lysippus alludes, Melantius's punishment comes to pass for reasons curiously remote from anything he says or does in the play. Amintor's suicide is the direct result of Aspatia's death—for which one can hardly blame Melantius. And, of course, the ending would be further unconventional in allowing the man supposedly "curs'd" by God to survive. For the concept of divine intervention, in short, there is only the authority of Lysippus, who may be presumed to regard it as a doctrine highly desirable to inculcate in one's subjects. That characters die for love is what the play shows us, indeed insists that we see.

Fletcher's *Bonduca* (1613) resembles *Cupid's Revenge* and *The Maid's Tragedy* in being calculated to make tears drop "as fast as the Arabian trees / Their medicinable gum." It differs, however, in introducing instances in which death is heroic, not merely pathetic. Such is the suicide of Penyus, a Roman centurion, who has disgraced himself by refusing to lead his regiment into combat with the Britains. This refusal may be partly motivated by pride—he resents having his general "command" him to come—but also is based on his conviction that the enemy forces are so vastly superior that certain slaughter awaits those foolish enough to venture themselves in battle. He is mistaken, and the Romans triumph without him. What is left for him is to make a noble death partial recompense for his uncharacteristic cowardice. Encouraged by soldiers who call him "brave Captain," "Most excellent Commander," he dies lest he cease to merit such honorifics:

> Then to keep 'em
> For ever falling more, have at ye, heavens, [*Stabs himself.*]
> Ye everlasting powers, I am yours: The work's done,
> That neither fire, nor age, nor Eating envie
> Shall ever conquer. Carry my last words
> To the great General: kisse his hands, and say,
> My soul I give to heaven, my fault to justice
> Which I have done upon my self: my vertue,
> If ever there was any in Poor Penyus,
> Made more, and happier, light on him. I faint.
> And where there is a foe, I wish him fortune.
> I die: lie lightly on my ashes, gentle earth.
>
> (4.3.163–74)[19]

The act, which restores his self-respect, is presented as an appropriate—even admirable—response to the plight in which Penyus finds himself. Though much in the scene is sentimental, we are meant to feel in this speech what T. S. Eliot called "the greatness in defeat of a noble but erring nature."[20] As the Roman officer Drusus says in the lines that conclude the scene:

> Fare well, great Penyus,
> Thou thunder-bolt, fare-well. Take up the body:
> To morrow morning to the Camp convey it,
> There to receive due Ceremonies. That eye
> That blindes himself with weeping, gets most glory.
>
> (211–15)

Queen Bonduca and her two daughters commit suicide rather than fall into the hands of the Romans. The younger daughter is at first pathetic rather than heroic, begging her mother to accept the Romans' offer of mercy. Her sister, however, assures her that they will go "to the blessed, / Where we shall meet our father . . ." (4.4.106–7); "Where eternal / Our youths are, and our beauties; where no Wars come, / Nor lustful slaves to ravish us" (110–12). "That steels me," the girl replies; "A long farewel to this world" (112–13)—whereupon she stabs herself. (Was ever "long farewel"

so brief?) Her older sister, courageous from the start, addresses
herself to the Romans:

> The next is mine.
> Shew me a Romane Lady in all your stories,
> Dare do this for her honour: they are cowards,
> Eat coals like compell'd Cats: your great Saint Lucrece
> Di'd not for honour; Tarquin topt her well,
> And mad she could not hold him, bled.
>
> (114–19)

So much for Portia and Lucrece. She continues her vaunts until her
mother urges her to "make haste" (126). Finally, still addressing the
Romans, she brings her part to its end:

> would ye learn
> How to die bravely, Romanes, to fling off
> This case of flesh, lose all your cares for ever?
> Live as we have done, well, and fear the gods,
> Hunt Honour, and not Nations with your swords,
> Keep your mindes humble, your devotions high;
> So shall ye learn the noblest part, to die. [*Dyes.*]
>
> (127–33)

Bonduca herself, after quaffing poison from a cup, mocks the Romans for failing of their object:

> Ye fools,
> Ye should have ti'd up death first, when ye conquer'd,
> Ye sweat for us in vain else: see him here,
> He's ours still, and our friend; laughs at your pities;
> And we command him with as easie reins
> As do our enemies. I feel the poison.
> Poor vanquish'd Romanes. . . .
> . . . .
> If you will keep your Laws and Empire whole,
> Place in your Romane flesh a Britain soul. [*Dyes.*]
>
> (141–47; 152–53)

Death, Tamburlaine's ultimately treacherous "servant," is here de-
picted as Bonduca's friend—yet a friend she can command. Her
death is in all respects as remote from the pathetic as possible.

In dramatizing the three suicides in the scene, then, Fletcher
progressively intensifies the element of the heroic. The younger
daughter serves as a foil to her sister; yet though the latter's con-

duct is heroic, her language verges at times on the hysterical: it is
rhetoric to be spoken with dilated pupils. Bonduca, however, combines a heroic attitude toward death with a self-mastery that enables her to speak as impressively as she acts.

Despite the emphasis on the heroic in this scene and in the death
of Penyus, one might argue that Fletcher is chiefly interested in the
heroic as a means of making the most of the pathetic.[21] For the fifth
act of *Bonduca* has for its main dramatic interest the noble suffering
of the "Britain" general Caratach and his nephew Hengo. Hengo, a
valiant boy, may be said to play a role comparable to figures such as
Urania and Aspatia. For his death is pure pathos, as extreme in its
way as the heroic suicide of Bonduca.

Hengo's death is a notable instance of Fletcher's delight in dramatic contrasts. Not only is it set off by its relationship to the other
deaths in the play; it is preceded by a comic interlude in which one
soldier asks another to kill him, then begs for (and receives) his life
(5.3.19–98). Then *"Enter Caratach and Hengo on the Rock."* Caratach spies the provisions which Judas, a Roman soldier, has placed
nearby to lure him to destruction:

> Courage my Boy, I have found meat: look Hengo,
> Look where some blessed Britain, to preserve thee,
> Has hung a little food and drink: cheer up Boy,
> Do not forsake me now.
>
> (99–102)

Though faint for lack of food, Hengo volunteers to descend:
"Come, tie me in your belt, and let me down"; but, just as he seizes
the meat and bottle, Judas pierces him with an arrow. Caratach
hurls a stone at Judas, knocking out his brains. But nothing he can
do will save Hengo's life. "Shall I draw it [the arrow]?" he asks; and
the boy replies:

> Ye draw away my soul then. I would live
> A little longer; spare me heavens, but onely
> To thank you for your tender love. Good Uncle,
> Good noble Uncle weep not.
>
> (143–47)

Surely if Caratach did not weep at this, he would weep at nothing.
Relentlessly, the dialogue continues:

> *Caratach.*　　　　　　　Oh my chicken,
> 　My deer Boy, what shall I lose?

Hengo.   Why, a child,
That must have died how-ever: had this 'scap'd me,
Fever or famine: I was born to die, Sir.

(147–50)

Macduff, in lines one imagines Jonson numbered among those
Shakespeare should have blotted, not only alludes to the loss of his
"pretty chickens" but gives them a "dam." As used by Caratach, in
any event (both here and in line 113), the term is ludicrous rather
than pathetic.

Like Bonduca's younger daughter, Hengo is comforted with talk
of the hereafter, where he and Caratach will "enjoy together that
great blessedness / You told me of" (154–55). Then he grows
feebler: "I grow cold, / Mine eyes are going" (155–56). Brave, pious,
and noble, the boy takes leave of his uncle and dies:

Hengo.   Pray for me;
And noble Uncle, when my bones are ashes,
Think of your little Nephew. Mercie.
Caratach.   Mercie.
You blessed angels take him.
Hengo.   Kisse me: so.
Farewell, farewell. [*Dies.*]

(156–60)

It is a death reminiscent of Aspatia's not only in its concentrated
pathos, but in its relative avoidance of the painful. Though the
arrow is said to hurt ("Oh how it pricks mee" [130]), Hengo's life
ebbs tranquilly. Slowly, with almost no apparent discomfort, he
ceases to be.

In *Valentinian* (1614), Fletcher concentrates on the heroic possibilities of death—so much so, indeed, that he relegates to an
offstage death the one character who would have afforded him an
opportunity for wringing tears from his audience. This is Lucina,
the wife of Maximus, who expires from grief after being raped by
Valentinian. What might have been dramatized is reported:

When first she enter'd
Into her house, after a world of weeping,
And blushing like the Sun-set, as we saw her;
Dare I, said she, defile this [Maximus's] house with whore,
In which his noble family has flourish'd?
At which she fel, and stird no more.

(3.1.363–68)[22]

The suicides of Pontius and Aecius, on the other hand, provide some of the play's most memorable moments. Aecius, a Roman general, has cashiered Pontius for spreading sedition among the troops. Impelled by both the desire for revenge and Valentinian's promise that he will receive Aecius's position, Pontius intends to kill Aecius, but is won over by Aecius's nobility. For Aecius stands before him fearless, ready for death; nor will he defend himself from one sent by his emperor. Speaking as if he is about to execute Valentinian's command, Pontius readies himself to strike—but at the last moment turns his sword against himself:

> For now Aecius,
> Thou shalt behold and find I was no traitor,
> And as I doe it, blesse me; die as I doe.
>
> (4.4.174–76)

The deed, which proves to Aecius that Pontius is "a Roman" (177), is not immediately followed by death. Instead, Pontius is permitted a long speech in which he attempts a partial justification of his past conduct (he never intended sedition, but acknowledges that Aecius's "patience" was nobler than his own soldierlike outspokenness). Aecius praises him for his virtue, and for what he has made of death: "Thou hast fashiond death, / In such an excellent, and beauteous manner, / I wonder men can live" (215–17). Pontius's remaining two speeches are brief (four lines each): in the first he asks for Aecius's hand—and his forgiveness—and warns him that he too must soon die. His final words are these:

> Dye nobly:——Rome farewell:
> And Valentinian fall, thou hast broke thy basis;
> In joy ye have given me a quiet death,
> I would strike more wounds, if I had more breath.
> [*He dyes.*]
>
> (223–26)

"Is there an houre of goodnesse beyond this? / Or any man would out-live such a dying?" exclaims Aecius (227–28). He cries out for Caesar's men to come and kill him. Since none will attempt the deed, he decides to emulate "strong Cato":

> Now for a stroak shall turne me to a Star:
> I come ye blessed spirits, make me room
> To live for ever in Elizium: [*Wounds himselfe.*]
> Doe men feare this? O that posterity

> Could learne from him but this, that loves his wound,
> There is no paine at all in dying well,
> Nor none are lost, but those that make their hell. [*Kills himselfe*.]
>
> (262–68)

Valentinian is poisoned by Aecius's servant Aretus, who first poisons himself so he may torment Valentinian by making him see the kind of agony that he will shortly experience. Delighting in his own anguish, Aretus describes what he suffers as being incomparably more terrible than the torments of the damned, but manifests almost total self-mastery. His is the death heroic and triumphant: "Feare, feare thou Monster, / Feare the just gods, I have my peace" (5.2.109–10).

Valentinian's death, though much unlike the pious and equable death of Aretus, is surprisingly impressive. If it is not heroic, neither is it the kind one might have expected. He has hitherto been portrayed as a monster; yet he dies as a man. Never before has he been brought so close to the audience. Addressing the gods, he confesses his guilt—but despises them if they refuse to grant him mercy. Indeed, unless they are merciful they are not gods. But if they are more than "dreames, and ghests, / And truly hold the guidance of things mortall" (127–28), he implores their forgiveness:

> Give me an howre to know ye in: Oh save me
> But so much perfect time ye make a soule in:
> Take this destruction from me; no ye cannot,
> The more I would beleeve, the more I suffer,
> My braines are ashes, now my heart, my eyes freinds;
> I go, I goe, more aire, more aire; I am mortall. [*He dyes*.]
>
> (135–40)

The desperate entreaty for more time reminds us of Faustus and a host of others before and after him.[23] It is what Everyman always says when soul and body are about to be sundered. But Valentinian is exceptional in that he cannot bring himself to believe in the existence of the gods he attempts to invoke. For him, unlike a figure such as Tourneur's D'Amville, there is no final realization that what has happened to him reflects the will of heaven (or, since the frame of reference is pagan, the gods). What his painful rush of words conveys is the anguish of a towering egotist who discovers at the last the reality of his own mortality. Nor does the play suggest that his death is anything other than the natural consequence of his deeds.[24]

In *Thierry and Theodoret* (1617),[25] the emphasis is again on the pathetic. Despite the title, the villainous Brunhalt dominates the play; the title figures—her sons—fall victim to her machinations. The death of Theodoret, which one might have expected to be given great prominence, is surprisingly perfunctory; stabbed by a hidden assassin, he speaks but a single line—and that is merely "Ha, did you not see one neere me?" (3.2.117).[26] The deaths of Thierry and his wife Ordella are what playgoers would have chiefly remembered. The scene in which they are restored to each other and die is at the heart of the play's emotional appeal.

Even by the standards of the day, this scene is an extraordinary one. It is, in a sense, the place where tragedy and tragicomedy converge, with the latter being subsumed by the former. Because Brunhalt has given Thierry a potion that renders him temporarily impotent when he marries Ordella, Ordella (blaming herself for his condition) resolves to take her life so Thierry may hope for children from another wife. Martell, described in the *dramatis personae* as Thierry's and Theodoret's "noble Kinsman," persuades her to preserve herself and let him deliver an account of her suicide to Thierry. (This device, also employed in Marston's *Malcontent,* leads the audience to expect a happy ending.) But during her absence Brunhalt strikes at Thierry again, this time with a handkerchief whose merest touch is death. By the time Ordella is brought into his presence he knows he is near his end.

Ordella, who is veiled, reveals herself to him; but Thierry cannot at first comprehend that she is still alive.[27] Instead, he believes he is being visited by her soul:

> Martell, I cannot last long, see the soule,
> (I see it perfectly) of my Ordella,
> The heavenly figure of her sweetenes there.
>
> (5.2.151–53)

Gradually, however, he is brought to an awareness of the truth:

Martell: She's alive Sir.
Thierry. In everlasting life I know it, friend;
   O happy, happy soule.
Ordella. Alas I live Sir
   A mortall woman still.
Thierry. Can spirits weepe too?
Martell. She is no spirit Sir, pray kisse her;——Lady,
   Be very gentle to him. [*She kisses him.*]
Thierry. Stay, she is warme,
   And by my life the same lips——tell me, brightnesse,

    Are you the same Ordella still?
Ordella.   The same Sir,
    Whom heavens and my good angell staid from ruine.
Thierry. Kiss me agen.
Ordella.   The same still, still your servant. [*Kisses him.*]
Thierry. 'Tis she, I know her now Martell.

                                        (163–73)

This is the stuff that happy endings are made of. Here, however, it is used for quite another purpose. Moments after these lines, Thierry abruptly informs Ordella that he is dying: "Love I must die, I faint, / Close up my glasses" (179–80). Only now do we discover the real reason for the preservation of Ordella:

    1. Doctor.   The Queene faints too, and deadly.
    Thierry. One dying kisse.
    Ordella.   My last Sir, and my dearest, [*Kisses him.*]
    And now close my eyes too.
    Thierry.   Thou perfect woman,——
    Martell. The kingdome's yours, take Memberge [Theodoret's daughter]
      to you,
    And keepe my line alive;——nay weepe not Lady,——
    Take me, I go.
    Ordella.   Take me too, farwell honor. [*Dies both.*]

                                          (180–85)

What poison does to Thierry grief does to Ordella. Though Ordella's death would have seemed less fantastic to seventeenth-century audiences than to us,[28] one must feel that the dramatists show themselves willing to dive into the bottom of the deep, to pluck up drowned Pathos by the locks.[29]

Little need be said of *The Bloody Brother* (1619).[30] As Bowers observes, "The first two acts are devoted to the rise of the villain [Rollo] to the throne, the third and fourth to the consolidation of his position by fresh atrocities, and the fifth to the blood revenge of his victims."[31] Only a few characters are given onstage deaths, and (as is common in plays of this sort) the emphasis is on the means by which death comes rather than how the dying take their farewell of the world.

Finally, there is *Sir John Van Olden Barnavelt* (1619), which Fletcher wrote in collaboration with Massinger.[32] Here the suicide of Leidenberge, who has betrayed Barnavelt's treasonous acts, mingles pathetic and heroic elements. His little son sleeps near him—a fact in itself certain to inject pathos—as he readies himself for death:

> Sleepe on, sweet Child, the whilst thy wreatched father
> Prepares him to the yron sleepe of death.
> Or is death fabled out but terrable
> To fright us from it? or rather is there not
> Some hid Hesperides, some blessed fruites
> Moated about with death.
>
> (3.6; 2:266)[33]

He calls on the souls of Cato and other noble Romans to observe his resolution and dispatch. But his imagery, linking as it does sexuality and death, is more like that of an Antony than a Cato:

> behold, and see me
> An old man and a gowne man, with as much hast
> And gladnes entertaine this steele that meetes me
> As ever longing lover did his mistris.
> —So, so; yet further, soe.
>
> (P. 266)

The boy cries out in his sleep. Leidenberge pauses, then realizes he must enlarge his wound still further:

> I bleed apace but cannot fall: tis here;
> This will make wider roome. Sleep, gentle Child,
> And do not looke upon thy bloody father,
> Nor more remember him then fitts thy fortune.
> . . . .
> I, now I faint; mine eies begin to hunt
> For that they have lost for ever, this worldes beutie—
> O oh, ô oh! my long sleepe now has ceizd me.
>
> (Pp. 266–67)

His son, hearing him "groane and cry," enters to find him dead.

The suicide of Leidenberge, then, is the act of a rather ordinary man who tries, with partial success, to die nobly. The execution of Barnavelt, with which the play concludes, is the death of an extraordinary figure, "a hero similar in some respects to Chapman's Byron—a once-great man who clings obstinately to the illusion that nothing he does can alter that greatness."[34] Through unquestionably guilty of treason, Barnavelt attempts, like Byron, to go to his death with the confident accents of one wholly innocent of the charges brought against him.[35]

When Barnavelt is informed that he must die, he replies: "I humbly thanck your honours: / I shall not play my last Act worst" (5.1; p. 301). Later, when his execution is imminent, a huge crowd gathers. "He will make a notable Speech, I warrant him," says one excited burgher (5.3; p. 307). Nor does Barnavelt's performance, when he mounts the scaffold, fall short of the expectations that the whole play has created and that these remarks directly prepare us for. Learning that the executioner who will strike off his head has won the right by defeating two other executioners at dice, he responds with sarcastic thanks to the "gentlemen" who are in charge. But when he sees Leidenberge's body hanging nearby he becomes, as a lord remarks, "much moved." Yet he soon regains his self-control and begins his oration from the scaffold. He has much to say of his services to the state; prompted to remember his treasons, he denies them. He does, he admits, regard himself as guilty of "one fault": "I dye for saving this unthanckfull Cuntry" (p. 312). He forgives the executioner, telling him, "When I speak lowdest, strike" (p. 313); he then takes his leave of the attending lords and asks favor for his wife and children. This done, he begins what will be his final speech:

> Commend my last breath to his Excellence [Orange];
> Tell him the Sun he shot at is now setting,
> Setting this night, that he may rise to morrow,
> For ever setting. Now let him raigne alone
> And with his rayes give life and light to all men.
> . . . .
> My last petition, good Cuntrymen, forget me:
> Your memories wound deeper then your mallice,
> And I forgive ye all.—A little stay me.—
>
> (P. 313)

Despite what appears an implicit acknowledgement of his guilt ("forget me"), the measured cadences of his lines testify to his self-possession as he goes to his ghastly death. Then, as he kneels and readies himself for the stroke, his words pour out with desperate energy:

> Honour and world I fling ye thus behind me,
> And thus a naked poore man kneele to heaven:
> Be gracious to me, heare me, strengthen me.
> I come, I come, ô gracious heaven! now, now,
> Now, I present—
>
> (P. 314)

"When I speak loudest, strike," he had told the executioner. The axe falls, severing his fingers as well as his neck. Yet Barnavelt, for all his guilt, has played his "last Act" so that his death becomes the final expression of his greatness. In its superb theatricality, it seems a death not so much endured as accomplished.[36]

5

Middleton and Massinger

To move from the plays just considered to the tragedies of Middleton is to move from the drama of emotional immersion to that of analysis and ironic distance. According to Samuel Schoenbaum, "The predominance of the Fletcherian school . . . created a most unfavorable situation for an artist with Middleton's gifts":

> He was by temperament a realist—but the new drama was wildly romantic. . . . He was interested in portraying a dark and frightening world in which a weak humanity struggles futilely against the terrible ironies that work against man's desires and aspirations—but the new mode stressed the artificial and the undisturbing, scarcely permitted the expression of a serious point of view.[1]

How hard—Schoenbaum seems to say—for Middleton to be Middleton. Yet one might argue that Fletcherian drama helped to sharpen Middleton's sense of his own quite different natural bent—that he first found his way by reacting against a kind of drama he found inimical.

The Second Maiden's Tragedy (1611), probably by Middleton,[2] is a curious compound of the Fletcherian and Middletonian modes. The main plot, as Schoenbaum notes, "show[s] the very considerable influence of Fletcherian melodrama";[3] in it a character designated only as the "Tyrant" seeks the love of the "Lady," who remains steadfast in her love for the rightful king, Govianus, whom the Tyrant has deposed. Finally, when the Tyrant has sent armed men to seize her, she resolves to die, and by Govianus's hand. He proves unequal to the task, however, fainting as he "*runs at her [with his sword]*" (3.3.148 s.d.).[4] Her heroic suicide follows. Apostrophizing Govianus's sword, she takes her leave of the world in a fashion (save for "hell's ministers") reminiscent of Marston's Sophonisba:

> Thou are my servant now; come, thou hast lost
> A fearful master, but art now preferred
> Unto the service of a resolute lady,
> One that knows how to employ thee, and scorns death

As much as great men fear it. Where's hell's ministers,
The tyrant's watch and guard? 'Tis of much worth,
When with this key the prisoner can slip forth!

(157–63)

She then kills herself, dying without another word.

In death as in life, the Lady is an image of perfect female virtue. Her death, both admirable and triumphant, is like no other in the play. The other main-plot characters who die—Sophonirus and the Tyrant—resemble her, however, in being highly schematic: they are unambiguously evil. Sophonirus, who attempts to pander for the Tyrant in Govianus's own house, is stabbed by Govianus. But he dies laughing to think how soon the Tyrant will possess the Lady:

How quickly now my death will be revenged,
Before the King's first sleep! I depart laughing
To think upon the deed.

(3.3.47–49)[5]

Even more melodramatic than Sophonirus's malevolent dying laughter is the Tyrant's death, for he dies after kissing the Lady's face, which Govianus has poisoned.[6] But Middleton (or whoever wrote the play) gives him only the most perfunctory "departing" words; dramatic interest is concentrated on the approbation accorded to Govianus's revenge by the ghost of the Lady and by the nobles.[7]

It is in the subplot that we see death presented in what may be called an anti-Fletcherian manner. Govianus has a brother, Anselmus, who prevails upon a friend to test the virtue of his wife. This man, Votarius, and the Wife fall in love and begin to engage in an affair. Ironically, however, Votarius becomes jealous on seeing his enemy, Bellarius, stealing through her house. Assuming that he too is the Wife's lover (in fact, his assignation is with her maid, Leonella), Votarius informs Anselmus that his wife was "yielding ere I left her last, / And wavering in her faith" (2.2.131–32). After the misunderstanding regarding Bellarius is cleared up, the Wife suggests to Votarius that they stage a scene to convince Anselmus she is not the "yielding" creature he now believes her to be. Votarius is to place Anselmus where he can hear all that is said, then enter the Wife's chamber like a confident would-be lover; she will defend herself with bitter words, and even with a rapier. Unknown to Votarius, she later decides that he should wear concealed armor so she "may feign a fury without fear" (4.1.113). Leonella, to whom she speaks, has already informed Anselmus that his wife and

Votarius are lovers; now she betrays the Wife's plot to Bellarius, who sees a chance to destroy his enemy:

> Forget of purpose
> That privy armour; do not bless his soul
> With so much warning, nor his hated body
> With such sure safety. Here express thy love.
> Lay some empoisoned weapon next her hand,
> That in that play he may be lost for ever.
>
> (158–63)

Thus, when the Wife thrusts at Votarius she not only surprises him by piercing his body but kills him:

> Madam!—Heart, you deal falsely with me. O, I feel it!
> Y'are a most treacherous lady! This thy glory?
> My breast is all a-fire—O!— [*Dies.*]
>
> (5.1.107–9)

Anselmus, coming from his place of concealment, takes the sword from his wife and kills Leonella for slandering her. But at this point Bellarius descends from the gallery to avenge the death of Leonella: *"They make a dangerous pass at one another. The Wife purposely runs between, and is killed by them both"* (121 s.d.). Though the action is in itself ambiguous, her dying words are not: "I come, Votarius!" (122). Yet Anselmus remains convinced of her virtue, and is enraged when Bellarius declares she was a whore. They fight, and Anselmus, fatally wounded, "ask[s] no more of destiny but to fall / Close by the chaste side of my virtuous mistress" (137–38). Crawling to where she lies, he is content to die: "I expire cheerfully and give death a smile" (143). (Given the nature of the play, one should probably take this literally.)

With Anselmus apparently dead, the focus shifts to Bellarius, who is dying from a wound given him by the sword he himself poisoned. Govianus and others enter, and Bellarius recounts all that has happened. His final words are these:

> As for the cunning lady, I commend her.
> She performed that which never woman tried:
> She ran upon two weapons and so died.[8]
> Now you have all, I hope I shall sleep quiet. [*Dies.*]
>
> (163–66)

No sooner has Bellarius finished than the long-silent Anselmus reveals that he has heard all. It is almost as if *Othello* had been turned inside out, with belief in Desdemona's purity followed by the revelation that Cassio was indeed her lover. Now Anselmus "repent[s] the smile / That I bestowed on destiny!" (170–71) and repudiates his wife. What is done with him could scarcely be more derisive:

> I fling thee thus from my believing breast
> With all the strength I have. . . .
> > > Now I sue
> To die far from thee; may we never meet!
> Were my soul bid to joy's eternal banquet,
> And were assured to find thee there a guest,
> I'd sup with torments and refuse that feast.
> O thou beguiler of man's easy trust!
> *The serpent's wisdom is in women's lust. [Dies.]*
> > > > > (172–73; 174–80)

Though the self-righteous Anselmus sees himself as pure victim in the eternal sexual melodrama of credulous man and serpentine woman, the audience knows better. Instead of Fletcherian emotional engagement, we are given a wittily ironic spectacle of human tawdriness.

Hengist, King of Kent, or The Mayor of Queenborough (1618),[9] requires little comment. The play is, as David M. Holmes has remarked, antiromantic throughout, with Middleton's "derisive treatment reach[ing] a peak in the catastrophe."[10] Here Vortiger, King of Britain, his wife Roxena, and his counselor Horsus are trapped in a burning castle, besieged by the sons of Constantius and their followers. What has brought Vortiger in such peril is not the murder of Constantius, but the fact he has married a pagan. Turning on Horsus, who was instrumental in bringing about this marriage, Vortiger stabs him—then hears Horsus laugh at him for being his cuckold: "Roxena, whom thou'st rais'd to thy own ruin, / She was my whore in Germany" (5.2.87–88).[11] The revelation leaves Vortiger, who has lost all because of Roxena, somewhat in the position of Anselmus. As he and Horsus strike at each other Roxena enters above; she is mad, and thinks that a flame is following her "in the figure of young Vortimer, the prince, / Whose life I took by poison" (101–2). The two men, exchanging insults, take no notice of her ("Toad! Pagan!" "Viper! Christian!"); finally, however, Horsus dies. Next to perish is Roxena:

> No way to 'scape? is this the end of glory?
> Doubly beset with enemies' wrath, and fire?

It comes nearer—rivers and fountains, fall!—
It sucks away my breath.

(111–14)

Moments later she plunges to her death, leaving Vortiger to express implacable hatred. "Help, help!" were her final words. "Burn, burn!" he begins:

> O mystical harlot,
> Thou hast thy full due! Whom lust crown'd queen before,
> Flames crown her now a most triumphant whore;
> And that end crowns them all! [*Falls.*]

(123–26)

Whether one takes this as lurid melodrama or as travesty,[12] *Hengist* is characteristically Middletonian in its ironic treatment of death.

More intricately ironic, if somewhat more sympathetic, is *Women Beware Women* (1621), in which seven characters die, all but one in the extraordinary scene that concludes the play. Leantio, who has lost his wife Bianca to the Duke, dies because he has become Livia's lover. Her brother, Hippolito, is infuriated that a mere factor (purchasing agent) should dishonor him by conducting an affair with his sister. Leantio, who has hitherto been more contemptible than sympathetic, shows surprising spirit. Struck and challenged, he draws his sword:

> Slave, I turn this to thee,
> To call thee to account for a wound lately
> Of a base stamp upon me.

(4.2.35–37)[13]

His courage is impressive, but he quickly falls to his more practiced adversary. His last thoughts are of Bianca:

> False wife! I feel now th' hast prayed heartily for me.
> Rise, strumpet, by my fall, thy lust may reign now;
> My heart-string and the marriage-knot that tied thee
> Breaks both together. [*Dies.*]

(42–45)

Though Leantio's death may have considerable impact on the stage,[14] Hippolito's grim comment emphasizes a derisory perspective: "There I heard the sound on't, / And never liked string better" (45–46). One is used to heart-strings breaking. But *audibly?*

After Leantio's death, the play moves from its predominantly realistic mode to a climax in which psychological probability is subordinated to dramatic design. In this ending, as R. B. Parker has observed,

> coincidence, dramatic irony, manipulation, and helplessness are emphasized to the point of farce: the characters are never less in control of their destinies; they are manipulated with absurd consistency to their improbable deaths; and the giddy speed with which this is accomplished seems to emphasize their helplessness and the author's manipulation. The effect is so nearly absurd that it quite insulates the characters from emotional sympathy.[15]

Yet as was the case with Leantio's death, Middleton mixes elements of the tragic: all is not dehumanized and derisive.[16] Isabella and Guardiano, who die wordlessly, may be passed over in silence. But the deaths of Livia and the Duke require some discussion. Livia, who is portraying Juno Pronuba in the masque ostensibly celebrating the Duke's marriage to Bianca, is killed by poisoned incense offered to her by Isabella.[17] Despite Livia's considerable prominence in the play, she is given but four lines, all unremarkable:

> Oh I am sick to th' death, let me down quickly;
> This fume is deadly. Oh 't has poisoned me!
> My subtlety is sped, her art has quitted me;
> My own ambition pulls me down to ruin. [*Dies.*]
>
> (5.2.130–33)[18]

The Duke, who drinks poison Bianca intended for his brother, the Cardinal, also dies rapidly and unmemorably. Handed Guardiano's confession, he asks the Cardinal to read it—"for I am lost in sight and strength" (184); "My heart swells bigger yet; help here, break't ope, / My breast flies open next" (189–90).[19]

Two characters, however—Hippolito and Bianca—are given death speeches of greater scope. Hippolito, who is shot with poisoned cupids' arrows, speaks at first in as perfunctory a fashion as Livia or the Duke: "Oh death runs through my blood; in a wild flame too. / Plague of those Cupids, some lay hold on 'em" (139–40). But a moment later he addresses those around him:

> Lust and forgetfulness has been amongst us,
> And we are brought to nothing. Some blest charity
> Lend me the speeding pity of his sword
> To quench this fire in blood. Leantio's death

Has brought all this upon us—now I taste it—
And made us lay plots to confound each other.

(146–51)

After explaining how these things have come to pass, he reaches
this orthodox moral: "'Tis the property / Of guilty deeds to draw
your wise men downward. / Therefore the wonder ceases" (164–66).
His pain growing intolerable, he rushes to his death: "Run and meet
death then, / And cut off time and pain [*Runs on a guard's halbert;
dies.*]" (167–168).[20]

Hippolito's lines about "lust and forgetfulness" have an arresting
eloquence. Yet here too, one must admit, Middleton is not interested in emphasizing the individual psychology of a character at
point of death. The lines are choral, not characteristic.

With Bianca, Middleton departs from his usual practice. Her
death is not only a conscious choice (which one may hardly say of
the pain-crazed suicide of Hippolito), but is prompted by her love
for the Duke. Kissing him, she apparently receives his final
breath:[21]

> Accursed error!
> Give me thy last breath, thou infected bosom,
> And wrap two spirits in one poisoned vapour.
> [*Kisses the Duke's body.*]
> Thus, thus, reward thy murderer, and turn death
> Into a parting kiss. My soul stands ready at my lips,
> E'en vexed to stay one minute after thee.
>
> (192–97)

Though she "feel[s] death's power within [her]" (201), her death is
protracted. At first, it seems that she will end by voicing orthodox
moral sentences:

> Thou hast prevailed in something, cursed poison,
> Though thy chief force was spent in my lord's bosom;
> But my deformity in spirit's more foul—
> A blemished face best fits a leprous soul.
>
> (202–5)[22]

But her next words express her love for the Duke, and contempt for
the Cardinal and the others who surround her:

> What make I here? These are all strangers to me,
> Not known but by their malice, now th' art gone;
> Nor do I seek their pities. [*Drinks from the poisoned cup.*]
>
> (206–8)

This decisive action is, however, followed by conventional moralizing:

> Leantio, now I feel the breach of marriage
> At my heart-breaking. Oh the deadly snares
> That women set for women, without pity
> Either to soul or honour! Learn by me
> To know your foes; in this belief I die:
> Like our own sex, we have no enemy, no enemy!
>
> (210–15)[23]

Learn by me: it seems that Bianca, even more than Webster's Vittoria, is to go to her death pointing a moral. Her present misery illustrates the dire consequences women must fear if they are false to their marriage vows; and to this misery Livia (who but a woman could have done it?) has brought her. Yet Bianca does not die with such unexceptionable sentiments on her lips. Her final lines are these:

> Pride, greatness, honours, beauty, youth, ambition,
> You must all down together, there's no help for 't.
> Yet this my gladness is, that I remove,
> Tasting the same death in a cup of love. [*Dies.*]
>
> (218–21)

The first two lines might almost have come from a morality play, but the couplet makes it plain that Bianca remains stubbornly heterodox. Far from repudiating her love for the Duke, she rejoices in having shared the fatal cup. (It is not the least irony of the play that Middleton grants to Bianca the death Shakespeare denied to Juliet.) If Bianca had not been betrayed, she would never have had the Duke. And the Duke, as she attests in action and in words, matters more to her than anything else. Her death, surely the most impressive in the play, brings her closer to being a tragic figure than one would have imagined possible.

Despite the emphasis Middleton gives to Bianca's death, it occurs in a play with a notably wide field of interest, and in a scene whose dehumanizing and derisive qualities have been remarked.[24] In *The Changeling* (with Rowley, 1622), a play with a narrower and more intense focus, all the action of the main plot culminates in the deaths of Beatrice-Joanna and De Flores. There is nothing derisory about their deaths, and their speeches—particularly those of De Flores—have the stamp of personal utterance. Significantly, both

deaths take place in a part of the play generally attributed to
Rowley.[25]

When De Flores brings Beatrice from Alsemero's closet, he has
already stabbed her fatally and is near death himself. "Come
forth," Alsemero has said, in rather Biblical accents, "you twins of
mischief!" (5.3.142).[26] De Flores answers colloquially and abruptly,
but concludes with an allusion thoroughly consonant with Alsemero's tone:

> Here we are; if you have any more
> To say to us, speak quickly, I shall not
> Give you the hearing else; I am so stout yet,
> And so, I think, that broken rib of mankind.
>
> (143–46)

De Flores, of course, is in a less painful position than Beatrice. He
is not only a man, but an outsider, with no apparent ties other than
to Beatrice. Beatrice, who has dishonored her father, hears him
express his amazement and anguish. As her reply indicates, he
must move toward her, perhaps reach out as if to touch her:

> O come not near me, sir, I shall defile you:
> I am that of your blood was taken from you
> For your better health; look no more upon't,
> But cast it to the ground regardlessly:
> Let the common sewer take it from distinction.
>
> (149–53)

Having, in effect, separated herself from her father, Beatrice goes
on to speak, with a kind of horrified honesty, of the man for whom
she feels she was always destined:

> Beneath the stars, upon yon meteor
> Ever hung my fate, 'mongst things corruptible;
> I ne'er could pluck it from him.
>
> (154–56)

Alsemero learns that he is a cuckold with a difference, since his
wife is "a stranger to [his] bed" (159). Diaphanta, her maid, took
her place—"while," as De Flores interjects, "I coupled with your
mate / At barley-break; now we are left in hell" (162–63).[27] De
Flores, who killed Piraquo to gain possession of Beatrice, has no
regrets. As usual, he takes the low rhetorical road, expressing
himself in an image of striking grossness:

> her honour's prize
> Was my reward; I thank life for nothing
> But that pleasure: it was so sweet to me
> That I have drunk up all, left none behind
> For any man to pledge me.
>
> (167–71)

Her father, understandably, calls him "Horrid villain!" and speaks of torturing him. But De Flores surprises his captors by drawing a knife and using it:

> I can prevent you; here's my penknife still.
> It is but one thread more, [*Stabs himself.*]—and now 'tis cut.
>
> (173–74)

His final thoughts are of the woman he has loved and destroyed:

> Make haste, Joanna, by that token to thee:[28]
> Canst not forget, so lately put in mind,
> I would not go to leave thee far behind. [*Dies.*]
>
> (175–77)

De Flores dies "likes himself," no more willing to be separated from Beatrice by death than in life. Beatrice herself, however, uses her last moments in a way that distances her from him. Instead of responding to what he has said, she asks Alsemero's forgiveness:

> Forgive me, Alsemero, all forgive;
> 'Tis time to die, when 'tis a shame to live. [*Dies.*]
>
> (178–79)

What surprises here is not the conventional morality—Beatrice's sense of guilt and her self-loathing have already been unforgettably expressed in this scene—but the mechanical quality of these lines. What a contrast between telling her father, "I am that of your blood was taken from you / For your better health," and this pallid request for her husband's forgiveness. It is as if Beatrice has drunk up all the dramatic vitality Rowley cares to give her.[29] In death as in life, De Flores dominates.

No Renaissance tragedian of comparable stature does so little with death as Philip Massinger. It is not, as T. A. Dunn has observed, that Massinger eschews the bloody and violent incidents so common in the dramas of his predecessors and contemporaries: his tragedies include "deaths *coram populo*, assassinations, sudden death, and fatal duels." What sets Massinger apart is that he is "positively perfunctory in getting them over with the minimum of fuss."[30] This perfunctoriness may be at least partially explained by Massinger's inability to give much life to his dramatic characters. "A 'living' character," as T. S. Eliot reminds us, "is not necessarily 'true to life.' It is a person whom we can see and hear, whether he be true or false to human nature as we know it."[31] And Massinger's characters, in Dunn's image, "are glove-puppets held in the grip of a rigid and purposeful puppet-master. Their only voice is his voice."[32]

Massinger is, moreover, relentlessly didactic. His greatest fault, as a tragic dramatist, lies in his inveterate moralizing; and his plays pay for it. *The Fatal Dowry* (with Field, 1619),[33] though a collaborative work, is thoroughly representative. Here Charalois, after discovering his wife's affair, compels her cowardly lover, Novall Jr., to fight with him. (One is reminded of Clermont D'Ambois and Montsurrey.)

> *Nouall Iunior.*   Since ther's no remedy
>   Despaire of safety now in me proue courage. [*They fight, Novall is slaine.*]

"How soone weak wrong's o'rthrowne!" comments Charalois (4.2.116–18).[34] Instead of taking vengeance on his wife, Charalois has her tried before her own father, who decrees that she must die, "Let her die then," says Charalois, stabbing her,

> Better prepar'd [spiritually] I am sure I could not take her,
> Nor she accuse her father, as a Iudge
> Partiall against her.
>
> (4.4.148–51)

And Beaumelle dies, not only expressing her satisfaction with the proceedings, but—the idea might have occurred to Fletcher—apparently embracing her husband-executioner:

> I approue his sentence,
> And kisse the executioner: my lust
> Is now run from me in that blood, in which
> It was begot and nourished.
>
> (151–54)

Charalois, in due course, is himself brought to trial for killing Novall Jr. He is acquitted, "notwithstanding you haue gone beyond / The letter of the Law" (5.2.324–25). But Pontalier, a kinsman and

dependent of Novall Jr., stabs him, and is in requital stabbed by
Charalois' friend Romont. "Then comes the lesson," Fredson
Bowers remarks, "Massinger has to teach."[35] For Charalois sees
himself as having been punished by God:

> . . . what's falne vpon me,
> Is by Heauens will, because I made my selfe
> A Iudge in my owne cause without their warrant.
>
> (332–34)

Pontalier acknowledges that he too suffers justly. And Charmi, who
has presided, points to the moral the play is designed to inculcate:

> We are taught
> By this sad president, how iust soeuer
> Our reasons are to remedy our wrongs,
> We are yet to leaue them to their will and power,
> That to that purpose haue authority.
>
> (338–42)

Moral-pointing of this order makes one long for the exuberant
anarchy of Fielding's *Covent Garden Tragedy,* which closes with
the lines: "From such examples as of this and that, / We all are
taught to know I know not what."[36]

The Virgin Martyr (with Dekker, 1620)[37] dramatizes death for
exemplary rather than monitory purposes, being based on the
legend of Saint Dorothea.[38] As Eugene M. Waith has noted, "The
basic problem of making a martyr's life not only instructive but
dramatically effective is that the fortitude to be admired must be
shown by the victim's calm endurance, while the villains occupy
most of the audience's attention with their nefarious activities."[39]
Death is, however, dramatized with progressively greater emphasis.
The two daughters of Theophilus are an instance of "positively
perfunctory" treatment of death. Having been converted by Dorothea, they spit at Jupiter's image and profess themselves Chris-
tians. They are given no dying words. Instead, the emphasis falls on
the fact that their father, urged on by Harpax (a devil in disguise),
kills them; he goes out *"with Harpax hugging him, laughing"*
(3.2.124 s.d.).[40] Dorothea's death is not the climax of the play, but
comes at the end of act 4. She is accompanied by her servant
Angelo, now revealed as an angel, who has been "sent to carry /
[Her] pure and innocent soule to ioyes eternall" (4.3.144–45). Also
with her is Antoninus, who languishes for her love.[41] She asks
Angelo to convert this love to heavenly love; he promises to do so,

adding that Antoninus and Dorothea will die at the same instant. Immediately, Antoninus feels himself transformed by "holy fire." Theophilus enters, and asks if Dorothea has any final words. "Nothing," she replies, "but blame / Thy tardinesse in sending me to rest":

> My peace is made with heauen, to which my soule
> Begins to take her flight, strike, O strike quickly,
> And though you are vnmou'd to see my death,
> Hereafter when my story shall be read,
> As they were present now, the hearers shall
> Say this of Dorothea with wet eyes,
> She liu'd a virgin, and a virgin dies. [*Her head strucke off.*]

"O take my soule along to waite on thine," says Antoninus, expiring as Angelo has promised (171–80).

The play culminates in the martyrdom of Theophilus, who dies witnessing to the faith he has so zealously persecuted. Like Dorothea, he welcomes death; he even complains that his torturers are not hurting him as much as he desires. Then—to the consternation of Harpax—

> *Enter Dorothea in a white robe, crownes vpon her robe, a Crowne vpon her head, lead in by [Angelo] the Angell, Antoninus, Caliste and Christeta following all in white, but lesse glorious, the Angel with a Crowne for him [Theophilus].* (5.2.219 s.d.)[42]

Thus "confirm'd," Theophilus puts off mortality:

> Oh now I feele thee, blessed spirits I come,
> And witnesse for me, all these wounds and scarres,
> I die a souldier in the Christian warres. [*Dies.*]
>
> (231–33)

When death ceases to be death, we are in a world beyond tragedy.

In the three tragedies he wrote without a collaborator, Massinger works with thoroughly conventional subjects. In *The Duke of Milan* (1621), a play often compared to *Othello*, Francisco convinces the title figure, Sforza, that Sforza's wife, Marcelia, has sought to seduce him. Francisco suggests that "to proue her temper to the height, / Say only that I am dead, and then obserue how farre / She'le be transported" (4.3.257–59).[43] Her response, as M. J. Thorssen notes, though "worldly-wise and aggressive," has the same consequences as the "innocent passivity" of Desdemona: "Genuinely outraged at being suspected of adultery, [she] openly expresses her anger at her husband's lack of trust, and in retaliation, insists that she did indeed love Francisco."[44] Sforza immediately stabs her. Too late, she proclaims her innocence, and discloses that Francisco had in fact sought to seduce her. The only nonexpository words she speaks are her farewell: "May heauen forgiue you" (312).

The murder of Marcelia, obviously indebted to *Othello,* may also remind us of the ironic reversal in *The Second Maiden's Tragedy,* in which a husband learns at the last that his apparently chaste wife is even falser than he had once feared her to be. In any event, Massinger goes to *The Second Maiden's Tragedy* for his play's spectacular denouement.[45] Sforza lapses into madness after his wife's death; his doctors, fearing he may kill himself, persuade him to believe that her wound is not fatal. But the body will soon putrefy, and they fear he will take his life on discovering the imposture. Their plight provides an opportunity for Francisco, who turns out to be avenging himself on Sforza for seducing his sister.[46] Posing as a Jewish physician and accompanied by his sister (also in disguise), he promises to make Marcelia's corpse seem to be alive. But he must, he adds, be left alone to practice his art.

Like Govianus in *The Second Maiden's Tragedy,* he poisons the corpse; like the Tyrant, Sforza kisses it. Revealing himself, Francisco tells Sforza to "looke on this face / Made old by thy base falshood, 'tis Eugenia" (5.2.233–34). The first part of his revenge was causing Sforza to murder his innocent wife; now his vengeance is complete:

> I haue giuen thee poison
> In this cup, now obserue me, which thy lust
> Carowsing deeply of, made thee forget
> Thy vow'd faith to Eugenia.
>
> (239–42)

He will go to his death well pleased:

> I leaue the world with glory; they are men
> And leaue behind them name and memory,
> That wrong'd doe right themselues before they die.
>
> (253–55)

Obviously, Massinger has lavished attention on the machinations of Francisco. By contrast, he shows little interest in dramatizing Sforza's response to impending death: the dominant tradition here is that of wittily ironic vengeance rather than the drama of character. Sforza's first words after hearing he has been poisoned place him among the ranks of Massingerian moralists. Asked by his mother, "How do you Sir?" he replies: "Like one, / That learnes to know in death what punishment, / Waites on the breach of faith" (243–45). And he falls into the stock language of one suffering from poison: "Now I feele / An Aetna in my entrailes! . . . I burne, I burne" (245–46; 248). But his final speech is in a different vein:

> I come death, I obey thee,
> Yet I will not die raging, for alas,
> My whole life was a phrensie. Good Eugenia
> In death forgiue me. As you loue me beare her
> To some religious house, there let her spend
> The remnant of her life, when I am ashes
> Perhaps shee'll be appeas'd, and spare a prayer
> For my poore soule. Bury me with Marcelia
> And let our Epitaph be—
>
> (256–64)

Who would have thought that Massinger would give Sforza such a death? Instead of anguished ravings, there is concern for Eugenia; and he dies, not in a platitude, but in midspeech. This too is a convention, of course—one thinks of Hotspur and Cleopatra. But as these examples suggest, it is a convention designed to create the greatest possible impression of realism.

The Roman Actor (1626) is like *The Duke of Milan* in its emphasis on the witty means by which characters die. The characters themselves, however—Paris and Domitianus Caesar—are permitted nothing resembling a final address to the world. Paris, appropriately cast as the title figure of *The False Servant,* is killed by Caesar in the course of its action. Massinger dispenses with him in a single line: "Oh, I am slaine in earnest" (4.2.283).[47] Caesar, overpowered by conspirators, speaks with comparable brevity: "'Tis done, 'tis done basely" (5.2.72).

The Unnatural Combat (1626) gives greater scope to death, but offers nothing like Sforza's final speech. Malefort Jr., mortally wounded by his own father, is not even given a death speech. (Massinger wishes to tantalize his audience by keeping the reason why Malefort Jr. desires his father's death as mysterious as possible.) Indeed, the son's last words precede the combat:

> Thou incensed Power,
> A while forbeare thy thunder, let me have

> No aid in my revenge, if from the grave
> My mother—

"Thou shalt never name her more," his father interjects (2.1.189–92).[48]

Theocrine, Malefort Sr.'s daughter, dies after being ravished by Montrevile, a character in some respects modeled on Massinger's own Francisco.[49] Malefort, after preventing Theocrine from marrying the man she loves, confides to Montrevile that he "languish[es] to / Enjoy her as a husband" (4.1.225–26). So that he will not be tempted by seeing her, he asks Montrevile to keep her at the fort he commands. Later, when Malefort decides not to "curbe [his] freedome" with the name of incest (5.2.39), Montrevile brutally restores her to him: *The souldiers thrust forth Theocrine, her garments loose, her haire disheveld* (5.2.185 s.d.). Echoing Beatrice-Joanna,[50] she insists that her father not approach:

> O come not neere me sir, I am infectious;
> To looke on me at distance is as dangerous
> As from a pinacles cloud-kissing spire,
> With giddy eyes to view the steepe descent,
> But to acknowledge me a certaine ruine.
>
> (198–202)

Beatrice-Joanna, of course, has some cause to speak as she does. Although Theocrine's sense of shame is understandable, she is an innocent victim. Nor does the prolix simile help matters. But her next speech, in which she accuses her father, rises to a higher level:

> Pray you turne away
> Your face and heare me, and with my last breath
> Give me leave to accuse you. What offence
> From my first infancie did I commit
> That for a punishment you should give up
> My Virgin chastity to the trecherous guard
> Of Goatish Montrevile?
>
> (205–11)

Malefort is so stunned that he needlessly asks her to tell him what Montrevile did. "Abus'd me sir by violence," she replies, "and this told / I cannot live to speake more":

> may the cause
> In you finde pardon, but the speeding curse

> Of a ravish'd maid fall heavie, heavie on him.
> Beaufort my lawfull love, farewell for ever. [*Dies.*]
>
> (212–16)

All is calculated to increase Malefort's anguish. His incestuous passion has brought her to this.

Theocrine's rape and death, horrible though they are, are chiefly significant in terms of their impact on Malefort. What happens to her is part of his punishment. As Dunn observes, "It may be very reasonably maintained that when Massinger sacrifices the innocent he gets a *quid pro quo* in a more impressive sanction for his moral lesson. It may be good that one good man or woman should die for the good of the moral."[51] Such is the case with Theocrine. Indeed, Theocrine's fate is later shown to be something more than the natural consequence of her father's miscalculations. Through her, Heaven is punishing him.

This is made relentlessly clear by what follows. Montrevile appears above and mocks Malefort, but is interrupted by a soldier who brings word that the fort is under attack. Suddenly, a storm begins; Lear-like, Malefort remarks that he feels a greater tempest within himself. Then, like Richard III, Malefort receives a terrible visitation:

> *Enter the Ghost of young Malefort, naked from the wast, full of wounds, leading in the shadow of a Ladie, her face leprous.* (271 s.d.)

Unlike the ghosts who appear to Richard, these ghosts do not speak. But their gestures answer Malefort's questions:

> You come to launce my sear'd up conscience? Yes,
> And to instruct me, that those thunderbolts,
> That hurl'd me headlong from the height of glory,
> Wealth, honours, wordly happinesse, were forg'd
> Upon the anvile of my impious wrongs
> And cruelty to you? I doe confesse it.
>
> (280–85)

He confesses that, in order to marry a second wife (Theocrine's mother), he poisoned his first. This is why his son sought to kill him—and why the combat ended as it did:

> . . . thou being my sonne,
> Were't not a competent judge mark'd out by heaven

> For her revenger, which thy falling by
> My weaker hand confirm'd.
>
> (294–97)

As he asks himself if it is too late to save himself through penance or repentance, the ghosts vanish without a gesture. Malefort now turns to blaming fate and the stars:

> What's left to doe then? I'll accuse my fate
> That did not fashion me for nobler uses:
> Or if those starres crosse to me in my birth,
> Had not deni'd their prosperous influence to it,
> With peace of conscience like to innocent men,
> I might have ceas'd to be, and not as now,
> To curse my cause of being. [*He's kill'd with a flash of lightning.*]
>
> (300–306)

So perishes Malefort Sr., struck down by the "incensed Power" alluded to by his son (2.1.189). "The unique catastrophe," as Bowers notes, ". . . is a logical progression to the last step in the dramatic portrayal of the religious contention that all revenge should be left to God."[52] But the Q.E.D. fashion in which Massinger dramatizes this idea makes an instance of divine intervention such as the death of D'Amville in *The Atheist's Tragedy* seem almost subtle. Whether or not Massinger remembered D'Amville, he is certainly thinking of the last moments of Faustus. Marlowe, of course, dramatizes Faustus's last moments with total integrity. He has no need to extinguish him with a thunderbolt; what happens to him grows out of the action of the play. And how thoroughly Massingerian is Malefort's final soliloquy. Faustus speaks like Faustus; Marlowe has disappeared into his dramatic character. Malefort has no voice of his own, and dies to point a moral. As usual, Massinger submits himself to the didactic element.

6
Ford and Shirley

Middleton's death scenes tend to be harshly ironic, even derisive, with dehumanized characters dying as befits them; Massinger rarely does much with the last moments of his protagonists. In Ford, however, one finds an almost obsessive concentration on how characters confront death. The manner in which his protagonists die is the definitive "performance" of their lives. And, whether or not they are morally admirable, their deaths are designed to astonish and impress.

Love's Sacrifice (1632), the least successful of Ford's extant tragedies,[1] dramatizes four deaths. The first, that of Ferentes, is presented with grotesque humor. Ferentes is stabbed in the course of a masque by Colona, Julia, and Morona, all three of whom he has seduced and mocked. Before he can determine the extent of his wounds the women enter unmasked, each bearing a child he has fathered. Each hurls back at him the insult she had received:

> *Colona.* I was too *quickly wonne,* you slaue.
> *Morona.* I was *too old,* you dogge.
> *Iulia.* I (and I neuer shall forget the wrong)
>   I was not *faire enough,* not *faire enough*
>   For thee, thou monster; let me cut his gall. [*She stabs him.*]
>   Not *faire enough!* oh scorne! not *faire enough?*
>
> (1880–85)[2]

The women are most unusual revengers;[3] and Ferentes, instead of offering the sort of sober self-judgment Massinger would have equipped him with, expires echoing Mercutio ("I am pepper'd") and scattering jests and insults:

> Pox vpon all Codpeece extrauagancy.
> I am pepper'd—oh, oh, oh—Duke forgiue me.
> Had I rid any tame beasts, but Barbary wild Colts,
> I had not bin thus jerk'd out of the saddle.
> My forfeit was in my blood, and my life hath answer'd it.

Vengeance on all wild whores, I say,—oh 'tis true;
Farewell generation of Hackneyes.—ooh. [*Dyes.*]

(1889–95)

After such rhetoric—especially the witty variation on the biblical, and Shakespearean,[4] "generation of vipers"—the Abbot's moralizing seems somewhat inadequate: "Here's fatall sad presages, but 'tis iust, / He dyes by murther, that hath liu'd in lust" (1903–4).

The death of Biancha reflects the extravagances of Fletcherian dramaturgy. Biancha, Duke Caraffa's wife, is passionately in love with Fernando, his young favorite. The Duke surprises them exchanging kisses during a nocturnal meeting, and has Fernando taken away by guards. Instead of attempting to mollify her husband, Biancha offers an outrageous defense of her behavior:

Can you imagine, Sir, the name of Duke
Could make a crooked leg, a scambling foot,
A tolerable face, a wearish hand,
A bloodlesse lip, or such an vntrimm'd beard
As yours, fit for a Ladies pleasure, no:
I wonder you could thinke 'twere possible,
When I had once but look'd on your Fernando,
I euer could loue you againe?

(2436–43)

The speech is reminiscent of Marcelia's deliberate provocation of her husband in *The Duke of Milan,* but more obviously out of character.[5] Unlike Marcelia, however, Biancha denies being guilty of adultery—not because of her fidelity to Caraffa, but because Fernando refused to comply with her amorous desires:

I must confesse I mist no meanes, no time,
To winne him to my bosome; but so much,
So holily, with such Religion,
He kept the lawes of friendship, that my sute
Was held but, in comparison, a iest.

(2485–89)

Since Fernando's chaste forbearance has been motivated by his respect for Biancha's marriage vows, not his fidelity to the Duke, this account of his conduct seems calculated to save his life. But the Duke, who remains unconvinced by her denial of adultery, tells her to ready herself for death. She will, she replies, "to the point / Of thy sharpe sword, with open brest . . . runne / Halfe way thus naked" (2527–29); but she again asks that he spare his "noble

friend" Fernando: "For life to me, without him, were a death"
(2533).[6] Instead of killing her, Caraffa drops the sword. But, goaded
by his sister, he stabs Biancha with his dagger. Now Biancha, who
has already conducted herself in a fashion reminiscent of Fletcher's
awe-inspiring women, dies like one of his tender creatures of pathos:

> 'Tis brauely done; thou hast strucke home at once:
> Liue to repent too late: Commend my loue
> To thy true friend, my loue to him that owes it,
> [M]y Tragedy to thee, my hart to—to—Fernand-oo oh. [*Dies.*]
>
> (2546–49)

Fernando and Caraffa die in what has been called "the silliest
final scene in Jacobean tragedy."[7] Caraffa, now convinced of
Biancha's chastity, visits her tomb. But she is not alone: *"One goes
to open the Tombe, out of which ariseth Fernando in his winding
sheet, onely his face discouered; as Caraffa is going in, he puts him
backe"* (2763–65 s.d.). Finding that Fernando is adamant about
denying him entry, Caraffa orders his guards to "drag him out"
(2795). But before they can do so Fernando drinks poison:

> I haue out-stript thy plots:
> Not all the cunning *Antidotes of Art*
> Can warrant me twelue minutes of my life:
> It workes, it workes already, brauely, brauely.—
> Now, now I feele it teare each seuerall ioynt:
> O royall poyson? trusty friend? split, split
> Both heart and gall asunder. . . .[5]
>   well search'd out
> Swift nimble venome, torture euery veyne.
> I, come Biancha,—cruell torment feast,
> Feast on, doe; Duke farewell. Thus I—hot flames
> Conclude my Loue—and seale it in my bosome, oh—[*Dies.*]
>
> (2799–2809)

The familiar rhetoric of death might have been written by scores of
Ford's contemporaries. What is unusual is not the description of
what the poison does to the body, but the speaker's attitude toward
pain. As Ronald Huebert observes, "Fernando seems to stretch the
moment of death to its maximum length. He does not merely
describe the sensation of pain. He uses the imperative mood to
invite and demand the mingled agony and ecstasy of dying."[8]
Whether or not Huebert is correct about "ecstasy," the passage is
shocking in its masochism.

Similarly masochistic is the death of Caraffa, whose suicide follows almost immediately. Calling Fernando "a friend vnmatch't" (2815), he asks to be buried with Biancha and Fernando in a single monument. He then stabs himself:

> Oh that these thicke streames
> Could gather head, and make a standing poole,
> That jealous husbands here might bathe in blood.
> So; I grow sweetly empty; all the pipes
> Of life vn-vessell life; now heauens wipe out
> The writing of my sinne: Biancha, thus
> I creepe to thee—to thee—to thee Bi—an—cha. [*Dyes.*]
>
> (2835–41)

Caraffa's death is the last—and most inadequately motivated—of "love's sacrifices." Ferentes falls an unwilling sacrifice to his lustful and cynical exploitation of women; Biancha, detected in what Caraffa believes to be an adulterous relationship with Fernando, dies trying to save her lover's life. These deaths are not problematic in terms of Elizabethan dramatic convention. Caraffa's death is another matter. He resembles Fernando both in dying to rejoin Biancha, and in the pleasure he appears to take in pain. Unlike Fernando, however, he is punishing himself—a fact that in itself might appear to make his attitude toward suffering more understandable. As Huebert remarks, "Caraffa's need for pain seems to be linked to his desire for forgiveness. He has after all murdered the chaste Biancha, and he welcomes pain as a form of self-imposed penance."[9] But Biancha's virtue consists either of stopping short of a passionately desired physical consummation, or of failing to seduce Fernando; even Caraffa has no reason to regard her as such a paragon. His death, then, seems contrived—and it is probably significant that his last two lines (and the accompanying action) are redolent of Fletcherian pathos.[10]

Death is given no less emphasis and considerably greater scope in *'Tis Pity She's a Whore* (1632), Ford's most violent play, which dramatizes the deaths of six characters. Bergetto, a comic "innocent" or fool, is reminiscent of Ferentes in that his death produces some grotesque humor. (Bergetto, however, is the victim of a mistake: Grimaldi, who stabs him, thinks he is taking vengeance on Soranzo, his rival for Annabella; and the poison in which he dips his rapier is supplied by Richardetto, whose wife, Hippolita, Soranzo has whored.) "O help, help, here's a stitch fallen in my guts," Bergetto cries out; "O for a flesh-tailor quickly" (3.7.8–9);[11] "I am sure I cannot piss forward and backward, and yet I am wet before and behind" (11–12); "my belly seethes like a porridge-pot" (18). But his final speech, in which he expresses his concern for Richardetto's niece, whom he had intended to marry, is not devoid of dignity:

> Is all this mine own blood? nay then, goodnight with me; Poggio [his servant], commend me to my uncle, dost hear? Bid him for my sake make much of this wench—O, I am going the wrong way sure, my belly aches so—O fare-well, Poggio—O——O—— [*Dies.*]
>
> (3.7.29–33)

The effect of all this is more complex than one might have expected. A character whose primary function has been to elicit derisive laughter is to a degree humanized by death.

Hippolita's death is the ironic consequence of her own plot to murder Soranzo. Vasques, Soranzo's servant, pretends to be in league with her but sees to it that she drinks the poisoned wine she has intended for his master. Pain and vengefulness dominate her final moments:

> . . . had that slave
> Kept promise—O, my torment!—thou this hour
> Hadst died, Soranzo.—Heat above hell-fire!—
> Yet ere I pass away—cruel, cruel flames!—
> Take here my curse amongst you: may thy bed
> Of marriage be a rack unto thy heart—
> Burn, blood, and boil in vengeance; O my heart—
> My flame's intolerable!—May'st thou live
> To father bastards, may her womb bring forth
> Monsters, and die together in your sins
> Hated, scorned and unpitied!—O—O— [*Dies.*]
>
> (4.290–300)

It is a death that without the exclamatory "breaks," would have far greater force. But Ford seems to be trying to achieve the sort of dramatic effect one associates with Middleton: the almost mechanically inserted references to physical suffering dehumanize and distance, making Hippolita's death something that an audience observes without any expenditure of sympathetic involvement.

The death of Annabella is, by contrast, almost pure pathos. Unlike Shakespeare's Desdemona, who strives desperately to save her own life (see chapter 8), Annabella meets death with what Robert Davril describes as "une sorte de paisible abandon qui fait jaillir la pitié."[12] Giovanni, who means to kill her in order to frustrate Soranzo's intended revenge, tells her to pray:

> Pray, Annabella, pray; since we must part,
> Go thou white in thy soul, to fill a throne
> Of innocence and sanctity in Heaven.
> Pray, pray my sister.
>
> (5.5.63–66)

Instead of readying her soul for death, Annabella invokes heavenly protection: "Then I see your drift; / Ye blessed angels, guard me!" (66–67). Yet she herself takes no action. Giovanni asks her to kiss him; she does so. Some ten lines later he asks for a second kiss: "Kiss me again—forgive me." "With all my heart," she replies (78). Though the dialogue has established that Giovanni means to kill her, Annabella is too dazed to comprehend what is about to happen. This is most clearly shown by her response to his ominous "Farewell": "Will you be gone?" (79). After "one other kiss" (83), he stabs her: "Revenge is mine; honour doth love command" (86). Her reaction is the shocked "O brother, by your hand?" (87). Her last words mingle prayer and reproach:

> Forgive him, Heaven—and me my sins; farewell,
> Brother, unkind, unkind—mercy, great Heaven!—O—O! [Dies.]
>
> (91–92)

The scene of Annabella's death is dominated by Giovanni, whose hypertrophic egotism is the more evident when set against the trancelike state of the pathetically diminished Annabella. As Ralph J. Kaufmann remarks, "we can see very clearly that Giovanni is no longer *with* his sister. He acts unilaterally. He no longer possesses the love to share even his plans for a *Liebestod* with her. His selfishness has grown perfect, his love become an abstract and self-oriented thing."[13] In the play's final scene, as Derek Roper has noted, "It becomes clear that the shock of having killed his sister has pushed him over the line between what Kaufmann calls 'auto-intoxication' and madness."[14] While Soranzo and his guests prepare to feast, Giovanni enters with Annabella's heart on his dagger—"proud," as he tells Soranzo, "in the spoil / Of love and vengeance!" (5.6.11–12).[15] As if he expects his father to approve, he informs him that he "will yield up / How much I have deserved to be your son" (37–38). He recounts the story of incestuous love, including the fact that Annabella had become pregnant. Soranzo, still hoping that Giovanni may not really have killed Annabella, sends Vasques to fetch her; moments later Vasques returns, confirming that her heart has been ripped from her bosom. The news is fatal to Giovanni's father, who expires with grief: "Cursèd man!—

have I lived to—" (61). Giovanni's madness is plain from his approving comment: "Why this was done with courage" (66); as for himself, he is not stained, but "gilt in the blood / Of a fair sister and a hapless father" (67–68). It remains to complete his revenge on Soranzo.

> *Soranzo.* Inhuman scorn of men, hast thou a thought
>   T' outlive thy murders?
> *Giovanni.*   Yes, I tell thee yes;
> For in my fists I bear the twists of life.
> Soranzo, see this heart which was thy wife's:
> Thus I exchange it royally for thine, [*Stabs him.*]
> And thus, and thus; now brave revenge is mine.
>
> (69–74)

Vasques, seeing his master fall, attacks Giovanni but finds it necessary to summon the banditti whose intended role was to kill Giovanni and Annabella in the act of incest. These men, seconded by Vasques, prove too much for Giovanni:

> Oh, I can stand no longer; feeble arms,
> Have you so soon lost strength? [*Falls.*]
>
> (82–83)

Vasques turns to Soranzo, who expresses satisfaction to have "lived / To see my wrongs revenged on that black devil" (89–90); "let not that lecher live—O!" (92). Soranzo's dying words prove a needless admonition. Giovanni is already near death. "Whose hand gave me this wound?" he asks (95); Vasques claims credit for it: "Mine sir, I was your first man; have you enough?" (96). Giovanni, who dominates even in death, assures him that he has done for him only what he would have done to himself. Echoing one of Hieronimo's lines in the 1602 additions to *The Spanish Tragedy,* he taunts Vasques by asking about Soranzo: "Art sure thy lord is dead?" (99).[16] The Cardinal calls on Giovanni to "think on thy life and end, and call for mercy" (101). But Giovanni, who is glad to be dying, merely replies: "Mercy? Why, I have found it in this justice" (102). From his point of view, there is no repentance, nothing to repent. Though he has, as Roper observes, "recapture[d] lucidity," he remains "reckless and absolute, a true descendant of Tamburlaine and Faustus. His sweet earthly fruition, his perfect bliss and sole felicity, is the beautiful girl who happens to be his sister."[17] The only "grace" he seeks, even in death, is union with her:

O, I bleed fast;
Death, thou art a guest long looked-for, I embrace
Thee and thy wounds: O, my last minute comes.
Where'er I go, let me enjoy this grace,
Freely to view my Annabella's face. [*Dies.*]

(103–7)

Few Renaissance tragedies give death scenes greater prominence than *Love's Sacrifice* and *'Tis Pity She's a Whore*. Yet in *The Broken Heart* (1629) Ford focuses on the last moments of the dying in a way that makes this play his *ne plus ultra* in the representation of death. The three characters whose deaths are dramatized—Ithocles, Orgilus, and Calantha—die slowly and ritualistically. Each is accorded due weight. "With all," as Clifford Leech remarks, ". . . there is a sense that they are most supremely themselves in the moment of death, that this moment definitively marks their characters."[18] By their deaths they become what they are.

Before the action of the play begins, Ithocles has forced his sister Penthea to marry Bassanes rather than Orgilus, to whom she had been betrothed. It is for this that Orgilus kills him. The scene in which Orgilus takes his revenge begins just after Penthea has died from self-imposed starvation. Her body, face veiled, is brought on stage in a chair borne by her maids of honor, Chrystalla and Philema; two servants place chairs on either side of it. Ithocles and Orgilus enter as the servants are leaving: " 'Tis done; that [chair] on her right hand," one of them tells Orgilus (4.4.1).[19] Before proceeding Orgilus asks Philema and Chrystalla "How fares the lady?" "Dead!" "Dead!" "Starved!" "Starved!" they reply (3). The doubling of each word—like voice and echo—is the language of ritual. Even when their voices separate in the account they give of Penthea's last moments, their speeches are almost identical in style and length. To Chrystalla it falls to describe Penthea's final words and action: " 'O cruel Ithocles, and injured Orgilus!' / So down she drew her veil; so died" (9–10).

Sending Chrystalla and Philema away, Orgilus requests that Ithocles sit, indicating the chair with the "engine."[20] Once Ithocles is in his power, Orgilus gloats over him, mocking his "throne of coronation" (23); unveiling Penthea, he shows him "a beauty withered by the flames / Of an insulting Phaethon, her brother" (25–26). While dreaming of being married to the princess Calantha, Orgilus continues, Ithocles had no thoughts for the sister whose happiness he had destroyed. "As for my injuries,"

Alas, they were beneath your royal pity.
But yet they lived, thou proud man, to confound thee.
Behold thy fate, this steel.

(36–39)

All has gone according to Orgilus's design: to this point the scene is
in the tradition of witty vengeance, in which the cleverness of the
killer is more important than the response of the victim. But Ithocles's next words show that Ford is interested in something quite
beyond cunning ensnarement:

                    Strike home. A courage
As keen as thy revenge shall give it welcome.
But prithee faint not. . . .
Thou lookest that I should whine and beg compassion,
As loath to leave the vainness of my glories.
A statelier resolution arms my confidence,
To cozen thee of honour; neither could I,
With equal trial of unequal fortune,
By hazard of a duel; 'twere a bravery
Too mighty for a slave intending murder.
On to the execution.

(39–41; 43–50)

Impressed by this "goodly language" (52), Orgilus expresses admiration for the man that he is about to kill. What Orgilus has
conceived of as a murder becomes a sacrifice in which both men
participate. "Give me thy hand," says Orgilus. "Be healthful in thy
parting / From lost morality. Thus, thus, I free it" (58–59). "Yet, yet,
I scorn to shrink," replies Ithocles (59). In order to be "gentle even
in blood" (61), Orgilus must stab him again. And Ithocles dies
forgiving the man who has taken his life:

Nimble in vengeance, I forgive thee. Follow
Safety, with best success. O may it prosper!
Penthea, by thy side thy brother bleeds:
The earnest of his wrongs to thy forced faith.

(63–66)

Unlike Giovanni, who thinks only of union with Annabella, Ithocles renounces love (as well as ambition); his thoughts move from
the world's turbulence to the "peace" of heaven:

Thoughts of ambition, or delicious banquet,
With beauty, youth, and love, together perish

> In my last breath, which on the sacred altar
> Of a long-looked-for peace—now—moves—to heaven.
>
> (67–70)

The death of Orgilus, like that of Ithocles, desensationalizes the sensational; it too is a bloody ritual enacted in tranquility. Given his "choice / Of what death likes thee best" by Calantha (5.2.80–81), Orgilus chooses "To bleed to death" (99). He himself will lance the vein in one arm, but requests help with the other:

> Only I am a beggar to some charity
> To speed me in this execution,
> By lending th' other prick to th' other arm,
> When this is bubbling life out.
>
> (104–7)

Bassanes offers to assist him, and Orgilus thanks him: "Such courtesies are real which flow cheerfully / Without an expectation of requital" (110–11). Even more than Ithocles, he turns the necessity of his death into an occasion for enacting his own greatness:

> Reach me a staff in this hand. If a proneness
> Or custom in my nature from my cradle
> Had been inclined to fierce and eager bloodshed,
> A coward guilt, hid in a coward quaking,
> Would have betrayed fame to ignoble flight
> And vagabond pursuit of dreadful safety.
> But look upon my steadiness, and scorn not
> The sickness of my fortune, which since Bassanes
> Was husband to Penthea, had lain bed-rid.
> We trifle time in words. Thus I show cunning
> In opening of a vein too full, too lively.
>
> (112–22)

Bassanes, playing his part in the ceremony, opens the vein on Orgilus's other arm. "This pastime," he declares, "Appears majestical":

> Some high-tuned poem
> Hereafter shall deliver to posterity
> The writer's glory and his subject's triumph.
>
> (131–34)

There could be no clearer indication of how Ford wishes us to respond to Orgilus's words and actions: Orgilus is not (to anticipate

Eliot on Othello) "cheering himself up," but dying in a way that turns death into triumph. After speaking of those on whom he will "wait in death" (Calantha's father, Penthea, and Ithocles), he explains that he used "an engine" on Ithocles not out of fear, but because "I durst not / Engage the goodness of a cause on fortune, / By which his name might have out-faced my vengeance" (142–44). In saying this he acknowledges that he found it necessary to subordinate honor to vengeance. Then, recalling what the "oraculous" Tecnicus had foretold (4.2.139), he applies his words to his own death:

> *Revenge proves its own executioner.*
> When feeble man is bending to his mother,
> The dust 'a was first framed on, thus he totters.
>
> (147–49)

"Life's fountain is dried up," observes Bassanes. And Orgilus, apparently no longer able to remain upright, speaks for the last time:

> So falls the standards
> Of my prerogative in being a creature.
> A mist hangs o'er mine eyes. The sun's bright splendour
> Is clouded in an everlasting shadow.
> Welcome thou ice that sittest about my heart;
> No heat can ever thaw thee.
>
> (150–55)

These words (as was not the case with Ithocles, and his anomalous reference to heaven) are perfectly suited to both character and play. Orgilus's tragedy of depletion has run its course. But what he has made of his role raises it, in the context Ford creates, to the realm of high and "majestical" art. Indeed, as Huebert remarks, "The way the scene is organized, dramatically, stresses the emotions connected with dying: in the total excitement of the moment we almost forget that the suffering lover is also a criminal facing execution."[21] His death is, in a special sense, a rite of passage.

In the deaths of Ithocles and Orgilus, Ford combines stage sensationalism with dramatic ritual. The death of Calantha, though even more highly ritualized, is set apart by the absence of physical violence. For those who do not find Ford's "artificial" dramaturgy a barrier to emotional responsiveness,[22] the scene of her death is the most memorable and impressive in the play—the death that crowns the work.

The scene (5.3) is preceded by an unusually elaborate stage direction:

An altar covered with white. Two lights of virgin wax. Music of recorders; during which enter four bearing Ithocles on a hearse, or in a chair, in a rich robe, and a crown on his head; [they] place him on one side of the altar. After him enter Calantha in a white robe and crowned. . . .

Various others accompany her; she *"goes and kneels before the altar. The rest stand off, the women kneeling behind. Cease recorders during her devotions. Soft music. Calantha and the rest rise, doing obeisance to the altar."* After this wordless ritual has been performed, Calantha finally speaks, asking counsel in choosing a husband. "A woman," she declares, "has enough to govern wisely / Her own demeanours, passions, and divisions" (8–9). Upon being told that she should choose for herself, she turns to Nearchus, Prince of Argos, as if to treat of articles to be agreed to prior to their marriage. After Nearchus has promised to do what she requires, she refers to "the honours, titles, and preferments" so briefly possessed by her "neglected husband" (57–58). Nearchus asks what she means, and she replies:

> Forgive me. Now I turn to thee, thou shadow
> Of my contracted lord. Bear witness all,
> I put my mother's wedding ring upon
> His finger. 'Twas my father's last bequest.
> Thus I new-marry him whose wife I am.
> Death shall not separate us.
>
> (62–67)

Earlier, she had displayed astonishing Stoic discipline when she did not permit the successive revelations of the deaths of her father, Penthea, and Ithocles to interrupt the completion of the dance in which she and others were engaged (5.2). Now she reveals what was happening beneath her seeming equanimity:

> O my lords,
> I but deceived your eyes with antic gesture,
> When one news straight came huddling on another,
> Of death, and death, and death. Still I danced forward;
> But it struck home, and here, and in an instant. . . .
> They are the silent griefs which cut the heart-strings.
> Let me die smiling.
>
> (67–71; 75–76)

And, taking her farewell of Ithocles and proclaiming Nearchus her successor, she orders the singing of her funeral-hymn ("the song / I fitted for my end" [79–80]). To its strains she expires, dying with the concluding couplet: *"Love only reigns in death; though art / Can find no comfort for a broken heart"* (93–94).[23]

Calantha's death, as Thelma N. Greenfield has noted, is set apart from all others in the play, "represent[ing] a sensibility . . . so aristocratic that not old age, starvation, diabolic machine, or bloodletting but only repeated shock need be evoked to shatter it."[24] Yet this sensibility is wedded to a self-control so impressive that Calantha fashions her death into the most impressive "performance" of all. "When Calantha pronounces her own coronation-turned-abdication and marriage-funeral rites," Greenfield remarks, "the union of ritualized action and ritual language and the ceremonial paradoxes reach full strength. Fulfilling her personal destiny and her public duty at the same time, . . . Calantha harmonizes disparate elements that have hitherto in the play been at war."[25] One may add that the fashion in which Calantha presides over her death, her final words, and the song to which she dies combine to make death itself seem a voluntary cessation—as if life remains her subject until she licenses it to depart. Like Shakespeare's Cordelia, she seems a queen over her passions, however keenly they strike home. What the scene presents, then, is heroic deportment in a pathetic context; for as Eugene M. Waith has observed, "In only one respect, but an important one, does this quiet scene resemble those in more obviously heroic plays: it is clearly calculated to arouse the wonder of the spectators at the greatness of the heroine's spirit."[26] Though this is a long way from the wonder-working words and deeds of a Tamburlaine, we are nonetheless in the presence of the heroic.[27]

Shirley's tragedies suffer from the same defect one finds in Massinger. "Most of Shirley's heroes and heroines," writes Ben Lucow, "lack the complexity of Webster's or Ford's. They are, in fact, interchangeable from play to play."[28] What they can say is limited by what they are: the rather mechanical constructs of a playwright more interested in artful plotting than in the creation and revelation of character. Unlike Massinger, Shirley frequently places considerable emphasis on the dying words of his principal characters. Yet their speeches rarely seem to engage him. Greatness of utterance one has no reason to expect, but what they say tends to be wearisome, stale and flat, unprofitable to analyze.[29]

In *The Maid's Revenge* (1626), Berinthia's brother Sebastian, acting on their father's orders, kills her lover Antonio in a duel.[30] In vengeance, Berinthia stabs him while he is sleeping. "Oh stay thy hand," he cries out. But he is too late:

> —Berinthia! oh, thou'st done't.
> I wish thee heaven's foregiveness; I cannot
> Tarry to hear thy reasons: at many doors
> My life runs out. . . .
> Antonio, oh, Antonio, we shall now
> Be friends again. [*Dies.*]
>
>   (5.2; 1 : 181)[31]

Berinthia has already poisoned her sister Catalina and their maid, who now enter. After declaring what she has done to them and pointing to the corpse of Sebastian, she stabs herself. But she lingers on while the poison torments her two victims. Catalina speaks the grotesque rhetoric used by (among others) Webster's Flaminio when feigning death throes, and Ford's Bergetto when dying in earnest:

> . . . a cooler! a cooler! there's a smith's forge in my belly, and the devil blows the bellows. Snow-water! Berinthia has poisoned me . . . ; I must hence, hence; farewell! will you let me die so? Confusion, torment, death, hell!
>
>   (5.3; pp. 183–84)

Having expressed her delight at witnessing Catalina's suffering, Berinthia addresses her last words to their father:

> Your passion's fruitless;
> My soul is reeling forth, I know not whither.
> Oh, father!
> My heart weeps tears for you; I die. Oh, see
> *A Maid's Revenge* with her own Tragedy. [*Dies.*]
>
>   (P. 184)

And Catalina follows her: "Oh, I am gone; the poison now hath torn my heart in pieces."

It is all far from compelling, and wrought with apparent carelessness. Why should Berinthia weep tears for the father who commanded the killing of Antonio? Why is there no death speech or other indication of the maid's death? What is the intended effect of Catalina's grotesque ravings? One surmises that she speaks as she does for no better reason than that Shirley recalled Flamineo's words, for Vittoria is certainly the source for Berinthia's know-notwhithering soul.[32] In addition to being unimpressive in themselves, then, these deaths are highly derivative.

Love's Cruelty (1631), though more coherent, is otherwise comparable.[33] Here Clariana, who is married to Bellamente, has an affair with his best friend, Hippolito. Bellamente surprises them in bed together, but spares them. Renouncing his love for Clariana, Hippolito soon falls in love with another woman, Eubella, and plans to marry her. This is too much for Clariana, who sends him a letter in which she asks him to meet her privately so she can reveal a plot against his life. After she has pleaded in vain against his marriage, Bellamente again surprises them. While he goes to get help, Clariana stabs Hippolito and is stabbed in return. Happy to die, she thanks him for the wound he has given her and seems to request another:

> Thy sword was gentle to me; search't again,
> And thou shalt see how my embracing blood
> Will keep it warm, and kiss the kind destroyer. [*Falls.*]
>
>   (5.2; 2:264)

No one could miss the sexual aura of these lines—or their traditional nature.[34] But if Clariana here echoes heroines such as Aspatia, her last lines are reminiscent of passages in Heywood and Webster:

>   —Oh! forgive me,
> Good heaven! I have wrong'd thee, Bellamente.
> Oh wives, hereafter, mean your hearts to them
> You give your vows: what mist weighs down
> My eyes already! oh, 'tis death, I see,
> In a long robe of darkness, is preparing
> To seal them up for ever. 'Twere no death,
> If we could lose our sins as we do breath. [*Dies.*]
>
>   (P. 265)[35]

Hippolito dies less volubly, expiring in the presence of Eubella: "My wound hath had a happy patience. / Farewell!" (p. 266); and Bellamente, asked by the Duke to explain what has happened, adds yet another to the ranks of the grief-slain in Stuart drama:

> Pray give me leave, because you shall not suffer
> In the expectation, you shall have it all
> Together; this Hippolito, and that Clariana—
> Hark! there 'tis. [*Falls, and dies.*]
>
>   (P. 267)

Ford, in *The Broken Heart,* makes Calantha's death a kind of monument of patrician magnificence; here the convention does little more than dispose of what to do with Bellamente.

Enough has been seen of Shirley's characteristic way with death to pass over both *The Duke's Mistress* (1636) and *The Politician* (1639) and conclude with his two most celebrated death-marked plays, *The Traitor* (1631) and *The Cardinal* (1641).

The Traitor, "essentially a formula play," with "nothing in it that had not, by 1631, been proved successful,"[36] dramatizes five deaths. Three of these are accomplished with Massingerian dispatch. The two deaths to which Shirley accords extended presentation, Amidea's and the Duke's, are in the Fletcherian tradition. Amidea, wholly good, is slain by Sciarrha to prevent her from becoming the Duke's mistress. Told by Lorenzo that he will be executed for Pisano's murder unless he persuades Amidea to yield to the Duke, he refuses to buy his life so basely. But when Lorenzo informs him that his execution will be followed by the ravishment of Amidea, Sciarrha feigns compliance, saying his sister will be at the Duke's "dispose" that night. Though he means to save Amidea's honor, Sciarrha decides to test her virtue[37] by pretending that he will kill her unless she acquiesces. In order to keep him from staining himself with a sister's blood, she pretends that she will do so. And on hearing that she "will obey the duke" (5.1.133), he stabs her. Dying, she reveals the truth:

> Oh let me see the wound.
> 'Tis well, if any other hand had done it.
> Some angel tell my brother now I did
> But seem consenting.
>
> (134–37)

Though she assures Sciarrha that "you may believe my last breath" (138), Shirley draws out her death for another forty lines. After she has explained herself more fully, Sciarrha tells her that he intended to kill her when, having rejected his spurious request, she was "nearest heaven" (157). Florio then *"breaks open the door,"* and asks: "How came this wound?" Amidea replies:

> I drew the weapon to it.
> Heaven knows my brother love'd me. Now I hope
> The duke wo'not pursue me with new flames.
> Sciarrha, tell the rest. Love one another
> The time you live together. I'll pray for you

In heaven. Farewell. Kiss me when I am dead.
You will else stay my journey. [*She dies.*]

(172–78)

Amidea, of course, has no motive for her lie: Sciarrha's life has been
doomed unless she yields to the Duke. As Carter notes,

> So set was the pattern of the noble woman, that in her death Amidea is
> forced by convention to declare, "I drew the weapon to it," and so win
> the audience's heart with a dying, noble lie. Desdemona's similar lie . . .
> is dictated by her desire to save Othello. Since Sciarrha's life is already
> forfeit, Amidea has no reason to take upon herself this guilt, except that
> the . . . audience would have expected it of her.[38]

Here we have a clear instance of a convention using a dramatist,
rather than the reverse.

The Fletcherian pathos of Amidea's death is, by the familiar
principle of schematic contrast, counterbalanced by the horrific
death of the Duke, who has played Lustful Tyrant to her Noble
Innocent. Here too we see how mindlessly Shirley borrows from his
predecessors. In accordance with Sciarrha's instructions, Florio
tells Lorenzo that Amidea has agreed to come to the Duke's chamber—though out of modesty she wishes to be admitted privately.
Lorenzo promises that even he will not look on her. The play's final
scene (5.3) begins with *"Amidea discover'd in a bed prepar'd by two
Gentlewomen."* Florio dismisses them but leaves soon after the
arrival of the Duke. What has been the point of the stratagem
conceived by Sciarrha and executed by Florio? One might expect,
remembering *The Revenger's Tragedy* and *The Duke of Milan,* that
poison has been applied to Amidea's face. But this is not the case.
Sciarrha promised to deliver his sister to the Duke, and has kept his
word. Indeed, the only connection between Sciarrha's machinations and the Duke's death is that the Duke has dismissed his train
in order to enjoy his secret rendezvous with Amidea. For the
Duke's murder is the work, not of Sciarrha or Florio, but of
Lorenzo and his creature Petruchio. Discovering that Amidea is
dead, the Duke cries out for them to kill him—a piece of verbal
extravagance they respond to by stabbing him.[39] He begs for mercy,
then for time to pray; Lorenzo expresses regret over the state of his
soul but stabs him again. Now the Duke ceases to beg. Like
Berinthia, he expresses uncertainty "whither" he must go:

> No tear prevail? O whither must I wander?
> Thus Caesar fell by Brutus. I shall tell

> News to the world I go to, will not be believ'd.
> Lorenzo kill'd me.
>
> (5.3.66–69)

"Will it not?" says Lorenzò, who then stabs a third time. Now the Duke has reached what proves to be his final speech:

> I am coming, Amidea, I am coming.—
> For thee, inhuman murderer, expect
> My blood shall fly to heaven, and there inflam'd
> Hang a prodigious meteor all thy life.
> And when, by some as bloody hand as thine,
> Thy soul is ebbing forth, it shall descend
> In flaming drops upon thee. Oh, I faint!
> Thou flattering world, farewell. Let princes gather
> My dust into a glass, and learn to spend
> Their hour of state. That's all they have, for when
> That's out, time never turns the glass again. [*Dies.*]
>
> (71–81)

The whole speech makes up in length what it lacks in depth or conviction. The first line pays homage to the *Liebestod* tradition, notably the death of Cleopatra, but sounds absurd on the lips of Shirley's Duke. Then there is protracted but equally unpersuasive vengeful rant, followed by the conventional farewell to the world, with the self as monitory example. Taken as a whole, the speech seems not so much constructed as laminated.

Finally, there is *The Cardinal*, "the last important tragedy of the English Renaissance."[40] Of the five characters whose deaths are dramatized,[41] two—seconds in the duel between Columbo and Hernando—perish without speaking. Columbo himself, mortally wounded, forgives Hernando rather after the fashion of Ithocles in *The Broken Heart:* "Give me thy hand, when shall we meet again?" To which Hernando, displaying a wit rarely encountered in Shirley's tragedies, replies: "Never, I hope" (4.3.80–81). Columbo then rapidly expires: "I feel life ebb apace, yet I'l look upwards, / And shew my face to heaven" (82–83).

In killing Columbo, Hernando is taking vengeance on behalf on Rosaura, whose husband, Alvarez, Columbo murdered in the revels following their marriage. Hernando meets his own death later in the play when he intervenes to keep the Cardinal, Columbo's uncle, from raping her. Though the Cardinal cries out for his servants, Hernando has time to stab him before they arrive, but is soon mortally wounded:[42]

> So, now we are even;
> Where is the Dutchess [Rosaura]? I would take my leave
> Of her, and then bequeath my curse among you. [*Hernando falls.*]
>
> (5.3.181–83)

After several brief speeches expressing his satisfaction at having stabbed the Cardinal, Hernando bids the world farewell; "I have preserv'd the Dutchess from a rape, / Goodnight to me and all the world for ever" (193–94).

The Cardinal, feeling himself near death, expresses great remorse for his wicked life. The play's ending seems at hand. But Shirley, committed to the Fletcherian dramaturgy of surprise and shock, is merely setting us up for his masterstroke. The Cardinal informs Rosaura that he is "lost" if she will not forgive him for a crime of which she is as yet unaware: "I must confess more than my black intents / Upon your honour, y'are already poyson'd" (210–11). He then offers her an antidote, which he mixes with wine and tastes himself; thus assured of its efficacy, she drinks. The supposed antidote, of course, is really poison, and the Cardinal gloats over his successful vengeance. But if the Cardinal has his revenge, it is undercut by a familiar irony. "I knew I could not live," he says (271)—only to hear a surgeon say his wounds are not mortal. Thus the Cardinal fulfills his own prognostication that he would die by poison; the witty contriver is "caught . . . in [his] own Engin" (275):

> no humane art can now resist it,
> I feel it knocking at the seat of life,
> It must come in; I have wrackt all my own
> To try your charities, now it would be rare,
> If you but waft me with a little prayer,
> My wings that flag may catch the wind; but 'tis
> In vain, the mist is risen, and ther's none
> To stear my wandring bark. [*Dies.*]
>
> (278–85)

Here is yet another rising of Websterian mist.[43] But surely Shirley is also remembering Shakespeare's Prospero, who remarked that "the rarer action is / In virtue than in vengeance" (*Tempest* 5.1.27–28), and who told the audience in the Epilogue:

> Gentle breath of yours my sails
> Must fill, or else my project fails,
> Which was to please. Now I want
> Spirits to enforce, art to enchant,

And my ending is despair,
Unless I be reliev'd by prayer.

(11–16)

But not even Shirley's petty pilfering from Prospero can keep the Cardinal's speech from foundering.

Rosaura's death speech receives much less emphasis. Addressing herself to the king, she merely says:

The minute's come that I must take my leave too.
Your hand great Sir, and though you be a King
We may exchange forgiveness, heaven forgive,
And all the world. I come, I come Alvarez. [*Dies.*]

(270–93)

Despite its brevity, the speech, like that of the Cardinal, is the work of a playwright who relies more on memory than imagination.[44]

The death speech, having risen from its unpromising beginnings to become one of the most striking features of Renaissance tragedy, becomes in Shirley little more than a mechanical exercise. Essentially formulaic by his time, it is further vitiated by Shirley's proclivity for inserting borrowed phrases in inhospitable contexts. Since in other respects Shirley is thoroughly representative, there is nothing to be gained by examining the death speech in the works of his less talented contemporaries. Yet as Ford demonstrates a gifted dramatist with a serious and sympathetic interest in human action and suffering could still infuse the words of the dying with life. Ford's most notable characters, in William Faulkner's phrase, "stand up and cast a shadow."[45] Speaking and enacting what they are, they die like themselves. The characters of Massinger and Shirley cast no shadows. What has not lived cannot die. The great age of English tragedy has ended.

The history of the death speech epitomizes that of Renaissance tragedy. Horrific or sentimental melodrama, or the drama of dispassionate analysis, may survive, even flourish, primarily on the basis of plot. (So too, of course, may comedy.) But expressive and highly individualized language, spoken by passionate, vivid characters, is at the heart of the greatest Renaissance tragedies. These plays were written by poetic dramatists, "single nature's double name,"[46] in whom drama and poetry could become one flesh. Such playwrights are, by their nature, rare. But they are the ones who can get the most out of death.

To Shakespeare, and his so potent art, I now turn.

Why, what is pomp, rule, reign, but earth and dust?
And live we how we can, yet die we must.

(16–28)

Though the conclusion is pious enough, the lines in which Warwick takes obvious pleasure in recalling his past greatness express the fascination pomp, rule, reign, and glory hold for him even at the edge of death. Oxford and Somerset enter and reveal that his brother, Montague, has been slain. "Sweet rest his soul!" responds Warwick. "Fly, lords, and save yourselves, / For Warwick bids you all farewell, to meet in heaven" (48–49). With these words he dies, in the company of those who love him. Unlike Clifford, his body is saved from ignominy: *"Here they bear away his body"* (50 s.d.).

The death of Prince Edward stands in much the same relation to Rutland's as does Warwick's to Clifford's. Again the approach is markedly contrastive. In place of the terrified and pitiful Rutland, Shakespeare gives us the suicidally courageous Prince Edward, who dies after calling the Yorkist victors traitors:

Lascivious Edward, and thou perjur'd George,
And thou misshapen Dick, I tell ye all
I am your better, traitors as ye are,
And thou usurp'st my father's right and mine.

(5.5.34–37)

Retaliation is so swift and lethal that he never speaks again:

King Edward. Take that, the likeness of this railer here [Queen Margaret, the Prince's mother]. [*Stabs him.*]
Gloucester. Sprawl'st thou? take that, to end thy agony. [*Richard stabs him.*]
Clarence. And there's for twitting me with perjury. [*Clarence stabs him.*]

(38–40)[21]

The last death in the play, King Henry's, is unusual in at least two respects. For one thing, Henry is in the midst of a "prophetic" speech regarding the evils Richard will wreak on England. "I'll hear no more," Richard interjects;

Die, prophet, in thy speech: [*Stabs him.*]
For this, amongst the rest, was I ordain'd.

(5.6.57–58)

The pious Henry, unlike anyone else in these plays, dies praying for his own murderer: "O God forgive my sins, and pardon thee!" (60). And if Henry dies in character, Richard kills in it:

> What? will the aspiring blood of Lancaster
> Sink in the ground? I thought it would have mounted.
> See how my sword weeps for the poor king's death!
> O may such purple tears be alway shed
> From those that wish the downfall of our house!
> If any spark of life be yet remaining,
> Down, down to hell, and say I sent thee thither—
> [*Stabs him again.*]
> I, that have neither pity, love, nor fear.
>
> (61–68)

Richard is so vividly realized that he, not his virtuous but pallid victim, creates the main impression of Henry's death.

The first audiences of *Richard III* (1592–93)[22] would have had every reason to expect a play rivalling, if not surpassing, the bloodiness of *3 Henry VI*. Yet Shakespeare sets the bloody Richard in a remarkably unsanguinary play. There are, indeed, only two onstage deaths—those of Clarence and Richard. More surprisingly still, not even Richard is given a conventional death speech.

Rivers, Grey, Hastings, and Buckingham are all executed off-stage; Edward IV dies there, as does Anne; and Tyrell provides an account, derived from Dighton and Forrest, of the murder of the princes. Rivers and Gray remember Margaret's prophecy before they are led forth to die (1.3); Buckingham will do the same (5.1);[23] in both instances characters are of less interest as individuals than as a means of emphasizing the play's pattern of retributive justice. The same may be said of Hastings, who refers to Margaret's curse before moralizing upon his downfall:

> O momentary grace of mortal men,
> Which we more hunt for than the grace of God!
> Who builds his hope in air of your good looks
> Lives like a drunken sailor on a mast. . . .
>
> (3.4.96–99)

Finely written though they are, these lines have little to do with Hastings as a dramatic character.

The deaths of both Clarence and Richard are prepared for by passages of extraordinary psychological penetration. Clarence, who has no knowledge that he is about to be murdered at Richard's instigation, has a dream that uncannily presages the death which is even now approaching:

> Methoughts that I had broken from the Tower
> And was embark'd to cross to Burgundy,
> And in my company my brother Gloucester,
> Who from my cabin tempted me to walk
> Upon the hatches. . . .
>   As we pac'd along
> Upon the giddy footing of the hatches,
> Methought that Gloucester stumbled, and in falling
> Strook me (that thought to stay him) overboard
> Into the tumbling billows of the main.
> O Lord, methought what pain it was to drown!
>
> (1.4.9–13; 16–21)

Clarence's subconscious fear of Richard, as Wolfgang Clemen observes, is one of the most remarkable aspects of these lines.[24] Before the scene is over, Clarence will learn from the murderers' own lips that Richard has sent them, beg for his life, and be struck down. He is then carried off to be drowned—if any life remains in him—in a butt of malmsey.

Richard's final moments are also preceded by what he regards as a dream (but which an audience perceives as having an objective existence).[25] After the ghosts of those he has slain have appeared to him, he wakes in terror:

> Give me another horse! bind up my wounds!
> Have mercy, Jesu! soft, I did but dream.
> O coward conscience, how dost thou afflict me!
>
> . . . .
> I shall despair; there is no creature loves me,
> And if I die no soul will pity me.
>
> (5.3.177–79; 200–201)

As Alan Hobson has remarked, "Striving to *be* a man without a conscience, Richard succeeds only in *appearing to be* a man without a conscience." In this soliloquy, however, "he seems for the first time to be really alone, and the words he speaks record, not his thoughts, but his feelings."[26] Richard's death, by contrast, is devoid of inwardness. He is shown on the field of battle; as in the dream, he needs a horse: "A horse, a horse! my kingdom for a horse!" (5.4.7). Catesby tries to rescue him: "Withdraw, my lord, I'll help you to a horse" (8). But Richard rejects Catesby's offer:

Slave, I have set my life upon a cast,
And I will stand the hazard of the die.
I think there be six Richmonds in the field;
Five have I slain to-day in stead of him.
A horse, a horse! my kingdom for a horse!

(9–13)

Richard's celebrated line is so familiar that its meaning is usually
taken for granted. Few critics, I suspect, would quarrel with Harold
C. Goddard's interpretation: "The King's final words are a confession that the worldly kingdom, to the attainment of which he has
sacrificed everything, is worth less than the few seconds by which
another horse might postpone his doom."[27] Yet if Richard were
merely thinking of protracting his life, he would not have answered
Catesby as he did. Obviously, Richard is declaring, with all possible
vehemence, that he wants a horse; equally obviously, he is trying to
keep his kingdom. The exchange offer is merely rhetorical. Given a
horse, he may yet find and kill Richmond: the battle—and the
kingdom—may be riding upon a horse. In any event, these are
Richard's last words. In the next scene he and Richmond enter, and
Richard is killed: "The bloody dog is dead" (5.5.2). The emphasis is
not on Richard, but the brave new world to come.

Titus Andronicus (1593–94)[28] is similarly experimental in its presentation of death. Of the eight characters whose deaths are dramatized, not one is accorded a death speech. This conscious emphasis
on silent death is highly unusual, although *The Spanish Tragedy*
offers an obvious precedent. To some extent, Shakespeare seems to
have been guided here by his sense of ironic propriety. Chiron and
Demetrius not only rape Lavinia and cut off her hands, but cut out
her tongue; bereft of words, she can communicate only by actions.[29] She moves and suffers in silence. And it is to silence that
Chiron and Demetrius are reduced before Titus cuts their throats:
"Stop close their mouths," he commands, "let them not speak a
word" (5.2.164). In the final welter of violence, Titus first kills
Lavinia: "Die, die, Lavinia, and thy shame with thee, / And with thy
shame thy father's sorrow die!" (5.3.46–47). He places the blame
for her death on Chiron and Demetrius, and explains that there is
no need to send for them:

Why, there they are, both baked in this pie;
Whereof their mother daintily hath fed,
Eating the flesh that she herself hath bred.
'Tis true, 'tis true, witness my knive's sharp point.

(60–63)

Saturninus avenges Tamora—"Die, frantic wretch, for this accursed deed!"—and Lucius avenges Titus: "Can the son's eye behold his father bleed? / There's meed for meed, death for a deadly deed!" (64–66). All deaths seem instantaneous.[30] Of those who survive the play, the weeping grandson of Titus and the villainous Aaron are set in stark contrast. The boy, grief-stricken, finds speech impossible. Not so Aaron ("Ah, why should wrath be mute and fury dumb?" [184]). In this play, however, silence can have its own eloquence.[31]

In *Romeo and Juliet* (1595–96),[32] death is, with one exception, so sudden that there is time for few words or none. Paris merely exclaims:

> O, I am slain! [*Falls.*] If thou be merciful,
> Open the tomb, lay me with Juliet. [*Dies.*]
>
> (5.2.72–73)

Romeo's long speech before he commits suicide is obviously designed to heighten the pathos of what is already a highly charged situation. While in one sense we know Juliet will not awake in time, there is always an element of irrational hope. But once he takes his farewell and acts, death follows almost instantaneously:

> Eyes, look your last!
> Arms, take your last embrace! and lips, O you
> The doors of breath, seal with a righteous kiss
> A dateless bargain to engrossing death!
>
> . . . .
>
> Here's to my love! [*Drinks.*] O true apothecary!
> Thy drugs are quick. Thus with a kiss I die. [*Dies.*]
>
> (112–15; 119–20)

The poison is conventional; the celerity with which it works is not.[33] Romeo, of course, acts with characteristic rashness. Juliet's suicide is an act performed in the fulness of knowledge. Finding the cup in Romeo's hand, she first thinks of sharing it with him:

> Poison, I see, hath been his timeless end.
> O churl, drunk all, and left no friendly drop
> To help me after? I will kiss thy lips,
> Haply some poison yet doth hang on them,
> To make me die with a restorative.
> Thy lips are warm.
>
> (162–67)

She then stabs herself with Romeo's dagger, dying even more rapidly than he did:

> O happy dagger, [*Taking Romeo's dagger.*]
> This is thy sheath [*Stabs herself.*]; there rust, and
> let me die. [*Falls on Romeo's body and dies.*]
>
> (169–70)

All these deaths are in keeping with the headlong pace of the play. Tybalt's death is even swifter: *"They fight; Tybalt falls"* (3.1.131 s.d.). The exceptional death is that of Mercutio, who remains voluble after Tybalt has stabbed him: " 'Tis not so deep as a well, nor so wide as a church-door, but 'tis enough, 'twill serve. Ask for me tomorrow, and you shall find me a grave man. I am pepper'd. . . . A plague a' both your houses!" (3.1.96–100). If Romeo and Juliet die like lovers, exhibiting the fatal fixity of death-marked love, there is nothing archetypal or generic about Mercutio's death. He can only be said to die like Mercutio—a character with a unique and instantly recognizable voice. But Mercutio, of course, dies offstage.

Before examining what Shakespeare does with death in his later tragedies, I wish to return, briefly, to several of his histories: *King John* (1594–96), *Richard II* (1595), *1 Henry IV* (1596–97), and *2 Henry IV* (1598).[34]

King John, if indeed as late as 1596,[35] does remarkably little with the two opportunities it offers. Arthur, leaping from the wall of his prison, risks his life in a desperate attempt to escape from John:

> As good to die and go, as die and stay. [*Leaps down.*]
> O me, my uncle's spirit is in these stones,
> Heaven take my soul, and England keep my bones! [*Dies.*]
>
> (4.3.8–10)

The death of John, who has been poisoned by a monk, is as dilatory as Arthur's is sudden. He is brought on stage near death and describes his torment in the physiological language so common in Renaissance drama:

> There is so hot a summer in my bosom
> That all my bowels crumble up to dust.
> I am a scribbled form, drawn with a pen
> Upon a parchment, and against this fire
> Do I shrink up.
>
> (5.7.30–34)

Asked how he fares, he replies:

> Poison'd—ill fare! Dead, forsook, cast off,
> And none of you will bid the winter come

> To thurst his icy fingers in my maw,
> Nor let my kingdom's rivers take their course
> Through my burn'd bosom. . . .
>   I do not ask you much,
> I beg cold comfort.
>
>   (35–39; 41–42)

There is little here but a show of *copia;* even the pun, which would come naturally from Richard II, seems merely clever. His last words, spoken a few minutes later, are to Faulconbridge:

> The tackle of my heart is crack'd and burn'd,
> And all the shrouds wherewith my life should sail
> Are turned to one thread, one little hair.
> My heart hath one poor string to stay it by,
> Which holds but till thy news be uttered,
> And then all this thou seest is but a clod
> And module of confounded royalty.
>
>   (52–58)

His death, to apply a phrase from the play (3.4.108), is as tedious as a twice-told tale.

The last words of John of Gaunt and of Richard in *Richard II* also contrast volubility and extreme brevity. Gaunt, whose dying words fill much of 1.2, prophesies, in language too familiar for quotation, what will become of Richard, warns him of his peril, and accuses him of murdering Thomas of Woodstock. He is then borne from the stage to die. Gaunt's speeches are essentially proleptic and thematic; eloquent though some of them are, they do not justify their presence by illuminating Gaunt, but by calling attention to Richard's misrule and the destruction into which he is rushing. Richard's death occurs at an intensely dramatic moment, when he has just killed two would-be murderers. He is then struck down by Exton:

> That hand shall burn in never-quenching fire
> That staggers thus my person. Exton, thy fierce hand
> Hath with the King's blood stain'd the King's own land.
> Mount, mount, my soul! thy seat is up on high,
> Whilst my gross flesh sinks downward, here to die. [*Dies.*]
>   (5.5.108–12)

In this play which begins and ends with a king stained by his kinsman's blood, in which Richard falls and Bolingbroke rises, these lines resemble Gaunt's with respect to thematic emphasis.[36]

But they also heighten our sense of the character of Richard, who seems never so much a king as at the moment of his death. By deed and word he shows himself, as Exton acknowledges, "As full of valure as of royal blood" (113).

The *Henry IV* plays place dramatic emphasis on only one death—that of Hotspur.[37] Here, surely as notably as in any play written by this date, a character's dying words have the personal accents of an imagined self. In a rush of words (speaking "thick," as is his wont), he expresses his anguish for the honor that has been lost and won:

> O Harry, thou hast robb'd me of my youth!
> I better brook the loss of brittle life
> Than those proud titles thou has won of me.
> They wound my thoughts worse than thy sword my flesh.
>
> (*1 Henry IV*, 5.4.77–80)

But Shakespeare, making use of the convention that the dying may become gnomic and even prophetic, extends the compass of Hotspur's thoughts:

> But thoughts, the slaves of life, and life, time's fool,
> And time, that takes survey of all the world,
> Must have a stop. O, I could prophesy,
> But that the earthy and cold hand of death
> Lies on my tongue.
>
> (81–85)

The vision of life articulated in these lines is, one must feel, too Macbeth-like to come naturally from Hotspur. Even the knowledge of his own impending death seems no reason for so radical a revaluation of what he must leave behind.[38] But Shakespeare gives him fewer than three lines in this vein. Instead of dying while taking grim measure of the futility of life or foretelling the future, Hotspur is surprised by death while speaking of the fate of his own body:

>   No, Percy, thou art dust,
>   And food for— [*Dies.*]
>
> (85–86)

"For worms," supplies Hall, who goes on to provide a balanced estimate of the man he has killed. As was not the case at the end of *3 Henry VI*, victor and victim share equally in creating our final impression of the scene.

King Henry does not die onstage, but what Shakespeare does

with his last moments is one of the extraordinary achievements of *2 Henry IV*. After Hal has explained to his father's satisfaction why he took the crown,[39] Henry opens his mind to him. Briefly alluding to the "by-paths and indirect crook'd ways / I met this crown" (4.5.183–85), he goes on to speak of the threat posed by his former allies. For the first time he reveals that the politic purpose of his intended pilgrimage was to give people something to do "lest rest and lying still might make them look / Too near unto my state" (211–12). He suggests that Hal employ an analogous strategy:

> Therefore, my Harry,
> Be it thy course to busy giddy minds
> With foreign quarrels, that action, hence borne out,
> May waste the memory of the former days.

> (212–15)

Knowing that he is about to die does not alter the way Henry sees the world or himself; he merely permits himself to be candid with his son and heir. The last words he speaks, delivered in the presence of Hal, Prince John, and the Earl of Warwick, mark a return to his habitual mode of utterance. On hearing from Warwick that the room in which he first fainted is called "Jerusalem," he declares that

> It hath been prophesied to me many years,
> I should not die but in Jerusalem,
> Which vainly I suppos'd the Holy Land.
> But bear me to that chamber, there I'll lie,
> In that Jerusalem shall Harry die.

> (236–40)

It is as if the purpose of his pilgrimage had been pious acquiescence to the will of God—as if he had meant to die there. What has become of the man who has just spoken of pilgrimage as a political ploy? The two Jerusalems are not more distinct than the two Henrys, private and public. His final speeches reinforce our sense of this fundamental dichotomy.

In *Julius Caesar* (1599), Shakespeare gives dramatic emphasis to the dying moments of several characters, each with his own distinct claim on our sympathies. The first is Caesar, who suffers in silence the onslaught of his assassins until stabbed by Brutus: "*Et tu, Brute?*—Then fall Caesar!" (3.1.77). Shakespeare's discretion is nowhere more evident; for the alternative account, in which Caesar says "And thou my sonne,"[40] would make patricide overt in a play that needs to keep it (at most) symbolic, and perhaps would have disqualified Brutus as a tragic protagonist. The use of Latin is one of those daring strokes that it is now easy to take for granted. But the shocking effect of these words could have been achieved only by departing from "Roman English": Caesar addresses Brutus in what is made to seem the intimacy of a private language. After this laconic, resonant, poignant half-line, Caesar's final words, "Then fall Caesar!" (77), make his death appear almost an act of willing abdication—as if the work assassins' swords have begun is completed by the recognition of such intimate betrayal. Caesar never seems greater—or more sympathetic—than at the moment of his death.

The deaths of Cassius and Brutus are almost as powerfully rendered as that of Caesar. Cassius, who has sent Titinius to determine if the soldiers who occupy his own camp are friends or foes, depends on Pindarus ("My sight was ever thick" [5.3.21]) to inform him of what ensues.[41] Watching from a hilltop, Pindarus reports that Titinius has just been captured. "O, coward that I am, to live so long," Cassius cries out in self-blame, "To see my best friend ta'en before my face!" (34–35). He has not, of course, seen Titinius taken—nor has Pindarus, who has been misled by equivocal appearances. But with characteristic rashness, Cassius decides that the time has come to die. His bondsman Pindarus is given the task of aiding him in suicide:

> . . . with this good sword,
> That ran through Caesar's bowels, search this bosom.
> Stand not to answer; here, take thou the hilts,
> And when my face is cover'd, as 'tis now,
> Guide thou the sword. [*Pindarus stabs him.*]
>   Caesar, thou art reveng'd,
> Even with the sword that kill'd thee. [*Dies.*]
>
> (41–46)

Within moments, Titinius and Messala return with the news that Brutus has triumphed over Octavius. And Titinius, after placing on Cassius's brow the garland sent by Brutus, kills himself with Cassius's sword. Rash, choleric, envious Cassius, we are reminded by the circumstances of his death, is one of the play's most notable "lovers."[42] And to his worth Titinius testifies with his own life.

For Brutus, suicide comes when it must, as the necessary alternative to ignominious capture. Like Cassius, he seeks assistance in death; but requests, in turn, from three "friends" what Cassius commands of his bondsman. Each time he is refused. Brutus bids them, and Strato, who has just awakened, farewell:

> Countrymen,
> My heart doth joy that yet in all my life
> I found no man but he was true to me.
> I shall have glory by this losing day
> More than Octavius and Mark Antony
> By this vile conquest shall attain unto.
> So fare you well at once, for Brutus' tongue
> Hath almost ended his live's history.
> Night hangs upon mine eyes, my bones would rest,
> That have but labor'd to attain this hour.
>
> (5.5.33–42)

Here, in what is perhaps the most affecting illustration of the idea, Shakespeare shows how much the "nobility" of Brutus depends on his capacity to overlook or suppress what he would prefer not to see. In North's Plutarch, Brutus merely expresses joy "that not one of my frends hath failed me at my neede";[43] Shakespeare's Brutus makes the astonishing declaration that *no man* has been false to him. What Mark Antony promised and performed has, apparently, no place in Brutus's mind. As for his own sense of "glory," he remains (like Plutarch's Brutus) convinced of his moral superiority to his adversaries. But as Reuben A. Brower notes, "Shakespeare has seen what Plutarch barely recognized, that a person of such gentleness and such abstract purity of intention could not act the part of conspirator and political murderer without pain."[44] Hence the sleeplessness that afflicts Brutus throughout the play. And his lines here convey an enormous weariness, a sense of death as release from the exigencies of life, not as the triumphant departure of one who harbors no lingering misgivings. Only in death will Brutus cease to be "with himself at war" (1.1.46).

Telling the others that he "will follow" (5.5.43), Brutus asks Strato to remain with him:

> I prithee, Strato, stay thou by thy lord.
> Thou art a fellow of a good respect;
> Thy life hath had some smatch of honor in it.
> Hold then my sword, and turn away thy face,
> While I do run upon it. Wilt thou, Strato?
>
> (44–48)

Brutus's courteous and humane nature, his concern for honor (he would not wish to be aided in his "honorable" death by someone ill-fitted for the task), and his self-mastery are equally evident. In contrast to Cassius, who covers his face, Brutus desires to see the sword that will take his life. But even at this moment he thinks of Strato's feelings: to direct him not to look is to spare him all he can. And after a ritual handshake, Brutus gains the death he seeks:

> Farewell, good Strato. [*Runs on his sword.*] Caesar, now be still,
> I kill'd not thee with half so good a will.
>
> (50–51)

Indeed, he did not: this sudden release of pent energies, this running on the sword, is perhaps the most heart-whole action Brutus has performed. Since we rarely see Brutus in action, the two stabbings, so markedly in contrast, almost serve to define what he has *done* in the play.

One other death deserves mention—that of Cinna the poet. It is like nothing else in Shakespeare. Here we have the death of a man who has not previously appeared in the play—has not even been spoken of. Despite an ominous dream, Cinna is on his way to attend Caesar's funeral:

> I dreamt to-night that I did feast with Caesar,
> And things unluckily charge my fantasy.
> I have no will to wander forth of doors,
> Yet something leads me forth.
>
> (3.3.1–4)

A mob of the plebeians subjects him to intimidating interrogation; on hearing that his name is Cinna, someone suggests that they "tear him to pieces, he's a conspirator" (28). In Plutarch, this mistake with respect to Cinna's identity leads to his death.[45] But Shakespeare gives Cinna time to explain who he is: "I am Cinna the poet, I am Cinna the poet"; "I am not Cinna the conspirator" (29, 32). The truth is irrelevant. The mob, needing a victim, will "tear him for his bad verses" (31), and because his name is Cinna: "Tear him, tear him!" (35). The emphasis is on mob psychology, not on the character of Cinna. Shakespeare has, however, moved far beyond what he did with the interrogation of Joan of Arc.

8
Shakespeare (2)

Hamlet (1600–1601) is, among other things, a play in which death is motive and cue for revenge.[1] Indeed, what the Ghost of old Hamlet says of his murder (1.5.59–79) is more powerful than the onstage deaths of many characters in the drama of the period. As for deaths that are represented, not merely described, Polonius is permitted only "O, I am slain" (3.4.25). If his death while eavesdropping is ironic, so too is his singular brevity.

Until late in act 5, *Hamlet* is largely a play of violence deferred, of energies turned inward. But during the fencing bout between Hamlet and Laertes, after each has wounded the other with the poisoned rapier, Gertrude suddenly falls. The wine she has drunk to Hamlet's fortune has, as we know, marked her for death. But Claudius, a player king desperately playing for time, tries to pretend that she has merely fainted at the sight of blood. For the only time since falling, the Queen speaks:

> No, no, the drink, the drink—O my dear Hamlet—
> The drink, the drink! I am pois'ned. [*Dies.*]
>
> (5.2.309–10)

What the Queen suffers is brought home to us with extraordinary force: hers is an agony made palpable by wrenched, spasmodic bursts of language. She dies, moreover, attempting to warn her son. Her words point the way toward vengeance.

The death of Claudius, by poisoned rapier and poisoned wine, belongs to Hamlet. He is at his most impressive; Claudius dies caught in his own toils, vainly clutching at life, no mighty opposite at last. If "this action of our death . . . / Shewes all a man," what Claudius's final moments reveal is his essential smallness. Claudius's love for Gertrude has been, perhaps, his most appealing characteristic; at least he is no hypocrite there. But as Shakespeare prepares us for Claudius's death, we see the King withdrawing into the circle of himself. Since he cannot preserve Gertrude without betraying himself, he watches her drink: "It is the pois'ned cup, it is too late" (292), he remarks to himself. He never speaks to her again. After her death, while Laertes speaks of the poison on his rapier, Claudius remains silent, as if the unmasking of his plot has paralysed him. The play spares him nothing. Not for him the desperate, partially redeeming courage of Richard III or Macbeth. In a direct encounter he seems out of his element, impotent; symbolically, at least, he wears no sword. His last words, "O, yet defend me, friends, I am but hurt" (324), spoken after Hamlet has stabbed him, complete the process of his diminution. Claudius, who has lied to others, now lies to himself. For the poison, as he knows, is mortal. The master realist cannot face the reality of his own death. Then Hamlet is upon him, quenching further speech. Claudius dies in the midst of his sins, deprived of any opportunity to express repentance or remorse. For both Hamlet and the audience, his death is profoundly satisfying.

Laertes dies after asking Hamlet to exchange forgiveness with him (329–31). Hamlet's next words—"Heaven make thee free of it [my death]! I follow thee. / I am dead, Horatio. Wretched queen, adieu!" (332–33)—are a striking instance of the play's unconventional use of conventions. An audience would expect Hamlet to die. But of course the speech continues:

> You that look pale, and tremble at this chance,
> That are but mutes or audience to this act,
> Had I but time—as this fell sergeant, Death,
> Is strict in his arrest—O, I could tell you—
> But let it be. Horatio, I am dead,
> Thou livest. Report me and my cause aright
> To the unsatisfied.
>
> (334–40)

Again, the lines seem Hamlet's last; yet when Horatio attempts to drink off the remaining poison, Hamlet has strength enough to seize the chalice from him. It is as if his anguish at the thought of ill repute enables him to wrest time from death:

> As th' art a man,
> Give me the cup. Let go! By heaven, I'll ha't!
> O God, Horatio, what a wounded name,
> Things standing thus unknown, shall I leave behind me!
> If thou didst ever hold me in thy heart,
> Absent thee from felicity a while,
> And in this harsh world draw thy breath in pain,
> To tell my story.
>
> (342–49)

Nor is this the end. The "warlike volley" with which Young Fortinbras greets the ambassadors to England turns Hamlet's mind to thoughts of the succession:

> O, I die, Horatio,
> The potent poison quite o'er-crows my spirit.
> I cannot live to hear the news from England,
> But I do prophesy th' election lights
> On Fortinbras, he has my dying voice.
> So tell him, with th' occurrents more and less
> Which have solicited—the rest is silence. [*Dies.*]
>
> (352–58)

Such, then, are the last moments of Hamlet: forgiveness for Laertes, concern for his own reputation and the future welfare of the state. Unlike such protagonists as Brutus, Hamlet's is a self too various to be adequately represented by a few moments, even those before death. Yet in a sense he too dies "like himself," though it is a self achieved rather than merely enacted. After a just and satisfying revenge, Hamlet dies exhibiting qualities of mind and spirit that turn the last of life's "occasions" into a kind of triumph. "Now cracks a noble heart. Good night, sweet prince, / And flights of angels sing thee to thy rest!" (359–60)—Horatio's valediction, choral as well as personal, gives shape and direction to what an audience must leave unexpressed. In his death Hamlet has proved, in Fortinbras's phrase, "right royal," dying like the king he has never become.[2]

At the end of *Hamlet,* Fortinbras remarks on the indecorum of the scene: "Such a sight as this, / Becomes the field, but here shows much amiss" (5.2.401–2). In *Troilus and Cressida,* however (1601–2), a play which with ironic propriety begins with an armed Prologue (a warlike figure for a play of war), Shakespeare defeats expectation by dramatizing only a single death—that of Hector.[3] And Hector, surely the most appealing character in the play, falls in a way that sullies him. After an inconclusive combat with Achilles, Hector notices a man wearing exceptionally fine armor; when the man flees, he pursues and kills him, only to find that the sumptuous armor concealed something hideously vile:

> Most putrified core, so fair without,
> Thy goodly armor thus hath cost thy life.
>
> (5.8.1–2)

It is a moment almost purely symbolic, in which emblematic meaning assumes the prominence usually accorded verisimilitude.[4] What prompts Hector's words can be no ordinary adversary: beneath the splendid exterior he finds, at the least, a body ravaged as by syphilis or the plague. Hector, who has declared that it is "mad idolatry / To make the service greater than the god" (2.2.56–57), perishes in committing such idolatry. His honor, which is revealed as making no distinction between outward show and inner worth, leads him to his death; the armor he has coveted is like the golden casket in *The Merchant of Venice,* which contains "a carrion Death" (2.7.63). Disarming, he becomes easy prey for Achilles' Myrmidons: "Strike, fellows, strike, this is the man I seek. [*Hector falls.*]" (5.8.10).[5]

Othello (1604) does even more with death than *Hamlet.* Desdemona is given, in effect, two deaths—one wrenchingly pathetic, the other heroic. Responding to Othello's declaration that Cassio is dead, she speaks with unintentional ambiguity: "Alas, he is betray'd and I undone!" (5.2.76). To Othello this can mean only one thing: "Out, strumpet! weep'st thou for him to my face?" (77). She begs to be allowed to live in banishment, then that he will "kill [her] to-morrow" (80); "But half an hour!" (82); "But while I say one prayer!" (83). Othello is inexorable: "It is too late." Word and action fuse as he *"Smothers her"* (83 s.d.).

That Desdemona is terrified, frantically clutching at life, makes these moments all the more harrowing. (One recalls the final minutes of Marlowe's Faustus.) The effect is heightened in the first Quarto (1622) by an additional line: "O Lord, Lord, Lord!" which is spoken while Othello attempts to smother her (85).[6] But Desdemona's death is daringly protracted. After hearing Emilia calling for him, Othello notices that Desdemona is still alive, and acts to end her suffering: "So, so" (89). Desdemona's death now seems an established fact;[7] the dramatic focus shifts to Othello's sense of what it means to live without her—and to his impending interview with Emilia. Suddenly, after Emilia has entered with the news that Roderigo has been slain and Cassio injured, Desdemona speaks: "O falsely, falsely murder'd" (116). But there is no accusation of Othello. In place of the terror we have already witnessed is complete self-mastery—and a love so great that she will attempt to shield her murderer:

Desdemona. A guiltless death I die.
Emilia. O, who hath done this deed?
Desdemona. Nobody; I myself. Farewell!
    Commend me to my kind lord. O, farewell! [*Dies.*]

(122–25)

It is a death testifying to selfless and superbly irrational devotion. Like the "kind lord" by whose hands she dies, she is (though in a different sense) "great of heart."

Much of the dramatic impact of Desdemona's death comes from what Shakespeare does with Emilia. Even as Othello is killing Desdemona, we know—or sense—that he will soon have to live with the truth of what he has done. Hardly is Desdemona dead than Emilia launches into an impassioned defense of her, culminating in her revelation that she herself gave the handkerchief to Iago. Her own death resembles that of Desdemona in its selflessness and utter fidelity. Stabbed by Iago for refusing to hold her tongue, she asks to be placed "by my mistress' side" (5.2.237). Her next words are addressed to Desdemona, whose "Willow" song she echoes:

> What did thy song bode, lady?
> Hark, canst thou hear me? I will play the swan,
> And die in music. [*Sings.*] "Willow, willow, willow."
>
> (246–48)

Her last thoughts are of Desdemona and her innocence:

> Moor, she was chaste; she lov'd thee, cruel Moor;
> So come my soul to bliss, as I speak true;
> So speaking as I think, alas, I die. [*Dies.*]
>
> (249–51)

In the years since T. S. Eliot's "Shakespeare and the Stoicism of Seneca" (1927), Othello's last words have been so frequently discussed that one almost hesitates to quote them. Yet one must not bate Othello his "word or two":

> Soft you; a word or two before you go.
> I have done the state some service, and they know't—
> No more of that. I pray you, in your letters,
> When you shall these unlucky deeds relate,
> Speak of me as I am; nothing extenuate,
> Nor set down aught in malice. Then must you speak
> Of one that lov'd not wisely but too well;
> Of one not easily jealous, but being wrought,
> Perplexed in the extreme; of one whose hand,
> Like the base [Indian],[8] threw a pearl away
> Richer than all his tribe; of one whose subdu'd eyes,
> Albeit unused to the melting mood,
> Drops tears as fast as the Arabian trees
> Their medicinable gum. Set you down this;

And say besides, that in Aleppo once,
Where a malignant and a turban'd Turk
Beat a Venetian and traduc'd the state,
I took by th' throat the circumcised dog,
And smote him—thus. [*He stabs himself.*]

. . . .
I kiss'd thee ere I kill'd thee. No way but this,
Killing myself, to die upon a kiss. [*(Falls on the bed and) dies.*]

(338–56; 58–59)

Eliot, of course, is nothing if not critical: Othello is "*cheering himself up.* He is endeavouring to escape reality, he has ceased to think about Desdemona, and is thinking about himself. Humility," Eliot gravely reflects, "is the most difficult of all virtues to achieve; nothing dies harder than the desire to think well of oneself. . . . [Othello] takes in the spectator, but the human motive is primarily to take in himself. I do not believe that any writer has ever exposed this *bovarysme,* the human will to see things as they are not, more clearly than Shakespeare."[9]

Eliot's attitude toward Othello is not only symptomatic of what Helen Gardner calls our age's "distaste for the heroic,"[10] but unworkable in the theater. As Nevill Coghill has remarked, "If Shakespeare had wished to convey the 'terrible exposure of human weakness' that Mr Eliot sees in Othello's speech, he could very easily have made this simple purpose plain, unless he was a bungler, or quite indifferent to the effect he was creating. For if Mr Eliot is right, the better this speech is spoken and acted, the more it must deceive the audience; and this is, in effect, conceded by Mr Eliot, who says Othello 'takes in the spectator.' "[11]

But dramatists were deceivers ever. "Tragedy, by means of legends and emotions, creates a deception in which the deceiver is more honest than the non-deceiver, and the deceived is wiser than the non-deceived."[12] And the speech the "honest" Shakespeare gives Othello conveys, not self-deception, but "the recovery of his real self through the return to the rhetoric that he had made his own."[13] There is appropriate self-respect in his reference to his past services to Venice; and the play supports his contention that his jealousy was induced, not innate. Were it otherwise, what need for a "demi-devil" as potent as Iago? But if, like Hamlet and many other Renaissance protagonists, he wishes his life and conduct to be properly understood, he has not ceased to think of Desdemona. No one, I think, has described what Othello says and means better than Gardner: "His error he cannot explain. He sees it in an image which asserts her [Desdemona's] infinite value and his supreme good fortune, which in ignorance he did not realize. . . . The tears he weeps now are not 'cruel tears,' but good tears, natural and healing. He communicates this by an image drawn from his life of adventure." Every inch Othello, he is ready to die:

> As he nerves himself to end everything, there flashes across his mind an image from his past which seems to epitomize his whole life and will "report him and his cause aright"; an act of suicidal daring, inspired by his chosen loyalty to Venice. With the same swiftness he does justice on himself, traducer and murderer of his Venetian wife. As, at their re-union, after the tempest, his joy stopped his speech, so now his grief and worship express themselves finally in an act, the same act: he dies "upon a kiss."14

Othello gathers to greatness, dying as he has lived. In his end is his beginning.

King Lear (1605), though a play in which many persons die, dramatizes only three deaths. The first to die, the nameless servant who attempts to aid Gloucester, is struck down by Regan:

> O, I am slain! My lord, you have one eye left
> To see some mischief on him [Cornwall]. O! [*He dies.*]
>
> (3.7.81–82)

Beginning and ending with a cry, the speech tells us of his pain as well as his concern for Gloucester, whose remaining eye will be gouged out in direct response to his words. The second character to die, the "serviceable villain" Oswald, comes by his death through his ruthless opportunism. Coming upon Gloucester and the dis-guised Edgar, he arrogantly proclaims:

> That eyeless head of thine was first fram'd flesh
> To raise my fortunes. Thou old unhappy traitor,
> Briefly thyself remember; the sword is out
> That must destroy thee.
>
> (4.6.227–30)

To his astonishment, however, he is dashed to the ground by Edgar's cudgel:

> Slave, thou hast slain me. Villain, take my purse:
> If ever thou wilt thrive, bury my body,
> And give the letters which thou find'st about me
> To Edmund Earl of Gloucester; seek him out

> Upon the English party. O untimely death!
> Death!

> (4.6.246–51)

Oswald too evinces fidelity to another, proving, in Edgar's phrase, "As duteous to the vices of [his] mistress / As badness would desire" (253–54). Yet his death is kept from touching us. Indeed, Shakespeare makes his last four words faintly ludicrous.

Then there is Lear, whose death is the last—and most terrible—of the play's peaks of pain, its culminating passion.[15] Before Lear dies we have witnessed what might almost be described as the death of Cordelia; like Lear we may harbor the delusion that "this feather stirs, she lives!" (5.3.266). And Lear, charged with more emotion than nature can endure, reaches the end of his dark journey:

> And my poor fool is hang'd! No, no, no life!
> Why should a dog, a horse, a rat, have life,
> And thou no breath at all? Thou'lt come no more,
> Never, never, never, never, never.
> Pray you undo this button. Thank you, sir.
> Do you see this? Look on her! Look her lips,
> Look there, look there! [*He dies.*]

> (306–12)[16]

Lear's death, is quite simply, incomparable, like the play itself. As Maynard Mack has observed, the protagonist's death "is usually in Shakespeare climactic and distinctive, has sacrificial implications, dresses itself in ritual, springs from what we know to be a Renaissance mystique of stoical self-dominion." One expects a "salute to death." But in this respect (as in others) *Lear* violates the Shakespearean norm:

> How differently death comes to Lear! Not in a moment of self-scrutiny that stirs us to awe or exaltation or regret at waste, but as a blessing at which we must rejoice with Kent, hardly more than a needful afterthought to the death that counts dramatically, Cordelia's.[17]

Lear's death seems to me both distinctive and climactic (surely it is odd to describe it as "hardly more than a needful afterthought"). But it is strikingly "modern" in its emphasis on the private and the personal. Lear is not concerned with having his actions—or even sufferings—correctly apprehended; he does not care how people will speak of him. His mind is not on the king who has gone from everything to nothing, but on Cordelia.

Macbeth (1606) resembles *Lear* in dramatizing only a few of its many deaths. Yet in this bloody play filled with "strange images of death" (1.3.97), we are made to imagine much that we do not see. Hence it is almost shocking to be reminded that Banquo, Macduff's son, Young Siward, and Macbeth are the only characters who die on stage.

What is at least equally remarkable is how little emphasis is given to the last words of these characters. With the exception of *Titus Andronicus,* no Shakespearean tragedy is so perfunctory in this respect. Banquo's death overtakes him before he can do more than cry out:

> O, treachery! Fly, good Fleance, fly, fly, fly!
> Thou mayst revenge. O slave! [*Dies. Fleance escapes.*]
>
> (3.3.17–18)

The safety of his son and his desire for vengeance are the two concerns that define him. The last words of Macduff's son are similarly brief, expressing only the boy's futile hope that his mother may escape:

> He has kill'd me, mother:
> Run away, I pray you! [*Dies.*]
>
> (4.2.84–85)

Young Siward dies wordlessly (5.7.11 s.d.); and so—in defiance of dramatic convention—does Macbeth (5.8.34 s.d.).[18]

In one sense Shakespeare's denial of a death speech to Macbeth is reminiscent of *Richard III,* whose villainous protagonist suffered the same curtailment. But Richard, as Emrys Jones has noted, occupies a historically determined role:

> To Tudor audiences the real significance of Richard III was his destined role as antagonist to Richmond/Henry VII. In fighting Richmond to the death at Bosworth he was, or so he might seem to be a hundred years later, opposing the establishment of the Tudor dynasty, trying to avert the coming reigns of Henry VII, his son, and his three grandchildren.[19]

Despite efforts to characterize *Macbeth* as a "royal play" designed to please King James,[20] one must be skeptical of the idea that it gives much prominence to the origins of the Stuart dynasty. The historical future does not loom so large, nor does it require Macbeth's diminishment.

Macbeth seems rather an instance of a protagonist who, having

already taken his final measure of the world, cannot be imagined as
having anything to add. His vision of human experience, in which
life is "a tale / Told by an idiot . . . / Signifying nothing" (5.5.26–
28), is spoken when and as it must be, in response to his wife's
death. This is the language of inward and private experience
(though Seyton is present, the effect is almost that of a soliloquy),
not of the battlefield. His last words, addressed to his destined
slayer, precede the fatal "laying on":

> I will not yield,
> To kiss the ground before young Malcolm's feet,
> And to be baited with the rabble's curse.
> Though Birnan wood be come to Dunsinane,
> And thou oppos'd, being of no woman born,
> Yet I will try the last. Before my body
> I throw my warlike shield. Lay on, Macduff,
> And damn'd be him that first cries, "Hold, enough!"
>
> (5.8.27–34)

Desperate courage is all that remains. The life that Macbeth strives
to save signifies nothing; with his "blind brow / above an empty
heart,"[21] he has no need of further speech. There is nothing to
express.

In *Coriolanus* (1607–8) the protagonist is again denied the conventional "salute to death." In this play Shakespeare returns to the
technique employed in *Troilus and Cressida:* only one death—that
of Coriolanus—is dramatized; and like Hector he is slaughtered by
those incited by his formidable but dishonorable rival.

Radically different from Macbeth in most ways, Coriolanus resembles him in being incapable of any last-minute perceptions or
discoveries. For Macbeth, the final shape of reality is that described
in "To-morrow, and to-morrow, and to-morrow." Coriolanus,
goaded by Aufidius, responds as we know he must:

> Measureless liar, thou hast made my heart
> Too great for what contains it. "Boy"? O slave!
> . . . .
> Cut me to pieces, Volsces, men and lads,
> Stain all your edges on me. "Boy," false hound!
> If you have writ your annals true, 'tis there
> That, like an eagle in a dove-cote, I
> [Flutter'd][22] your Volscians in Corioles.
> Alone I did it. "Boy"!
>
> (5.6.103–4; 111–16)

Moments later the conspirators draw their swords and stain them,
and Aufidius treads on the body. But Coriolanus has spoken and
died "like himself." Character and dramatic context necessitate the
sacrifice of Coriolanus's dying words. Nonetheless, the last six lines
quoted above are obviously spoken by one who knows he is confronting death. Their suicidal daring gives them greater force than
they could have had at any other point in the play. If he could speak
after the assassins have struck, he could at best repeat them.

Macbeth and *Coriolanus* make death as sudden as it is violent.
Terrible wounds spill life in moments, leaving time for no more than
a brief outcry. *Antony and Cleopatra* (1606–7), as different from
these plays as Nile from Acheron or Tiber, carries on what might be
called an Egyptian dalliance with death. No other of Shakespeare's
plays gives comparable scope to the words and actions of the dying.

Of the characters whose deaths are dramatized, the first is Enobarbus. Having left Antony for Octavius, Enobarbus soon realizes
the baseness of his action. Then Antony sends "thy treasure, with /
His bounty overplus" (4.6.20–21)—a magnanimous gesture which
"blows" Enobarbus's heart. Invoking the moon (which, constant in
change, is ever the same), he calls for death:

> O sovereign mistress of true melancholy,
> The poisonous damp of night dispunge upon me,
> That life, a very rebel to my will,
> May hang no longer on me. Throw my heart
> Against the flint and hardness of my fault,
> Which being dried with grief will break to powder.
>
> (4.9.12–17)

His last thoughts are of his own turpitude and Antony's nobility:

> O Antony,
> Nobler than my revolt is infamous,
> Forgive me in thine own particular,
> But let the world rank me in register
> A master-leaver and a fugitive.
> O Antony! O Antony! [*Dies.*]
>
> (4.9.18–23)

Mysteriously, through no act of self-violence, he receives the death
he seeks. "Love hath reason, Reason none," confesses Reason in
The Phoenix and the Turtle (47): Enobarbus learns that fidelity to
Antony, though arrant folly in worldly terms, is wiser in the way
that matters most. To leave Antony is an act of moral suicide, of

self-violation. Instead of wishing what most men wish—a noble memory—Enobarbus's self-loathing is so intense that he desires to become a fixed figure of notoriety.

Enobarbus's death, of course, serves to magnify Antony, whose own death will soon follow. What it attests to is clear enough. The death of Antony, a curious compound of deception, self-deception, and magnanimity, epitomizes the ambiguities and tensions of the play. After his final defeat, Antony is readying himself for suicide: "Nay, weep not, gentle Eros, there is left us / Ourselves to end ourselves" (4.14.21–22). Then Mardian arrives, bringing word of Cleopatra's death: her last words, according to the cunning report, were " 'Antony, most noble Antony!' " (30). Almost immediately, Antony, "No more a soldier" (42), resolves to join her in death:

> Where souls do couch on flowers, we'll hand in hand,
> And with our sprightly port make the ghosts gaze.
> Dido and her Aeneas shall want troops,
> And all the haunt be ours.
>
> (51–54)

It is a consummation devoutly to be wished, wonderfully in character in its insistence that the lovers will be accorded center stage throughout eternity. Yet this potent imaginative projection, which expresses Antony's vision of the future, mars what it does. Not only is Antony an anti-Aeneas, governed by passion rather than a sense of duty: to many in Shakespeare's audience, Antony would have seemed strangely deluded. For, as has often been noted, Antony is our only source for the idea that Dido and Aeneas are lovers in Elysium.[23] In the *Aeneid,* when Aeneas encounters Dido in the underworld she will not speak to him; adamantly irreconcilable, she returns to her husband: "At length she flung herself away and, still his foe, fled back to the shady grove, where Sychaeus, her lord of former days, responds to her sorrows and gives her love for love" (6.472–74).[24] Time, too, becomes utterly subjective:

>   Since Cleopatra died
> I have liv'd in such dishonor that the gods
> Detest my baseness.
>
> (55–57)

Only moments have passed since the news of Cleopatra's death was brought; yet for Antony, as for Juliet, "in a minute there [may be] many days" (*Romeo and Juliet* 3.5.45).[25] The audience, especially as it knows that Cleopatra is alive, is likely to be more objective. Antony's situation is ironic, his decision precipitant.

Eros, called upon to play the part that Pindarus played for Cassius, is reminded of his oath: "When I did make thee free, swor'st thou not then / To do this when I bade thee? Do it at once" (81–82). But unlike Pindarus, Eros prefers taking his own life to that of his "master," "captain," and "emperor." Again we see that Antony inspires devotion in those closest to him. Who would die for Caesar? Eros dies for love, admirably.

Antony pays tribute to Eros ("Thrice-nobler than myself!" [95]), whose valiancy he will emulate. But he is also thinking of Cleopatra's heroic death:

> My queen and Eros
> Have by their brave instruction got upon me
> A nobleness in record; but I will be
> A bridegroom in my death, and run into't
> As to a lover's bed.
>
> (97–101)

The image is, appropriately, amatory, linking this speech to Antony's initial response to Cleopatra's death. But with an ineptitude that would have been unimaginable in Othello, Antony bungles his suicide, his very force entangling itself with strength. "Let him that loves me strike me dead," he implores his guardsmen (108). None is willing to be the death of Antony. Then Diomedes enters, bearing word that Cleopatra's death is a fiction. Neither now nor later does Antony descend to recrimination. He merely asks to be carried to Cleopatra.[26]

Antony's first concern is to comfort her: "Peace! / Not Caesar's valor hath o'erthrown Antony, / But Antony's hath triumph'd on itself" (4.15.13–15). Like Othello (and Romeo and Juliet), he desires a final kiss:

> I am dying, Egypt, dying; only
> I here importune death awhile, until
> Of many thousand kisses the poor last
> I lay upon thy lips.
>
> (18–21)

After these almost reverential lines (the kiss is like a sacrifice, her lips an altar), he is borne aloft to Cleopatra and speaks of her future without him. Clearly, he does not entirely trust her: "One word, sweet queen: / Of Caesar seek your honor, with your safety" (45–46); she can, he (wrongly) believes, trust Proculeius. Then come his final words:

> The miserable change now at my end
> Lament nor sorrow at; but please your thoughts
> In feeding them with those my former fortunes
> Wherein I liv'd, the greatest prince o' th' world,
> The noblest; and do now not basely die,
> Not cowardly put off my helmet to
> My countryman—a Roman by a Roman
> Valiantly vanquish'd. Now my spirit is going,
> I can no more.
>
> (51–59)

Antony's account of his suicide is usually taken as another instance of his capacity for self-deception. Indeed, as Foreman remarks, "his contention that his valor, not Caesar's, has triumphed seems as good an example as any of what Eliot describes as cheering oneself up. . . . [S]ince Antony killed himself on the basis of a lie, and didn't do it very neatly, his assertion here [14–15; 55–58] may seem a little forced, his death a little shabby."[27] Antony, in short, dies better pleased with himself than circumstances warrant, a Roman Bovarist who takes in himself but fails to take in the audience.

Yet Foreman's use of "may seem" is significant. In *Antony and Cleopatra* fundamentally different possibilities are often simultaneously present.[28] And what if Antony's counterversion of reality is not imputed to self-deception?

It seems at least equally possible that what Antony tells Cleopatra is *splendide mendax,* a conscious falsehood in the service of a noble purpose. Nowhere else is the greatness of Antony more evident than in these moments with Cleopatra. What he says—and does not say—reveals a magnanimity vastly transcending even that displayed by his treatment of Enobarbus. As noted earlier, he does not rebuke her for sending Mardian, nor so much as mention the matter. Instead, he speaks as if Cleopatra had played no part in bringing about his death—as if the force that drove his sword was sheer *Romanitas*. Of course we know better. "The scene of [Antony's] death," as Foreman observes, "makes him a richer, more complex figure than the valiant Roman he claims to be in his final speech."[29] But one need not conclude that his spurious account of his death is the work of a falsifying ego. Like other speeches in this scene, it may arise from his protective concern for

Cleopatra. For it may be in some sense his last gift to her, an effort to please her thoughts, feed her heart.[30]

What Antony actually believes is impossible to determine. He is fully capable of self-deception, the magnanimity I have suggested, or even some combination of the two. The play does not answer such questions so much as pose them. As Adelman has remarked,

> Nothing goes unquestioned in this play. In most literature there is a convention that character is knowable as it rarely is in life, that characters act in accordance with certain constant, recognizable, and explicable principles which we and they can know. This convention does not operate in *Antony and Cleopatra*. There the characters do not know each other, nor can we know them, any more clearly than we know ourselves.[31]

Antony's dying words are a good instance of this breach of convention. He is to the last a dramatic character, playing a part; we never see into his heart's core.

The death of Antony, according to Cleopatra, leaves "nothing . . . remarkable / Beneath the visiting moon" (4.15.67–68). Nonetheless, she does not choose to follow him in death until she has assessed what the future holds. Her deepest motivation, like that of Antony, is essentially inscrutable.

The stages by which Cleopatra comes to her death suggest something of its complexity. Moments after Antony's death she alludes to suicide. "We'll bury him; and then, what's brave, what's noble, / Let's do't after the high Roman fashion, / And make death proud to take us" (4.15.86–88). This suggests a suicide comparable to Antony's, as described by himself. At her next appearance she is shown reflecting on the nobility of suicide. The act has become more than a triumph over oneself, like Antony's; it is the definitive victory over the mutable world:

> My desolation does begin to make
> A better life. 'Tis paltry to be Caesar;
> Not being Fortune, he's but Fortune's knave,
> A minister of her will: and it is great
> To do that thing that ends all other deeds,
> Which shackles accidents and bolts up change.
>
> (5.2.1–6)

Yet her resolve is not tested at this point. Instead, she is taken prisoner while she speaks with Proculeius; although she draws a dagger, she is swiftly disarmed.

This initiates another phase in Cleopatra's progress to death. Her situation, as she envisions it, resembles that of Macbeth: she could not tolerate being the main exhibit in Caesar's triumph. As she declares to Proculeius,

> Know, sir, that I
> Will not wait pinion'd at your master's court,
> Nor once be chastis'd with the sober eye
> Of dull Octavia. Shall they hoist me up,
> And show me to the shouting varlotry
> Of censuring Rome?
>
> (52–57)

Such is the future in its most appalling shape. Moments later, after Dolabella has replaced Proculeius as her guard, Cleopatra speaks of the past: "I dreamt there was an Emperor Antony. / O, such another sleep, that I might see / But such another man!" (76–78). Disregarding Dolabella's attempts to interrupt, she proceeds to share her "dream":

> His face was as the heav'ns, and therein stuck
> A sun and moon, which kept their course, and lighted
> The little O, th' earth. . . .
> His legs bestrid the ocean. . . .
>   In his livery
> Walk'd crowns and crownets; realms and islands were
> As plates dropp'd from his pocket.
>
> (79–81; 82; 90–92)

The inestimable loss she has suffered is emphasized even more than her nightmare of the future. But if her "size of sorrow" draws her towards death, the future exercises a power no less compulsive.

For Cleopatra's motives are characteristically complex. Her grief, as we know, is real. Yet the panegyric on Antony, hyperbole hyperbolized, flies so defiantly in the face of truth that one may suspect it to be less designed to hold the mirror up to Antony than to body forth her sense of loss. And what's Dolabella to her, that she should wish to make him share her "dream"? His significance may be his possible usefulness. No sooner does she perceive how deeply her words have affected him than she asks what Caesar intends to do with her. For Caesar too has his dream. As Dolabella discloses, he means to lead her in triumph.

In the interview with Caesar that immediately ensues Cleopatra is deferential, politic, acting as if she knew nothing of Caesar's

purpose. Everything Caesar does is calculated to make her preserve her life. She has, he declares at parting, no cause for despair:
"We intend so to dispose you as / Yourself shall give us counsel.
Feed, and sleep" (186–87). "My master, and my lord!" is her
officious reply (190).

The injunction to feed and sleep is particularly offensive, suggesting as it does a mode of life that is base, ignoble. "What is a man,"
asks Hamlet, "if his chief good and market of his time / Be but to
sleep and feed? a beast, no more" (4.4.33–35). Cleopatra, readying
herself for death, intends to act nobly: "He words me, girls, he
words me, that I should not / Be noble to myself" (191–92). Yet she
knows that such self-betrayal would be profitless. Whatever Caesar
says, he plans to lead her in triumph.

Cleopatra acts at once, sending Charmian to summon the means
of death that has been provided. While Charmian gives the final
word, Dolabella reports that "Caesar through Syria / Intends his
journey, and within three days / You with your children will he send
before" (200–202). From one point of view the information is irrelevant. Death is on the way. But what Dolabella reveals makes suicide
easier to embrace. Gross derision, cruel mockery, are only three
days and a journey away. What waits in Rome is intolerable even to
imagine. Most impious of all,

> The quick comedians
> Extemporally will stage us, and present
> Our Alexandrian revels: Antony
> Shall be brought drunken forth, and I shall see
> Some squeaking Cleopatra boy my greatness
> I' th' posture of a whore.
>
> (216–21)

Given the choice between such a life and death, Cleopatra will not
waver.

But Cleopatra would be less than herself if she could not make
suicide into something more positive. It is, she declares, "the way /
To fool their preparation, and to conquer / Their most absurd
intents" (224–26). She will die like Cleopatra, victorious. She thinks
of the day she conquered Antony:

> Show me, my women, like a queen; go fetch
> My best attires. I am again for Cydnus
> To meet Mark Antony.
>
> (227–29)

The rustic comes in with the figs; she protracts the conversation, as if relishing it. Then it is time to die:

> Give me my robe, put on my crown, I have
> Immortal longings in me. . . .
>   Methinks I hear
> Antony call; I see him rouse himself
> To praise my noble act. I hear him mock
> The luck of Caesar, which the gods give men
> To excuse their after wrath. Husband, I come!
>
>   (280–81; 283–87)

Like Hamlet, Cleopatra is too complex to be represented by a single speech. Yet it is remarkable how much of her infinite variety Shakespeare manages to distill into these lines. The fig-bearer has said that the asp's bite is "immortal," meaning deadly (247); Cleopatra simultaneously alludes to his blunder and invests the word with astonishing sublimity. Her motives for suicide are complex: she desires union with Antony; but no less exigent is her desire to rob Caesar of his triumph (and spare herself the humiliation of participating in it). Antony draws her toward death; Caesar drives her from life. The shocking domesticity of "Husband!" reveals her embracing yet another role—and transcending its potential limitations. What might otherwise seem merely sentimental becomes a kind of emotional shorthand for suggesting the depth and permanence of her commitment to Antony.

Yet Cleopatra's thoughts are never far from the erotic, the most artfully natural of her natural habitats. Iras is the first to die, dropping wordlessly after Cleopatra has kissed her farewell:

> If thou and nature can so gently part,
> The stroke of death is as a lover's pinch,
> Which hurts, and is desir'd.
>
>   (294–96)

Love and death are joined in another sense a moment later. Like Antony, she envisions union after death. But what if Iras reaches Antony before she does? "If she first meet the curled Antony, / He'll make demand of her, and spend that kiss / Which is my heaven to have" (301–3). Yet her thoughts are not only on this undomestic Antony; she is also conscious of beguiling Caesar, who will prove "an ass / Unpolicied!" (307–8). Only in yielding to a death that is euphoric, almost orgasmic, does the latter motive disappear:

Dost thou not see my baby at my breast,
That sucks the nurse asleep? . . .
As sweet as balm, as soft as air, as gentle—
O Antony!—Nay, I will take thee too:
  [*Applying another asp to her arm.*]
What should I stay—[*Dies.*]

                           (309–13)

Unlike Antony, who closes his life with a kind of Roman control ("Now my spirit is going, / I can no more"), Cleopatra gives the impression that she is surprised by death. She might say more. The same is true of Charmian, who dies directing our attention to Cleopatra:

1 Guard. What work is here, Charmian? Is this well done?
Charmian. It is well done, and fitting for a princess
  Descended of so many royal kings.
  Ah, soldier! [*Charmian dies.*]

                           (325–28)

The final words, which suggest the ineffability of Cleopatra (how, really, is one to justify her action in a phrase or two?) also reach out to the man addressed. The intimate, human quality of "Ah, soldier!" is a world apart from Dryden's *All for Love,* where this plangent exclamation is replaced by the soldierlike "Yes, 'tis well done, and like a queen, the last / Of her great race: I follow her" (5.1.501–2).[32] Dryden's speaker, one feels, has her say; Shakespeare's implies much that she cannot say, for which only *Antony and Cleopatra,* taken as a whole, provides adequate utterance.[33]

Cleopatra, whom everything becomes, goes beyond Antony—or anyone else in Renaissance drama—in transmuting death to victory. Unlike Antony, she does not act prematurely, nor in response to a lie. And she does it "beautifully," directing and performing her death so that it becomes an aesthetic as well as personal triumph, "a work of art."[34] Antony's death, though undercut by various ironies, is also kept from seeming tragic. For as Harriett Hawkins observes, "how a tragic character ultimately feels about himself— how, looking back, he evaluates his life or confronts his death—is of crucial importance so far as the final impression left upon his audience is concerned."[35] Both protagonists of *Antony and Cleopatra* impose their own characters on death. They die as if to fulfill themselves, stepping from the flux of life into what they envision as a sustaining permanence. By refusing to see themselves

as tragic figures, Antony and Cleopatra encourage us to do like-
wise. And though "Octavian" critics may remind us that the lovers
are in fact deluded, poetry such as Antony and Cleopatra speak is
not so easily refuted. From the tension between the "facts" of the
plot and the lovers' intense subjectivity, "meaning" is generated;
yet the poetry is part of the meaning.[36] Consummation as much as
terminus, their deaths are like no others in Renaissance drama.[37]

Appendix: The Rhetoric of Death

Despite what would seem its obvious limitations, the convention by which the dying refer to the state of their own interior organs courses like quicksilver through Renaissance drama. Sometimes it is used self-consciously, in a way that suggests how thoroughly conventionalized such speeches had become. In the anonymous *Alphonsus, Emperor of Germany* (1594), for example, Alphonsus, pretending to be poisoned, calls for ice and snow to quench his fire:

> O most excessive pain, O raging fire!
> Is burning Cancer, or the Scorpion,
> Descended from the heavenly zodiac,
> To parch mine entrails with a quenchless flame?
> Drink, drink, I say, give drink, or I shall die!
> Fill a thousand bowls of wine! Water, I say,
> Water from forth the cold Tartarian hills!
> I feel th' ascending flame lick up my blood;
> Mine entrails shrink together like a scroll
> Of burning parchment, and my marrow fries.
> Bring hugy cakes of ice and flakes of snow,
> That I may drink of them being dissolved.
>
> (4.2.1–12)[1]

Since the audience has been informed that Alphonsus is merely attempting to divert suspicion from himself (he has just poisoned the King of Bohemia), it can be unusually objective about these lines. Yet one doubts that the speech is intended as parody; it seems rather to exemplify what audiences had come to expect from someone in the throes of death-by-poison.

In Chettle and Munday's *The Death of Robert, Earl of Huntington* (1598), Huntington (Robin Hood) feels that death is upon him:

> My dying frost, which no sun's heat can thaw,
> Closes the powers of all my outward parts:
> My freezing blood runs back unto my heart.[2]

169

This is, as such speeches go, notable for its brevity—although the death of Ampedo in Dekker's *Old Fortunatus* (1599) shows even greater restraint:

> Wanton farwell, I faint, deaths frozen hand
> Congeales lifes little Riuer in my breast.
>
> (5.2.152–53)[3]

But these two instances do not mean that audiences had tired of more copious treatments of death's impact on the body. In Chettle's *Hoffman, or A Revenge for a Father* (1602), for example, Otho, lingering in articulate anguish, thus describes the agony inflicted by the red-hot crown that has been placed on him:

> Oh Lorrique tortor, I feele an Aetna burne
> Within my braines, and all my body else
> Is like a hill of Ice, all these Belgique seas
> That now, surround vs cannot quench this flame
> Death like a tyrant seazeth me vnawares,
> My sinewes shrinke like leaues parcht with the sunne
> My blood dissolues, nerues and tendons fayle
> Each part's disioynted, and my breath expires
> Mount soule to heauen, my body burnes in fire.
>
> (226–34)[4]

Another head made more than uneasy by a crown is that of Sejanus in the anonymous *Claudius Tiberius Nero* (1607). But when Tiberius places a burning crown on Sejanus's head, Sejanus, in the six lines he speaks before expiring, makes only two brief references to his physical suffering (the speech is quoted in chapter 2). Instead, the emphasis is on Sejanus's vengeful fury. The effect of this shift in focus is that the audience is given something more dramatically engaging than the customary catalogue of depersonalized physiological details. But whatever its merits, the approach taken with the death of Sejanus remains unusual.

Heywood, in *The Brazen Age* (1611), provides Meleager with the almost obligatory language. Hardly has Althea fired the brand than the catalogue of torments begins:

> Still, still, there is an Aetna in my bosome
> The flames of Stix, and fires of Acheron
> Are from the blacke Chimerian shades remou'd,
> And fixt heere, heere. . . .

Moments later ("My flame increaseth still"), he feels that "The
Sunne hath cast his element on me, / And in my entrails hath he fixt
his Spheare." Then brand and life go out:

> Now 'gins my fire waste, and my naturall heat
> To change to Ice, and my scortch'd blood to freeze.
> Farewell, since his black ensigne death displayes,
> I dye, cut off thus in my best of dayes. [*He dyes.*][5]

Heywood, experienced writer that he was, gives the audience what
it expects.

Some dramatists, most notably Shakespeare, seem to have regarded the rhetoric of death as a convention more honored in the
breach than the observance. Only in *King John* (1594–96) does
Shakespeare make extensive use of it (see chapter 7). In *Romeo and
Juliet* (1595–96) and *Hamlet* (1600–1601), even characters who have
been poisoned say nothing about what is happening within their
bodies; and in *1 Henry IV* (1596-97), when Hotspur is dying from
Hal's sword-thrust, he makes only one brief reference to the
"earthy and cold hand of death" (5.4.84).[6] If one reflects how many
characters die in Shakespeare's plays, and how rarely they speak of
their physiological inner weather, Shakespeare's fundamental aver-
sion to the convention becomes evident.

Chapman and Webster seem to have felt much as Shakespeare
did. The Herculean protagonist of *Bussy D'Ambois* (1604), as one
might have expected, informs us about what is happening to his
"heart and liver" (5.3.184);[7] elsewhere, however, Chapman never
has a dying character speak this way. In *The White Devil* (1612),
when Bracciano is in agony after donning a poisoned helmet, he
cries out that his "brain's on fire" (5.3.4);[8] instead of expatiating he
lapses into madness; when he comes to his senses he is strangled.
Some grotesque lines spoken by Flamineo when he is pretending
that he has been shot are more conventional in being protracted:

> O I smell soot,
> Most stinking soot, the chimney is a-fire,—
> My liver's parboil'd like Scotch holy bread;
> There is a plumber, laying pipes in my guts.
>
> (5.6.141–44)

Since the audience has not been told that the pistols "held no
bullets" (150), it must assimilate the tone of these lines as best it
can.[9] But when Flamineo actually dies, he makes no reference to

the familiar topos of bodily suffering; nor does Vittoria at her death. In *The Duchess of Malfi* (1614), such speeches are entirely excluded.

Fletcher, Middleton, and Massinger also seem not to have shared the general enthusiasm for the rhetoric of death. Only in *Valentinian* (1614) does Fletcher use it, and there (see chapter 4) it is limited to a few lines. Middleton and Massinger similarly restrict its scope (see chapter 5). In *The Second Maiden's Tragedy* (1611), probably by Middleton, Votarius, pierced with a poisoned sword, says his "breast is all a-fire—O!—" (5.1.109)—and dies with no further ado.[10] *Hengist, King of Kent* (1618) and *The Changeling* (with Rowley, 1622) entirely omit references to physical suffering. *Women Beware Women* (1621) includes a number of them, but they are extraordinarily brief: Leontio refers to his broken "heart-string" (4.2.43);[11] Hippolito says, "death runs through my blood; in a wild flame too" (5.2.139), and calls for someone to "Lend me the speeding pity of his sword / To quench this fire in blood" (148–49); and the Duke exclaims: "My heart swells bigger yet; help here, break't ope, / My breast flies open next" (5.2. 189–90). All except Leontio have been poisoned, which makes Middleton's forbearance the more remarkable. (Bianca, also poisoned, dies speaking moral sentences instead of the expected language of suffering.) Massinger, who employs the convention once, in *The Duke of Milan* (1621), does so for only a few lines.

The dramatic practice of Middleton and Massinger might suggest that by the 1620s the rhetoric of death was going out of fashion. Such, however, is not the case. In Heywood's *The English Traveller* (1625), for example, an adulterous wife dies of grief:

> Swell sicke Heart,
> Euen till thou burst the ribs that bound thee in;
> So, there's one string crackt.[12]

Moments later she dies offstage. In Dekker's *The Noble Spanish Soldier* (1626), the King drinks poisoned wine and suffers the conventional effects:

> I feele no poyson yet, onely mine eyes
> Are putting out their lights: me thinks I feele
> Deaths Icy fingers stroking down my face;
> And now I'me in a mortall cold sweat.
>
> . . . .

I burne,
My braines boyle in a Caldron, O one drop
Of water now to coole me.

(5.4.72–75; 80–82)[13]

Such a speech might have been written as early as the 1590s.

Heywood and Dekker, one may say, are old-fashioned. But the young William Davenant makes extensive use of this kind of speech in his *The Tragedy of Albovine* (1628). Here Valdaura, stabbed by her husband, cries out: "I feel the frozen hand of death. Oh! oh! oh!"[14] And Paradine, like Alphonsus some thirty-five years before him, pretends to be poisoned:

Oh, oh! It scorches all my entrails up;
As if like Porcia I had swallowed coals.
I spit scum, such as o'er th' hot cauldron boils.

. . . .

I cannot rise. A stiff convulsion in
My sinews fetters all my limbs.

(Pp. 103–4)

"I spit scum" is a vile phrase. Yet the passage is not intended to be comic. The same thing is true in a later play by Davenant, *The Platonic Lovers* (1635), when Fredeline describes his poison-induced suffering:

How am I planet-struck, how suddenly
Depriv'd of strength. . . .
My sinews shrink, and bear me crooked when
I move, as I had been their load a hundred years.
Palsies and agues have possess'd my joints,
I quiver like a naked Russian in the snow;
And my dim eyes begin to glare and wink,
Like to a long-neglected lamp, whose oil
Is wasted to a drop.

(2:100)

Soon he will learn that the virulence of the potion will abate; yet the speech itself, despite the proliferation of similitudes, seems seriously intended.

A much greater playwright than Davenant, John Ford, uses the rhetoric of death in *Love's Sacrifice* (1632), *The Broken Heart* (1629), and *'Tis Pity She's a Whore* (1632), all discussed in chapter 6. Only in *The Broken Heart*, that strange and highly ritualized

ceremonial of thwarted love and emotional starvation, does the
convention yield impressive results. There the characteristic excesses of the speech can have no place—Ford's aristocratic Spar-
tans would never carry on so—and a singularly chastened language
of the body is used to speak of what the heart is, and of what it
suffers. In 'Tis Pity and Love's Sacrifice Ford sounds like a host of
his contemporaries.

Shirley, as one might expect, makes use of the rhetoric of death
on a number of occasions. In The Maid's Revenge (1626), Catalina,
poisoned by her sister, speaks in a way that echoes Flamineo's
pseudo-death (see chapter 6). A similarly grotesque speech occurs
in St. Patrick of Ireland (1639), when Rodamant, poisoned while
drinking to the Queen's health, describes his suffering:

> My royal love hath blown my bowels up. Oh, a cooler; would I were a
> while in the frozen sea! charity is not cold enough to relieve me; the
> devil is making fireworks in my belly.[15]

He goes on in this vein until he falls, but is recovered by St. Patrick.
Finally, in The Cardinal (1641), the title figure briefly alludes to
what poison is doing to him: "I feel it knocking at the seat of life"
(5.3.279).[16]

Several minor dramatists may be briefly mentioned. In Nabbes's
Hannibal and Scripio (1635), the suicide speech of Sophonisba,
who has poisoned herself, might have been written at any time after
about 1590 by anyone capable of writing blank verse:

> It begin's to worke
> With a full strength: my blood would serve to heate
> A Salamander, and convert his ice
> Into a flame. Aetna's but painted fire
> To that which burn's my marrow. Yet my lookes
> Are cherefull and erected.[17]

It is bad enough to speak these lines at all, but to do so while
looking cheerful! Hannibal, also dying by self-administered poison,
expatiates on what he suffers:

> Worke on, thou brave minister
> Of my last victory over my selfe;
> Quench thy unnatural flames with my scortcht bowels.
>   . . . .
> My heart, my heart!
> Quench it, Eridanus! but it would dry

Thy waters up. I'm wrapt in greater fires
Then the rash boy [Phaethon] thou choak'st.

(Pp. 268–69)

"Painted fire," it turns out, is the only fire Nabbes has at his disposal.

Thomas Rawlins's *The Rebellion* (with others, perhaps including Edward Sackville, 1636) is a work of comparable merit. One death is treated briefly: Raymond the Moor feels his "blood / Is frozen in [his] veins."[18] But the conventional account of what the approach of death does to the body is employed when Machiavel, the arch-villain of the play, reaches the verge of death:

> O, my once great heart
> Dissolves like snow, and lessens to a rheum,
> Cold as the envious blasts of Northern wind;
>
> .   .   .   .
>   my life
> Grows empty with my veins: I cannot stand; my breath
> Is, as my strength, weak; and both seiz'd by death.
> Farewell, ambition! catching at a crown,
> Death tripp'd me up, and headlong threw me down. [*Dies.*]

(P. 88)

The whole speech suggests assemblage rather than composition; Rawlins (like Nabbes) is content merely to mix the usual ingredients.

As a final instance there is Glapthorne's *Argalus and Parthenia* (1638), where Argalus informs Parthenia, his wife,

> I doe feele
> A marble sweat about my heart, which does
> Congeale the remnant of my bloud to Ice.[19]

Only in Ford, and only under the special circumstances provided by *The Broken Heart*, has the rhetoric of death contributed to the creation of death scenes of real distinction. The history of this convention—which should be recognized as a kind of linguistic addiction—testifies to the wisdom of those who, like Shakespeare, focused instead on the way the dying see themselves and the world they leave.

Notes

Introduction

1. *Selected Works of John Dryden,* ed. William Frost (New York and Toronto: Rinehart, 1955), p. 350.

2. *Pierce Pennilesse his Supplication to the Diuell, The Works of Thomas Nashe,* ed. Ronald B. McKerrow, rev. F. P. Wilson (Oxford: Clarendon Press, 1958), 1:212.

3. Quoted in E. K. Chambers, *The Elizabethan Stage* (Oxford: Clarendon Press, 1923; reprint, 1965), 2:309.

4. Gāmini Salgādo, trans., *Eye-Witnesses of Shakespeare: First Hand Accounts of Performances 1590–1890* (New York: Barnes and Noble, 1975), p. 30.

5. *Renaissance Self-Fashioning: From More to Shakespeare* (Chicago and London: University of Chicago Press, 1980), p. 2.

6. *Sir Walter Ralegh: The Renaissance Man and His Roles* (New Haven and London: Yale University Press, 1973), p. 15.

7. *Queen Elizabeth I: A Biography* (1934; reprint, Garden City, N.Y.: Doubleday, 1957), pp. 289–90.

8. John Buxton, *Elizabethan Taste* (London: Macmillan, 1963), p. 22.

9. *Sir Walter Ralegh,* p. 7.

10. Ibid., p. 20.

11. Ibid., pp. 20–21.

12. *Montaigne: Essays,* trans. John Florio, Everyman's Library (London: Dent; New York: Dutton, 1965), 2:112 (bk. 2, chap. 11: "Of Crueltie").

Chapter 1. Making Death Matter: Marlowe and His Predecessors

1. Vastly richer models were to be found elsewhere, notably in classical history and biography and Foxe's *Acts and Monuments* (1563). Indeed, as T. McAlindon has remarked, "Foxe's pages abound in heroic images that are likely to strike the student of Renaissance tragedy with a curious sense of *dejà vu*" (*English Renaissance Tragedy* [Vancouver: University of British Columbia Press, 1986], p. 19).

2. Except when otherwise noted, I have followed Alfred Harbage, *Annals of English Drama 975–1700,* rev. S. Schoenbaum (Philadelphia: University of Pennsylvania Press, 1964), for both dating and authorship. The date is that of probable first performance.

3. *Tudor Plays: An Anthology of Early English Drama,* ed. Edmund Creeth (Garden City: Doubleday, 1966).

4. *The Riverside Shakespeare,* ed. G. Blakemore Evans (Boston: Houghton Mifflin, 1974). Cf. the "death" of Rafe in *The Knight of the Burning Pestle,* ed. Sheldon P. Zitner, Revels Plays (Manchester: Manchester University Press, 1984), act 5, lines 329–41. The final line—"O, O, O, &c."—anticipates Hamlet's last utterances in the Folio; see below, chap. 8, n. 2.

5. *The Chester Mystery Cycle,* ed. R. M. Lumiansky and David Mills (Oxford: Oxford University Press, 1974). Cf. Christ's last words in the York Passion (248–60), those spoken by the Queen of Marseilles and by Mary in the Digby *Mary Magdalene* (1754–66, 2106–19), and by the title figure of *Everyman* (880–87); in *Medieval Drama,* ed. David Bevington (Boston: Houghton Mifflin, 1974).

6. *Medieval Drama,* ed. Bevington, Cf. Abel in the Wakefield *The Killing of Abel,* 328–29: "Veniance, veniance, Lord, I cry! / For I am slain, and not gilty"; and Lazarus in *Mary Magdalene,* 819–23:

> A, in woo I waltyr, as wavys in the wind!
> Awey is went all my sokour!
> A, deth, deth, thou art onkind!
> A, a, now bristit[h] min[e] hartt! This is a sharp shower!
> Farewell, my sisters, my bodely helth1

> (Both quoted from Bevington.)

7. *Seneca His Tenne Tragedies Translated into English,* ed. Thomas Newton, intro. T. S. Eliot (London: Constable; New York: Knopf, 1927), 2:234. (*Hercules Oetaeus* is usually regarded as non-Senecan; see Gordon Braden, *Renaissance Tragedy and the Senecan Tradition: Anger's Privilege* [New Haven and London: Yale University Press, 1985], p. 59 and p. 233, n. 36.)

8. See Scott McMillan, "The Figure of Silence in *The Spanish Tragedy,*" *ELH* 39 (1972): 27–48; and Carol McGinnis Kay, "Deception Through Words in *The Spanish Tragedy,*" *Studies in Philology* 74 (1976): 20–48. Both critics view Hieronimo's wordlessness as emblematically appropriate.

Other deaths may be briefly mentioned. Horatio has time only to speak a single line before he is hanged; Serberine dies instantly when shot; Pedringano is hanged while still expecting to be pardoned; Isabella does not speak again after stabbing herself. In Hieronimo's play, Hieronimo stabs Lorenzo; Bel-imperia stabs Balthazar, then herself. All deaths seem instantaneous, as does that of Castile, whom Hieronimo stabs immediately before his own suicide.

9. *The Works of Thomas Kyd,* ed. Frederick S. Boas (Oxford: Clarendon Press, 1901; reprint, 1954).

10. *The Shakespeare Apocrypha: Being a Collection of Fourteen Plays Which Have Been Ascribed to Shakespeare,* ed. C. F. Tucker Brooke (Oxford: Clarendon Press, 1908; reprint, 1967). Brutus is unique in the play in having a death speech proper; other characters either are struck down too suddenly for speech, or (with the numerous suicides) declare their intent and perform the action with instantaneous efficacy.

11. George Peele, *The Dramatic Works of George Peele,* gen. ed. Charles Tyler Prouty (New Haven: Yale University Press, 1952–70), vol. 2, ed. John Yoklavich.

12. Ed. Patricia Binnie in Revels Plays (Manchester: Manchester University Press; Baltimore: Johns Hopkins University Press, 1980). One may mention the death of Absalom in *David and Bethsabe;* see the edition of Elmer M. Blistein, *The Dramatic Works of George Peele,* vol. 3, lines 1529–44, where Absalom begs Joab for mercy but is wounded by him. Joab then leaves, and soldiers enter (Absalom does not speak to them); one of them dispatches him (1557).

13. *Death and Elizabethan Tragedy: A Study of Convention and Opinion in the Elizabethan Drama* (Cambridge, Mass.: Harvard University Press, 1940), p. 223. That Marlowe played the role Spencer attributes to him seems almost certain, even if one accepts E. A. J. Honigmann's "general chronology for [Shakespeare's] first plays" in his *Shakespeare's Impact on his Contemporaries* (New York: Barnes and Noble, 1982), p. 82.

14. Curt Zimansky, "*Doctor Faustus:* The Date Again," *Philological Quarterly* 41 (1962): 181–87, suggests that *Faustus* may have been written as early as 1589. See also MacD. P. Jackson, "Three Old Ballads and the Date of *Doctor Faustus*," *Journal of the Australasian Universities Language and Literature Association* 36 (1971): 187–200; and Keith Walker, ed., *Doctor Faustus* (Edinburgh: Oliver and Boyd, 1973), pp. 3–4.

15. For a discussion of dating, see H. J. Oliver, ed., *"Dido Queen of Carthage" and "The Massacre at Paris,"* Revels Plays (London: Methuen, 1968), pp. li–liii. "Proof of a 1592 date is impossible," Oliver concludes; yet "the presumption is strong."

16. All quotations from Marlowe are taken from the edition of Irving Ribner (New York: Odyssey Press, 1963).

17. *English Tragedy Before Shakespeare: The Development of Dramatic Speech,* trans. T. S. Dorsch (London: Methuen, 1961), pp. 282–83. Cf. The conspicuous lack of "dramatic immediacy" in the suicide of Agydas (3.2.90–106).

18. As J. B. Steane observes, in *Marlowe: A Critical Study* (Cambridge: Cambridge University Press, 1965), "Cosroe states too explicitly what he feels, and it registers as information rather than experience" (p. 100).

19. *Suffering and Evil in the Plays of Christopher Marlowe* (Princeton: Princeton University Press, 1962), pp. 90–91.

20. Ibid., p. 89.

21. The death of Sigismund is preceded by a speech (2.3.1–9) in which Sigismund speaks of God's having punished him and the Christian host for perjury. The lines have little dramatic force.

22. For a more favorable view of this passage (and others like it), see Stephen Greenblatt, *Renaissance Self-Fashioning: From More to Shakespeare* (Chicago: University of Chicago Press, 1980), p. 210: "... the dying in the play . . . speak of themselves in an oddly detailed, almost clinical language, as if to insist upon the corporeal reality of their experience."

23. *Death and Elizabethan Tragedy,* p. 227.

24. See F. P. Wilson, *Marlowe and the Early Shakespeare* (Oxford: Clarendon Press, 1953), pp. 54–55.

25. *Marlowe: A Critical Study,* p. 192.

26. As Harry Levin notes, "Marlowe seems to have naturally obtained that effect for which Brecht . . . consciously [strove]: alienation rather than identification, estrangement and not endearment" ("Marlowe Today," *Tulane Drama Review* 8 [1964]: 31). See also Michael Hattaway, "Marlowe and Brecht," in *Christopher Marlowe,* ed. Brian Morris, Mermaid Critical Commentaries (London: Benn, 1968), pp. 97–112.

27. On Edward's death, see Nicholas Brooke, "Marlowe the Dramatist," in *Elizabethan Theatre, Stratford-upon-Avon Studies* 9 (1966): 103; also Wilbur Sanders, *The Dramatist and the Received Idea: Studies in the Plays of Marlowe and Shakespeare* (Cambridge: Cambridge University Press, 1968), pp. 123–24.

28. For perceptive comments on Marlowe's desecration and pollution of "the holy office of kingship," see Philip Edwards, *Threshold of a Nation: A Study of English and Irish Drama* (Cambridge: Cambridge University Press, 1979), p. 64.

As Edwards observes, "we realise that we have been in the presence of sacredness only by our comprehending that what we see in the man in tattered robes soaked in ordure is the very image of desecration."

29. For a discussion of such speeches, see Appendix: "The Rhetoric of Death."

Chapter 2. Deaths Horrific and Exemplary

1. For a discussion of "The Reign of the Villain," see Fredson Thayer Bowers, *Elizabethan Revenge Tragedy 1587–1642* (Princeton: Princeton University Press, 1940), chap. 5.

2. Ed. M. L. Wine in Revels Plays (London: Methuen, 1973).

3. *"Arden of Feversham," Shakespeare Survey* 36 (1983): 130.

4. George Chapman, *The Plays of George Chapman: The Tragedies,* ed. Thomas Marc Parrott (1910; reprint, New York: Russell and Russell, 1961), vol. 2. For Cutwulf, see *The Works of Thomas Nashe,* ed. Ronald B. McKerrow, rev. F. P. Wilson (Oxford: Clarendon Press, 1958), 2 : 325–26.

5. Thomas Dekker, *The Dramatic Works of Thomas Dekker,* ed. Fredson Bowers (Cambridge: Cambridge University Press, 1953–61), vol. 4.

6. Ed. Reavley Gair in Revels Plays (Manchester: Manchester University Press, 1978).

7. Contrary to one's expectation, in view of *Thyestes,* Ovid's tale of Philomela, Procne, and Tereus, and *Titus Andronicus* (see below, chap. 7), Piero does not feast on his son. It is a rare instance of Marstonian restraint.

8. Gair (p. 39) believes the revengers mean to expiate their guilt. For the view that they regard themselves as guiltless, see Bowers, *Elizabethan Revenge Tragedy,* pp. 124–25.

9. With respect to the way in which Marston gives his audience "vicarious release of grievance, by criminal act in a just cause," T. A. Wharton observes that "no other dramatist of the period indulged these pleasures as fully and as sadistically as Marston in this play" ("Old Marston or New Marston," *Essays in Criticism* 25 [1975]: 367).

10. Malone Society Reprints, 1950 (1951).

11. Probably by Middleton. See David J. Lake, *The Canon of Thomas Middleton's Plays: Internal Evidence for the Major Problems of Authorship* (Cambridge: Cambridge University Press, 1975), pp. 136–62(a), and *Appendix II* (pp. 257–69); MacD. P. Jackson, *Studies in Attribution: Middleton and Shakespeare,* Salzburg Studies in English Literature: Jacobean Drama Studies, no. 6 (University of Salzburg, 1979), pp. 33–40; and Norman A. Britten, "Middleton's Styles: Adjectives and Authorship," in *"Accompaninge the Players": Essays Celebrating Thomas Middleton, 1580–1980,* ed. Kenneth Friedenreich (New York: AMS Press, 1983), pp. 53–54.

12. Ed. R. A. Foakes in Revels Plays (London: Methuen, 1966).

13. Foakes (p. xxi) considers the revengers' masque a probable instance of Marston's influence; see also his note at 5.1.181.

14. Cf. Eugène Ionesco, *Notes and Counter Notes,* trans. Donald Watson (New York: Grove Press, 1964), p. 228: "Take a tragedy, accelerate the movement, and you will have a comic play: empty the characters of all their psychological content, and again you will have a comic play." The kind of violence I speak of here (the deaths of Supervacuo et al.) certainly seems to impinge on the comic. (*The Jew of Malta,* of course, is a notable precursor.)

15. As Peter B. Murray remarks in *A Study of Cyril Tourneur* (Philadelphia: University of Pennsylvania Press, 1964), p. 201, "Antonio, the new duke, *condemns* Vindice and Hippolito for a crime of which he, too, may be morally guilty, and appears to be concerned primarily for his own welfare"; see also pp. 223–28. For a defense of Antonio, see Philip J. Ayres, *Tourneur: "The Revenger's Tragedy,"* (London: Arnold, 1977), pp. 29–31.

16. These lines, as Foakes notes, apparently allude "to the lords who joined with them in the revenge-masque" (p. 128).

17. T. S. Eliot, *T. S. Eliot: Selected Essays* (New York: Harcourt, Brace and World, 1950; reprint, 1960), pp. 161–62.

18. Ayres remarks that "even in his fall Vindice is able to leave the stage on a note of light-heartedness. Yet the play," he insists, "remains 'the revenger's tragedy' since Vindice, within a more serious dimension of the play, has been condemned as unfit to survive" (*Tourneur: "The Revenger's Tragedy,"* p. 41).

19. *Annals of English Drama* gives *Volpone*'s limits as 1605–6, *The Revenger's Tragedy*'s as 1606–7. Robert Ornstein, *The Moral Vision of Jacobean Tragedy* (Madison and Milwaukee: University of Wisconsin Press, 1965), p. 112, believes *Volpone* influenced *The Revenger's Tragedy*. He does not, however, read the ending of either play as I do.

20. Ed. Alvin Kernan (New Haven: Yale University Press, 1962).

21. Malone Society Reprints, 1914 (1915).

22. I quote from the 1607 text, as reproduced by University Microfilms (Ann Arbor, Mich., 1954).

23. Malone Society Reprints, 1911 (1912).

24. References are to act, scene, volume, and page in Robert Dodsley, ed., *A Select Collection of Old English Plays,* ed. W. Carew Hazlitt (London: 1874–76).

25. Ed. R. W. Van Fossen in Revels Plays (London: Methuen, 1961).

26. See Robert Ornstein, "Bourgeois Morality and Dramatic Convention in *A Woman Killed With Kindness,"* in *English Renaissance Drama: Essays in Honor of Madeleine Doran and Mark Eccles,* ed. Standish Henning, Robert Kimbrough, and Richard Knowles (Carbondale: Southern Illinois University Press, 1976), pp. 128–41 (esp. pp. 140–41). Cf. the deaths of Jane Shore and her husband in the last scene of Heywood's (?) and others' (?) *2 Edward IV.*

27. References are to act, scene, volume, and page in *The Plays of John Marston,* ed. H. Harvey Wood (Edinburgh: University of Edinburgh Press, 1934–39).

28. In his recent edition in Revels Plays (Manchester: Manchester University Press, 1984), Giorgio Melchiori argues for the presence of Lewis Machin as well as Marston and Barkstead ("Introduction," pp. 9–16). All quotations will be taken from this edition.

29. Ed. Irving Ribner in Revels Plays (London: Methuen, 1964). Ribner notes John Churton Collins's suggestion that this speech imitates Isabella's in *The Insatiate Countess.*

30. *Love and Death in Renaissance Tragedy* (Baton Rouge: Louisiana University Press, 1976), p. 322.

Chapter 3. Chapman and Webster

1. " 'Royal Man': Notes on the Tragedies of George Chapman," in *Shakespeare's Contemporaries: Modern Studies in English Renaissance Drama,* ed. Max Bluestone and Norman Rabkin (Englewood Cliffs, N.J.: Prentice-Hall, 1961), p. 231.

2. Ed. Nicholas Brooke in Revels Plays (London: Methuen, 1964). Brooke's edition is based on the 1607–8 quarto in preference to that of 1641; see his textual discussion, pp. lx–lxii, lxiv, lxxiv. On textual matters see also Robert P. Adams, "Critical Myths and Chapman's Original *Bussy D'Ambois*," *Renaissance Drama* 9 (1966): 141–61; also two essays by Albert B. Tricomi, "The Revised Version of Chapman's *Bussy D'Ambois:* A Shift in Point of View," *Studies in Philology* 70 (1973): 288–305; and "The Problem of Authorship in the Revised *Bussy D'Ambois, English Language Notes* 17 (1979): 22–29.

3. *The Herculean Hero in Marlowe, Chapman, Shakespeare and Dryden* (New York: Columbia University Press, 1962), p. 106. Waith is using Thomas Marc Parrott's edition of *Bussy* in *The Plays of George Chapman: The Tragedies* (London: Routledge and Kegan Paul, 1910), vol. 1, which follows the 1641 quarto. The 1607–8 text gives this passage greater emphasis: see Brooke's note, pp. 127–28; Adams, p. 157.

4. See Hereward T. Price, " 'Like Himself,' " *Review of English Studies* 16 (1940): 178–81; in Elizabethan usage, the phrase usually means: " 'like the great hero (king, etc.) that he is . . .' " (p. 180).

5. *Ideas of Greatness: Heroic Drama in England* (New York: Barnes and Noble, 1971), p. 129.

6. Brooke, p. 150, quotes and translates the relevant lines from *Hercules Oetaeus.* (As remarked in chap. 1, n.7, the play is probably not by Seneca.)

7. *The World's Perspective: John Webster and the Jacobean Drama* (New Brunswick: Rutgers University Press, 1983), p. 88. See also G. R. Hibbard, "Goodness and Greatness: An Essay on the Tragedies of Ben Jonson and George Chapman," *Renaissance and Modern Studies* 11 (1967): 38. Millar MacLure, *George Chapman: A Critical Study* (Toronto: University of Toronto Press, 1966), p. 114, interprets the passage as Bussy's realization that his "heroic energy . . . [has found] no worthy matter to work upon."

8. *Ideas of Greatness,* p. 129. Cf. Waith, *Herculean Hero,* p. 110: "This is the failure of a man like Tamburlaine, who must die, leaving much unconquered, and of one like Hercules, whose divine mission of purifying the world has not been fulfilled."

9. *George Chapman,* p. 125.

10. See, however, Jane Melbourne, "The Inverted World of *Bussy D'Ambois,*" *Studies in English Literature* 25 (1985): 393–95.

11. " 'Royal Man,' " p. 236.

12. MacLure, p. 125.

13. *Tragedies,* ed. Parrott (see above, n. 3), vol. 1.

14. MacLure, pp. 130–31.

15. For discussions of Clermont's defective Stoicism, see Allen Bergson, "The Worldly Stoicism of George Chapman's *Bussy D'Ambois* and *The Tragedy of Chabot, Admiral of France,*" *Philological Quarterly* 55 (1976): 43–64; Suzanne F. Kistler, " 'Strange and Far Removed Shores': A Reconsideration of *The Revenge of Bussy D'Ambois,*" *Studies in Philology* 77 (1980): 128–44; and Alexander Leggatt, "The Tragedy of Clermont D'Ambois," *Modern Language Review* 77 (1982): 524–36. If Chapman criticizes Clermont at all, he does so implicitly, when Tamyra chooses sequestration in a cloister rather than suicide: "Too easy 'tis to die" (209).

16. *Annals* gives limits of 1599–1607 for *Caesar and Pompey;* one scene (2.1) is said to have been "written 1610–1611."

17. *Tragedies,* ed. Parrott, vol. 2.

18. MacLure, p. 152.

19. One may compare what Jonson does with the onstage death of a Stoical Roman in *Sejanus* (1603) (ed. Jonas A. Barish [New Haven: Yale University Press, 1965]), where Silius commits suicide rather than have the Senate pass judgment and condemn him:

> It is not life whereof I stand enamored,
> Nor shall my end make me accuse my fate.
> The coward and the valiant man must fall;
> Only the cause and manner how, discerns them,
> Which then are gladdest when they cost us dearest.
> Romans, if any here be in this Senate,
> Look upon Silius, and so learn to die. [*Stabs himself.*]
>
> (3.332–39)

Here is a Stoic's death forcefully, but not shockingly, rendered—Cato without the entrails—a public suicide that has no basis is Tacitus. (Elsewhere in *Sejanus,* and in *Catiline* [1611], Jonson follows classical precedent in making death a matter for narration rather than dramatic representation.)

20. J. W. Lever, *The Tragedy of State* (London: Methuen, 1971), p. 75. As Lever notes, "At the end of the play there is only one man to whom [Caesar] turns, only one enemy he has reconciled. Pathetically he thanks him, saying 'You do me infinite honour.' The remark carries its own historical irony, for that man is Brutus."

21. *Tragedies,* ed. Parrott, vol. 1.

22. See Elias Schwartz, "Chapman's Renaissance Man: Byron Reconsidered," *Journal of English and Germanic Philology* 58 (1959): 623.

23. As G. R. Hibbard remarks, Byron "concludes not with self-abasement, but with self-assertion, preserving his greatness of soul to the last, and wringing a spiritual victory out of material and deserved defeat" ("Goodness and Greatness," p. 45). See also Alexander Leggatt, "Tone and Structure in Chapman's *Byron,*" *Studies in English Literature* 24 (1984): 325.

Parrott, in his "Notes" to *Byron's Tragedy* (2:623), expresses his certainty that this is "a 'tableau' ending, a curtain being drawn after the last line to conceal the figures of Byron kneeling on the scaffold and the hangman standing over him with his raised sword." Yet on-stage decapitation is far from unknown in Renaissance plays; several examples will be given in subsequent chapters, the one most closely resembling the death of Byron being that of Fletcher's and Massinger's Barnavelt.

24. *Annals* gives limits of 1611–1622?, and notes that "J[ames] Shirley revised the play in 1635."

25. *Ideas of Greatness,* p. 140.

26. "Chapman's Tragedies," *Jacobean Theatre, Stratford-upon-Avon Studies* 1 (1960; reprint, New York: Capricorn Books, 1967): 244.

27. *Tragedies,* ed. Parrott, vol. 1.

28. MacLure, p. 150.

29. Ed. John Russell Brown in Revels Plays, 2d ed. (London: Methuen, 1968). As Dieter Mehl observes, "All human sympathy is excluded by this method of presentation and this technique in itself is an indirect comment" (*The Elizabethan Dumb Show: The History of a Dramatic Convention* [Cambridge, Mass.: Harvard University Press, 1966], p. 141); see also J. R. Mulryne, "*The White Devil* and *The Duchess of Malfi,*" *Jacobean Theatre,* pp. 203–4.

30. The phrase is Nicholas Brooke's; see his *Horrid Laughter in Jacobean Tragedy* (London: Open Books, 1979), esp. pp. 28–69 (on Webster).

31. On the staging of Bracciano's death, see Peter Thompson, "Webster and

The Actor," in *John Webster,* ed. Brian Morris, Mermaid Critical Commentaries (London: Benn, 1970), pp. 33–34.

32. According to Charles Osborne McDonald, *The Rhetoric of Tragedy: Form in Stuart Drama* (Amherst: University of Massachusetts Press, 1966), p. 308, Vittoria does in fact tremble. But why believe Lodovico? What Vittoria says and does at this point in the scene is not indicative of weakness.

33. Line 227 indicates that Carlo will kill Zanche. It appears that Gasparo stabs Vittoria, Lodovico Flamineo. Lodovico's words might be taken as a command to all three of his companions—but why should he deny himself the pleasure of stabbing Flamineo, especially in light of lines 190–91?

34. Zanche is not given a death speech. See Brown's note, p. 182.

35. McDonald, certain that "Vittoria has broken down" (p. 308), takes credit for being the first critic he is aware of to realize that Flamineo's apparent commendation of his sister is "surely" ironic.

36. Coburn Freer, *The Poetics of Jacobean Drama* (Baltimore: Johns Hopkins University Press, 1981), p. 150.

37. See Brown, p. lvi.

38. Frederick S. Boas, *An Introduction to Stuart Drama* (Oxford: Oxford University Press, 1946), p. 198.

39. *The World's Perspective,* p. 131. For references to various interpretations of Vittoria's final words, see Larry S. Champion, *Tragic Patterns in Jacobean and Caroline Drama* (Knoxville: University of Tennessee Press, 1971), pp. 232–33 (n. 20).

40. Freer, *Poetics of Jacobean Drama,* p. 151, notes that "three lines of highly broken rhythms stop on *irrecoverably,* which recreates in itself the sound of a cough." Whether or not one accepts the idea of a coughing Flamineo, the stress on "irrecóverably" implies the action of bending over.

M. C. Bradbrook compares Flamineo's final speech and that of Chapman's Byron, observing that "the grand Marlovian sweep" of Byron's speech "does not make such demands on the actor as the free, shifting technique Perkins [the original Flamineo] used in Flamineo" (*John Webster: Citizen and Dramatist* [New York: Columbia University Press, 1980], p. 134).

41. *Poetics of Jacobean Drama,* pp. 147–48 (for the contrast), p. 151 (for Flamineo's speech).

42. *The Art of John Webster* (Oxford: Clarendon Press, 1972), p. 132.

43. *Poetics of Jacobean Drama,* p. 151.

44. Compare, for example, the strikingly different recent assessments of Charles R. Forker, *Skull Beneath the Skin: The Achievement of John Webster* (Carbondale and Edwardsville: Southern Illinois University Press, 1986), and Jonathan Dollimore, *Radical Tragedy: Religion, Ideology and Power in the Drama of Shakespeare and His Contemporaries* (Chicago: University of Chicago Press, 1984). For Forker, Flamineo's last words give "the sense of an identity fully achieved. . . . Actor and role become one" (p. 295); for Dollimore, Vittoria and Flamineo die "with the same dislocated identities" (p. 244).

45. Ed. John Russell Brown in Revels Plays (London: Methuen, 1964; reprint, 1969).

46. Brown, who regards the stage direction as "probably authorial," argues (pp. 110–11) that the two children who have remained with the Duchess, not merely the one who accompanied Antonio, are represented here. But he also notes a possible "dramatic point" in the fact that the Duchess speaks in lines 62–63 and 68 "as if she saw Antonio only."

47. For the suggestion that this visitation in a kind of charivari, see Inga-Stina

Ekeblad, "The 'Impure Art' of John Webster," *Review of English Studies,* n.s. 9 (1959); reprinted in *Elizabethan Drama: Modern Essays in Criticism,* ed. Ralph J. Kaufmann (New York: Oxford University Press, 1961), pp. 250–67.

48. *Love and Death in Renaissance Tragedy* (Baton Rouge: Louisiana State University Press, 1976), p. 244. As Stilling emphasizes, "it is a despair not of Christian faith but of romantic faith that [Ferdinand] tries consistently to effect."

49. *Themes and Conventions of Elizabethan Tragedy* (Cambridge: Cambridge University Press, 1935; reprint, 1964), p. 210. The lines are defended—unconvincingly—by Brown in Revels Plays, p. 109n.

50. Bosola will later express his intention to "execute thy last will; that's deliver / Thy body to the reverent dispose / Of some good women" (370–72). Yet the Duchess requested that her own women receive her body.

51. Freer, who remarks that "the ghoulishness of the final line is deftly underplayed by its brevity and the slightly askew rhyme" (*Poetics of Jacobean Drama,* p. 163), misquotes it as "Then they may feed in quiet."

52. *The World's Perspective,* p. 155.

53. Ibid., p. 158.

54. The similarity of these lines to Vittoria's in *The White Devil* (5.6.248–49) has often been remarked.

55. On the staging of these deaths, see Lois Potter, "Realism Versus Nightmare: Problems of Staging *The Duchess of Malfi,*" in *The Triple Bond: Plays, Mainly Shakespearean, in Performance,* ed. Joseph G. Price (University Park and London: Pennsylvania State University Press, 1975), p. 179.

56. See above, n. 40.

57. There is no need to consider the rather wooden suicide speech of Appius in *Appius and Virginia* (with Heywood? 1624).

Chapter 4. Beaumont and Fletcher

1. *The John Fletcher Plays* (London: Chatto and Windus, 1962), pp. 2–3; cf. Eugene M. Waith, *The Pattern of Tragicomedy in Beaumont and Fletcher* (New Haven: Yale University Press, 1952), pp. 2–3.

2. Thomas Stanley's "On the Edition" was printed in the 1647 Folio; I quote from *The Works of Francis Beaumont and John Fletcher,* ed. Francis Glover and A. R. Waller (1905–12; reprint, New York: Octagon Books, 1969), 1:xxvii.

3. Drawing on the research of Lawrence Stone and others, Marianne L. Novy gives a succinct account of the Elizabethan ideal of emotional control; see *Love's Argument: Gender Relations in Shakespeare* (Chapel Hill: University of North Carolina Press, 1984), pp. 8–10. As Novy notes (p. 9), the "model of emotional control" seems to have been "primarily a masculine ideal." Her book explores Shakespeare's plays as "symbolic transformations of ambivalence about gender relations," more specifically "the conflict between mutuality and patriarchy and the conflict between emotion and control" (p. 3).

4. In "*Hamlet:* Revenge and the Critical Mirror," *English Literary Renaissance* 8 (1978): 9–23, I suggest that plays such as *The Spanish Tragedy* offered audiences a much-needed antidote to society's *thou shalt not* attitude toward revenge: "Indeed, it could be argued that the religious temper of the age heightened the need for indulging the very instincts that were, by general agreement, immoral" (p. 14).

5. *Annals,* however, gives limits of *c.* 1607–12. For Beaumont's and Fletcher's respective shares, see Cyrus Hoy, "The Shares of Fletcher and His Collaborators

in the Beaumont and Fletcher Canon (III)," *Studies in Bibliography* 11 (1958): 90–91.

6. See John H. Astington, "The Popularity of *Cupid's Revenge*," *Studies in English Literature* 19 (1979): 219.

7. *The Dramatic Works in the Beaumont and Fletcher Canon,* ed. Fredson Bowers (Cambridge: Cambridge University Press, 1966–), vol. 2, ed. Bowers.

8. Hoy, *Studies in Bibliography* 11 (1958): 94, assigns only four scenes to Fletcher: 2.2, 4.1, 5.1–2.

9. Ed. Howard B. Norland (Lincoln: University of Nebraska Press, 1968).

10. *The John Fletcher Plays,* p. 125.

11. See William Shullenberger, " 'This For the Most Wrong'd of Women': A Reappraisal of *The Maid's Tragedy,*" *Renaissance Drama,* n.s. 13 (1982): 147.

12. Shullenberger, who so describes her (p. 147), argues that she "commits a crime which the patriarchal warriors of the drama implicitly dread, and in the act of murder, Evadne assumes herself some portion of the mystique which had rendered the king inviolable" (p. 147). According to Shullenberger's analysis, Melantius uses Evadne as his "instrument" because he is incapable of doing the deed himself: "The deep motive for Melantius' indirection and for Amintor's paralysis is the same: the king is taboo, . . . and the incalculable power of the Deity stands behind him" (pp. 146–47). Amintor, of course, actually believes in the mystique of kingship. I find no evidence that anyone else does. What does seem clear is that Melantius not unnaturally feels Evadne is the appropriate person to redeem the honor (her own, her family's, and Amintor's) she herself has stained.

13. Robert Ornstein, *The Moral Vision of Jacobean Tragedy* (Madison and Milwaukee: University of Wisconsin Press, 1965), notes "the unconscious, morbid sexuality of Aspatia's death wish" (p. 176).

14. According to Ronald Huebert, " 'An Artificial Way to Grieve': The Forsaken Woman in Beaumont and Fletcher, Massinger and Ford," *ELH* 44 (1977): 610, Aspatia's "borrowed robes indicate that in this society a woman may take decisive action only by assuming external masculine qualities." The assertion would be more persuasive if the play did not also contain Evadne.

15. Shullenberger, however, argues that "her pleas to Amintor to take her to bed reveal the glazed-over consciousness of one whose trauma has delivered her from ordinary reality" (p. 156).

16. Shullenberger considers Evadne's "self-murder striking for its clarity of will," and "an act of tragic courage" (p. 156). It is hard to see how she can be both the traumatized figure of the first description (see n. 15) and the heroic one of the second. Shullenberger also remarks that Evadne must kill herself "because no one else can approach her" (p. 147). Apart from the fact that suicide is obviously what the design of the play calls for, Amintor is the only person to encounter her after she kills the King. He is shocked by her deed, experiencing "anger" as well as "grief"; that he does not kill her hardly constitutes sufficient evidence for believing no one could.

17. *Poets on Fortune's Hill: Studies in Sidney, Shakespeare, Beaumont and Fletcher* (London: Faber and Faber, 1952), p. 196. Oddly, Shullenberger does not cite this passage, though he makes several references to Danby's discussion of the play. To Shullenberger, what is shocking about regicide in *The Maid's Tragedy* is that "no divine power, offended by the death of a legitimate monarch, exacts revenge," and that "the world does not collapse when its symbolic keystone is destroyed" (p. 151). What is shocking, I think, is that Beaumont and Fletcher created a play in which we never even entertain the possibility of such repercussions.

18. *Elizabethan Revenge Tragedy 1587–1642* (Princeton: Princeton University Press, 1940), pp. 175–76.

19. *The Dramatic Works in the Beaumont and Fletcher Canon*, vol. 4, ed. Cyrus Hoy.

20. "Shakespeare and the Stoicism of Seneca," in *T.S. Eliot: Selected Essays* (New York: Harcourt, Brace and World, 1950), p. 110.

21. Cf. Eugene M. Waith, *Ideas of Greatness: Heroic Drama in England* (New York: Barnes and Noble, 1971), p. 155: "Technically a tragedy, *Bonduca* shows how tragedy may become a celebration of virtue in which human weakness and limitation are dwelt on even less than in *Tamburlaine* or *Bussy D'Ambois*."

22. *The Dramatic Works in the Beaumont and Fletcher Canon*, vol. 4, ed. Robert K. Turner, Jr.

23. Perhaps in giving Valentinian the word "freinds" (139)—from him shocking in its human intimacy—Fletcher is remembering *Doctor Faustus:* "Sweet friends, what shall become of Faustus, being in hell for ever?" (5.2.50–51; ed. Irving Ribner [New York: Odyssey Press, 1963]).

24. As Clifford Leech has observed, "the gods play no active part here: as certainly as elsewhere in Fletcher's tragedies, the one thing of which he is aware is the conduct of men in a brightly-lit human world" (*The John Fletcher Plays*, p. 131).

25. Hoy, *Studies in Bibliography* 11 (1958): 85–106, gives Fletcher 1.1, 2.2–3, 4.1, 5.2; Beaumont act 3 and 5.1; and Massinger 1.2, 2.1, 2.4, and 4.2.

26. *The Dramatic Works in the Beaumont and Fletcher Canon*, vol. 3, ed. Robert K. Turner, Jr.

27. For a discussion of this scene in relation to its source, see my "Dramatic Variations on a Passage in Sidney's *Arcadia*," *Sidney Newsletter* 6 (1985–86): 3–12.

28. Cf. Juliana, in Fletcher's and Massinger's *The Double Marriage*, who expires from grief moments after discovering that the man she has mortally wounded is Virolet, her disguised husband. (The pathos of these deaths, characteristically, is counterbalanced by the heroic death of Marcia, who has betrayed her father because of her love for Virolet, at the play's end.) Other representative deaths of this sort include the Friar's in *Bussy D'Ambois*, Bellamente's in Shirley's *Love's Cruelty*, and—by far the most remarkable—Calantha's in Ford's *The Broken Heart*.

29. According to Frederick S. Boas, *An Introduction to Stuart Drama* (Oxford: Oxford University Press, 1946), p. 294, "There are few Stuart plays which glow at the end with so spiritual a light."

30. For Hoy's division of authorship among Fletcher, Chapman, Jonson, and Massinger, see *Studies in Bibliography* 14 (1961): 45–67; see also Bertha Hensman, *The Shares of Fletcher, Field and Massinger in Twelve Plays of the Beaumont and Fletcher Canon*, Salzburg Studies in English Literature: Jacobean Drama Studies, no. 6 (University of Salzburg, 1974), 2: 242–79.

31. *Elizabethan Revenge Tragedy*, p. 177.

32. For a discussion of authorial shares, see Hoy, *Studies in Bibliography* 9 (1957): 143–62.

33. References are to act, scene, volume, and page in *A Collection of Old English Plays*, ed. A. H. Bullen (1882–85).

34. Waith, *Ideas of Greatness*, pp. 155–56.

35. Waith notes that "the discrepancy between the character of the hero and his role is even more striking than in the case of Byron, about whom there is nothing petty" (*Ideas of Greatness*, p. 157).

36. Robert Boyle, whose note on *Barnavelt* is printed as Appendix 2 in Bullen, remarks that "there is no doubt that the audience wandered away in their thoughts from Sir John Van Olden Barnavelt, the saviour of his country from the Spanish yoke, as he professed himself in his defence on his trial, and Spain's determined enemy, to Sir Walter Raleigh, whose head had just fallen on the block" (pp. 434–35).

Chapter 5. Middleton and Massinger

1. *Middleton's Tragedies: A Critical Study* (New York: Columbia University Press, 1955), p. 57.

2. See Anne Lancashire, ed., *The Second Maiden's Tragedy,* Revels Plays (Baltimore: Johns Hopkins University Press, 1978), "Introduction," pp. 15–23; and "Appendix B," pp. 286–88.

3. Schoenbaum, p. 52.

4. Quotations are from Lancashire's edition.

5. Lancashire, following W. C. Hazlitt, inserts the stage direction *"Dies"* after "deed." But as she points out, Govianus's response ("'Tis thy banquet. / Down, villain, to thy everlasting weeping" [49–50]), suggests "a final sword-thrust" (p. 172). Surely the laughter to which Sophonirus refers would provoke some such action.

6. Lancashire (p. 26) notes the probable influence of *The Revenger's Tragedy.*

7. As Lancashire observes, "at the play's end the main-plot revenger-hero is triumphantly restored to the throne; whereas traditional revenge tragedy normally called for the death or punishment of the revenger, however just his cause" (p. 37).

8. "The phrase," Lancashire notes (p. 239), "is bawdily as well as literally meant." With respect to the latter sense, as David M. Bergeron remarks in "Art within Art in *The Second Maiden's Tragedy,*" *Medieval and Renaissance Drama in England* 1 (1984): 178, "One . . . wonders if the dramatist has self-satisfaction at having done something different." Certainly the play exhibits exceptional ingenuity in its presentation of death.

9. The idea that William Rowley contributed to *Hengist,* queried in *Annals,* is now usually rejected. See, e.g., David J. Lake, *The Canon of Middleton's Plays: Internal Evidence for the Major Problems of Authorship* (Cambridge: Cambridge University Press, 1975), p. 33.

10. *The Art of Thomas Middleton: A Critical Study* (Oxford: Clarendon Press, 1970), p. 139.

11. *The Works of Thomas Middleton,* ed. A. H. Bullen (1885), vol. 2.

12. According to Holmes, *Hengist* is "a travesty of the tragedy of ambition" (*The Art of Thomas Middleton,* p. 140).

13. Ed. J. R. Mulryne in Revels Plays (London: Methuen, 1975). Quotations are from this edition.

14. See Roma Gill, ed., *Women Beware Women,* New Mermaids (London: Benn, 1968), p. xx, for a quotation from Kenneth Tynan.

15. "Middleton's Experiments with Comedy and Judgement," in *Jacobean Theatre, Stratford-upon-Avon Studies* 1 (1960; reprint, New York: Capricorn Books, 1967): 198.

16. Parker, p. 197, calls attention to the presence of "elements of both these treatments [the tragic and the satiric] in the *denouement,*" but observes that "tragedy . . . keeps in a minor key, whereas the satire is savagely exaggerated."

17. For discussions of the masque and the symbolic propriety of the fashion in which death is meted out, see Inga-Stina Ewbank, "Realism and Morality in *Women Beware Women,*" *Essays and Studies* 22 (1969): 57–70; J. B. Batchelor, "The Pattern of *Women Beware Women,*" *Yearbook of English Studies* 2 (1972): 76–78; and Huston Diehl Hallahan, "The Thematic Juxtaposition of the Representational and the Sensational in Middleton's *Women Beware Women,*" *Studies in Iconography* 2 (1976): 66–84.

18. It seems odd that Livia should speak here of "ambition"; "presumably in aspiring to the part of Juno," suggests Parker (p. 162), "but perhaps with a hint of the old sense of 'vain-glory,' 'pomp' (*O.E.D.*, sense 2)."

19. I omit Mulryne's insertion of a stage direction indicating the Duke's death. See my discussion of Bianca's death.

20. The stage direction is explained in Mulryne's note, p. 164.

21. One is reminded of *The White Devil,* 5.3.26, where Bracciano warns Vittoria, "Do not kiss me, for I shall poison thee." Ed. John Russell Brown in Revels Plays, 2d ed. (London: Methuen, 1966).

22. Mulryne suggests that Bianca is "perhaps referring to the twisted features caused by poison; more likely, [she] tears at her face with her nails" (p. 166). Cf. Gill (see above, n. 14): "Possibly the poison she has kissed from the Duke's lips has burned into Bianca's own" (p. 111).

23. For a defense of this hypermetrical repetition, see Mulryne, p. 167.

24. Such plays as *Hengist* and *Women Beware Women,* and the subplot of *The Second Maiden's Tragedy* (assuming Middleton's authorship), remind one how much Middleton may have learned from the Marlowe of *The Jew of Malta.*

25. See N. W. Bawcutt, ed. in Revels Plays (London: Methuen, 1958; reprint, 1961), p. xxxix.

26. Quotations are from Bawcutt's edition.

27. For information about the game of barley-break, see Anne Pasternak Slater, "Hypallage, Barley-Break, and *The Changeling,*" *Review of English Studies,* n.s. 34 (1983): 436–37.

28. For *token* as both sexual intercourse and mortal wound, see Dorothea Kehler, *Explicator* 26 (1968): Item 41.

29. One might argue, however, that Beatrice might naturally have a keener sense of the defilement of her family's honor than that of this husband whom she barely knows, this "stranger to her bed."

30. *Philip Massinger: The Man and the Playwright* (Edinburgh: Thomas Nelson, 1957), pp. 95–96.

31. "Philip Massinger," in *T.S. Eliot: Selected Essays* (New York: Harcourt, Brace and World, 1950; reprint, 1960), p. 188.

32. *Philip Massinger,* p. 139.

33. According to Philip Edwards, "There can be little doubt that Acts I and V and all but the first scene of Act IV are by Massinger . . . and that Act III is begun by Massinger but continued by Field" (*The Plays and Poems of Philip Massinger,* ed. Edwards and Colin Gibson [Oxford: Clarendon Press, 1976], 1 : 1). All quotations from Massinger in this chapter except from *The Virgin Martyr* are from this edition; for the division of editorial responsibility, see "Preface," p. vi.

34. Edwards and Gibson, vol. 1.

35. *Elizabethan Revenge Tragedy 1587–1642* (Princeton: Princeton University Press, 1940), p. 191.

36. *The Works of Henry Fielding, Esq.,* ed. Leslie Stephen (1882), 9 : 197.

37. "Massinger's undoubted scenes," according to Cyrus Hoy, "are the whole of Act I; III.i; III.ii; IV.iii; V.ii" (*Introductions, Notes, and Commentaries to Texts*

in "The Dramatic Works of Thomas Dekker," ed. Fredson Bowers [Cambridge: Cambridge University Press, 1980], 3 : 193).

38. See Larry S. Champion, " 'Disaster with My So Many Joys': Structure and Perspective in Massinger and Dekker's *The Virgin Martyr," Medieval and Renaissance Drama in England* 1 (1984): 199–209.

39. *Ideas of Greatness: Heroic Drama in England* (London: Routledge and Kegan Paul, 1971), p. 165. "It is," Waith adds, "an acute form of the problem faced by Chapman with Clermont D'Ambois and Cato."

40. *The Dramatic Works of Thomas Dekker,* ed. Fredson Bowers (Cambridge: Cambridge University Press, 1953–61), vol. 3.

41. Champion discusses Antoninus as "a variation of the stock lovesick figure," whose function is to "instill interest into the life of a saint who perforce remains above the throes of human passion" (p. 204).

42. The second bracketed insertion (Theophilus) is my own.

43. Edwards and Gibson, vol. 1.

44. "Massinger's use of *Othello* in *The Duke of Milan," Studies in English Literaure* 19 (1979): 325.

45. See Gibson's "Introduction," p. 202.

46. "The curious withholding of the comparatively just motives for Francisco's vengeance," Bowers conjectures, ". . . may perhaps be laid to the influence of the growing disapproval of revenge" (*Elizabethan Revenge Tragedy,* p. 195). It is hard to see why.

47. Edwards and Gibson, vol. 3.

48. Edwards and Gibson, vol. 2.

49. See Bowers, *Elizabethan Revenge Tragedy,* p. 196.

50. See Gibson's "Introduction," pp. 181–82.

51. *Philip Massinger,* p. 144.

52. Bowers, *Elizabethan Revenge Tragedy,* p. 197.

Chapter 6. Ford and Shirley

1. The order of composition of *Love's Sacrifice, 'Tis Pity She's a Whore,* and *The Broken Heart,* the plays to be considered here, is uncertain. *Annals of English Drama* gives the following limits: *Love's Sacrifice* (1632?); *'Tis Pity* (1629?–1633); *The Broken Heart* (c. 1625–1633).

2. *John Fordes Dramatische Werke,* ed. W. Bang, *Materialen zur Kunde des älteren englischen Dramas,* no. 23 (1908; reprint, Vaduz: Kraus Reprint, 1963). Quotations are from Bang's text.

3. M. Joan Sargeaunt, *John Ford* (1935; reprint, New York: Russell and Russell, 1966), p. 112, notes that Ford is drawing on an episode in Sidney's *Arcadia.*

4. See *Troilus and Cressida, The Riverside Shakespeare,* ed. G. Blakemore Evans (Boston: Houghton Mifflin, 1974), 3.1.132–33. (All references to Shakespeare in this chapter will be to this edition.) There is also an echo of *The White Devil;* as Charles S. Forker notes in *Skull Beneath the Skin: The Achievement of John Webster* (Carbondale and Edwardsville: Southern Illinois University Press, 1986), p. 494, line 1893 echoes Vittoria's "O my greatest sin lay in my blood. / Now my blood pays for't" (ed. John Russell Brown in Revels Plays, 2nd ed. [London: Methuen, 1966], 5.6.240–41).

5. For an effort to defend Ford's dramaturgy here, see Donald K. Anderson, *John Ford* (New York: Twayne, 1972), p. 116.

6. This line suggests that Biancha still hopes to be spared—provided she can

save Fernando. Most critics, however, are certain she desires to die. See, e.g., Ronald Huebert, *John Ford: English Baroque Dramatist* (Montreal and London: McGill-Queens University Press, 1977), p. 49, where Biancha is described as being "willing to sacrifice herself with all the zeal of a Christian martyr."

7. Robert Ornstein, *The Moral Vision of Jacobean Tragedy* (Madison and Milwaukee: University of Wisconsin Press, 1965), p. 219.

8. *John Ford*, p. 50.

9. Ibid., p. 51.

10. On Ford's relationship to Fletcher, see Arthur C. Kirsch, *Jacobean Dramatic Perspectives* (Charlottesville: University Press of Virginia, 1972), chap. 7. (Kirsch, however, has a much lower regard for Ford than I do, seeing *'Tis Pity* and *The Broken Heart* rather as I do *Love's Sacrifice*.)

11. Ed. Derek Roper in Revels Plays (London: Methuen, 1975). Quotations are from this edition.

12. *Le drame de John Ford* (Paris: Didier, 1954), p. 312.

13. "Ford's Tragic Perspective," *Texas Studies in Literature and Language* 1 (1960); reprinted in *Elizabethan Drama: Modern Essays in Criticism*, ed. Kaufmann (New York: Oxford University Press, 1961), p. 369.

14. Introduction to *'Tis Pity She's a Whore*, p. liv.

15. According to Huebert's analysis (which I do not find convincing), Giovanni "performs the executioner's part in order to vindicate . . . his belief that incestuous love can be enobling, self-sacrificing, beautiful" (p. 147). As Kaufmann remarks in "Ford's Tragic Perspective," the act is "the perfect correlative of the frenzied, higher jealousy to which Ford is giving tragic expression" (pp. 370–71).

16. See the edition of Philip Edwards in Revels Plays (London: Methuen, 1959), p. 133: "But are you sure they are dead?" ("Fifth Addition," 2).

17. Introduction, pp. liv, lvi.

18. *John Ford and the Drama of His Time* (London: Chatto and Windus, 1957), p. 88.

19. Ed. T. J. B. Spencer in Revels Plays (Manchester and Baltimore: Manchester University Press and Johns Hopkins University Press, 1980). Quotations are from this edition.

20. See Spencer, "Appendix B: The trick-chair," pp. 224–28.

21. *John Ford*, p. 51.

22. Among those who regard Ford's "artificiality" as imposing such a barrier is Irving Ribner, *Jacobean Tragedy: The Quest for Moral Order* (London: Methuen, 1962). Ribner, like Kirsh (above, n. 10), points to the malign influence of Beaumont and Fletcher: Ford's imitation of them "lends a note of artificiality which renders *The Broken Heart* a far less moving work than *'Tis Pity* . . ." (p. 156). See also Tucker Orbison, *The Tragic Vision of John Ford*, Salzburg Studies in English Literature: Jacobean Drama Studies, no. 21 (University of Salzburg, 1974), p. 134: "The artificiality of the scene interferes with the verisimilitude necessary to the tragic vision."

23. "It should be noted," Charles O. McDonald observes, "that the singing of the dirge creates a rhetorical and musical parallel to that which is sung in the background in IV, iii, at Penthea's death" ("The Design of John Ford's *The Broken Heart:* A Study in the Development of Caroline Sensibility," *Studies in Philology* 59 [1962]: 155).

24. "The Language of Process in *The Broken Heart*," *PMLA* 87 (1972): 400.

25. Ibid., p. 404.

26. *Ideas of Greatness: Heroic Drama in England* (London: Routledge and Kegan Paul, 1971), p. 170.

27. The element of the heroic is equally strong in the title figure of *Perkin Warbeck* (possibly with Decker, 1633). In this case, however, Ford not only does not dramatize the death of his protagonist (Perkin is led off to execution), but ends the play before the sentence is carried out.

28. *James Shirley* (Boston: Twayne, 1981), p. 137.

29. See Juliet McGrath, "James Shirley's Use of *Language*," *Studies in English Literature* 6 (1966): 323–39, esp. 332–33.

30. For a summary of the play, see Robert Stanley Forsythe, *The Relations of Shirley's Plays to the Elizabethan Drama* (1914; reprint, New York: Blom, 1965), pp. 137–39.

31. *The Dramatic Works and Poems of James Shirley*, ed. William Gifford and Alexander Dyce, 6 vols. (1833; reprint, New York: Blom, 1966). References are to act, scene, volume, and page in this edition.

32. See *The White Devil*, 5.6.248–49, ed. John Russell Brown, 2d ed., Revels Plays (London: Methuen, 1966). For Webster's influence on Shirley in this and other instances, see Forker, *Skull Beneath the Skin* (cited above, n. 4), pp. 499–501.

33. For a summary of the play, see Forsythe, pp. 165–66.

34. For comments on the *Liebestod* motif, see Huebert, *John Ford* (cited above, n. 6), p. 184.

35. Cf. *A Woman Killed With Kindness*, ed. R. W. Van Fossen, Revels Plays (London: Methuen, 1961), sc. 13, lines 141–43. (Forsythe, pp. 164–72, discusses *A Woman Killed With Kindness* as an important "general source" for *Love's Cruelty*.) The mist is Websterian, having seeped into the play from *The White Devil*.

36. John Stewart Carter, ed., *The Traitor* (Lincoln: University of Nebraska Press, 1965), p. xiii. (All references will be to this edition.) For a summary of the play, see Forsythe, pp. 153–54.

37. Forsythe, p. 158, notes the influence of *The Revenger's Tragedy*, 2.1, and cites numerous analogues.

38. Introduction to *The Traitor*, p. xiv.

39. Forsythe, p. 163, notes that this closely resembles an incident in *Alphonsus, Emperor of Germany*.

40. Charles S. Forker, ed., *The Cardinal* (Bloomington: Indiana University Press, 1964), p. lxxi. (All references will be to this edition.)

41. For a summary of the play, see Forsythe, p. 185.

42. See Frank Manley, "The Death of Hernando in Shirley's *The Cardinal*," *Notes and Queries* 12 (1965): 342–43.

43. See Forker's editorial note to lines 284–85 (p. 116); and Forker, *Skull Beneath the Skin*, p. 499.

44. Forker (*The Cardinal*, p. 117) compares "I come, I come *Alvarez*" to Cleopatra's "Husband, I come!" (*Antony and Cleopatra*, 5.2.287). Rosaura's line may fairly be described as conventional; certainly the idea of union with the beloved makes more sense here than it did in *The Traitor*. But the lines about exchanging forgivenesses, which Forker compares with Laertes' words in *Hamlet* (5.2.329), are more problematical. Laertes has stabbed with a poisoned rapier the man who killed his father: both he and Hamlet have something to be forgiven, as well as to forgive. But Rosaura, though she has been injured by the King, who pardoned Columbo for murdering Alvarez, has never done anything to him that requires his forgiveness.

45. *Faulkner in the University: Class Conferences at the University of Virginia 1957–1958*, ed. Frederick L. Gwynn and Joseph L. Blotner (Charlottesville: University of Virginia Press, 1959), p. 47.

46. "The Phoenix and the Turtle," 39. For an acute discussion of poetic drama,

see Alan S. Downer, "The Life of Our Design: The Function of Imagery in the Poetic Drama," *The Hudson Review* 2 (1949); reprinted in *Modern Shakespearean Criticism: Essays on Style, Dramaturgy, and the Major Plays,* ed. Alvin B. Kernan (New York: Harcourt, Brace and World, 1970), pp. 30–44.

Chapter 7. Shakespeare (1)

1. "Shakespeare, Fletcher and Baroque Tragedy," *Shakespeare Survey* 20 (1967): 14.

2. E. A. J. Honigmann, however, has recently argued for "a general chronology for the first plays that may be outlined roughly as follows: 1586, *Titus Andronicus;* 1587, *Two Gentlemen of Verona;* 1588, *1 Henry VI, Taming of the Shrew;* 1589, *2 Henry VI, Comedy of Errors;* 1590, *3 Henry VI, Richard III;* 1591, *King John, Romeo and Juliet;* 1592, *Love's Labour's Lost* (*Shakespeare's Impact on His Contemporaries* [New York: Barnes and Noble, 1982], p. 88).

3. "Some Aspects of Style in the *Henry VI* Plays," in *Shakespeare's Styles: Essays in Honour of Kenneth Muir,* ed. Philip Edwards, Inga-Stina Ewbank, and G. K. Hunter (Cambridge: Cambridge University Press, 1980), p. 20; Clemen cites (p. 24, n. 38) the deaths of Mortimer (*1 Henry VI,* 2.5.3–16), Clifford (*3 Henry VI,* 2.6.1–20) and Warwick (*3 Henry VI,* 5.2.5–28).

4. In dating Shakespeare's plays I have followed the chronology given by G. Blakemore Evans, ed., *The Riverside Shakespeare* (Boston: Houghton Mifflin, 1974), pp. 47–56. All quotations from Shakespeare will be taken from this edition.

According to Stanley Wells in *William Shakespeare: The Complete Works,* ed. Wells and Gary Taylor (Oxford: Clarendon Press, 1986), p. 173, *1 Henry VI* is by Shakespeare "in collaboration with at least two other authors. . . . The passages most confidently attributed to Shakespeare are Act 2, Scene 4 and Act 4, Scene 2 to the death of Talbot at 4.7.32."

5. See above, Introduction.

6. *The Origins of Shakespeare* (Oxford: Oxford University Press, 1977), p. 158. For a more favorable estimate, see David Riggs, *Shakespeare's Heroical Histories: "Henry VI" and Its Literary Tradition* (Cambridge, Mass.: Harvard University Press, 1971), p. 110. See also Claire Saunders, " 'Dead in His Bed': Shakespeare's Staging of the Death of the Duke of Gloucester in *2 Henry VI,*" *Review of English Studies,* n. s. 35 (1984): 26.

7. "Preface to Shakespeare," in *Criticism: The Major Texts,* ed. Walter Jackson Bate, enl. ed. (New York: Harcourt Brace Jovanovich, 1975), pp. 208, 209.

8. Two other deaths receive perfunctory treatment—that of Horner at the hands of his apprentice (2.6), and Clifford at the hands of York. In the latter case one might have expected an extended death speech; yet Clifford only says *"La fin couronne les [oeuvres]"* (5.2.28).

9. Saunders, " 'Dead in His Bed,' " pp. 19–34, compares the memorially constructed Quarto *(The first part of the Contention),* where Gloucester's death is staged, to the Folio version. She concludes that "in *The Contention* the death of the Duke of Gloucester is just another in a series of brutal killings; in *2 Henry VI* it is the carefully manipulated focus for a meditation on death itself" (p. 34).

10. For the idea that this line may refer to smothering by a "dust-bed" made of straw, see Andrew S. Cairncross, ed., *2 Henry VI,* Arden Shakespeare, 3d ed. (London: Methuen, 1957; reprint, 1965), p. 98.

11. Saunders, who notes the linkage between the deaths of Gloucester and the Cardinal (pp. 29–30), remarks that "to the Elizabethans the death-bed was not

simply the ending of life: in Christian iconography it epitomized the moment at which the soul was separated from the body, the bed itself being the background against which the fight between Heaven and Hell for possession of that soul was staged" (p. 31).

12. Cf. Zabina in *Tamburlaine* (see above, chap. 1).

13. Jones, *Origins of Shakespeare,* p. 168, calls attention to Suffolk's "startling degree of class hatred" in this scene; he also points to evidence that suggests the lieutenant had once been one of Suffolk's retainers.

14. Cf. Mortimer in *Edward II* in *The Complete Plays of Christopher Marlowe,* ed. Irving Ribner (New York: Odyssey Press, 1963), 5.5.59–66. *Annals* gives the limits of composition for *Edward II* as 1591–93.

15. *The Devil's Party: Critical Counter-Interpretations of Shakespearian Drama* (Oxford: Clarendon Press, 1985), p. 82. As Hawkins later observes (p. 177), in Shakespeare's plays "the tendency for 'character to challenge story' is present from the beginning."

16. *Heroides,* 2.66 (Phyllis to her lover and betrayer Demophoon).

17. The scene runs 180 lines, with York being seized at line 60.

18. The molehill is also the locus for Henry VI's reflections in 1.4 ("Here on this molehill will I sit me down" [14]), the scene in which he witnesses the son who has killed his father and the father who has killed his son.

19. Saunders, " 'Dead in His Bed,' " notes that "the staging and language of the scene cannot fail to evoke the scene of Christ's Passion" (p. 27).

20. Clemen, "Some Aspects of Style in the *Henry VI* Plays" (see above, n. 3), comments on the cumulative effect of violence in these plays: "The magnification, the sharp light in which these stalking, depersonalised figures appear before our eyes make even more acute the final blurring of moral values. In the end, the issue is not clarified but confused. We do not know which side is right, for they are all wrong" (p. 22).

21. Cf. the strikingly similar murder of Arden in *Arden of Feversham* (see above, chap. 2). As is the case with Mortimer and Suffolk (above, n. 14), it is impossible to be certain where the indebtedness, if any, lies. (*Annals* gives limits of 1585–92 for *Arden.*)

22. Antony Hammond in his Arden edition of the play (London: Methuen, 1981), supports an early date for both the *Henry* plays and *Richard III:* "It seems . . . that Shakespeare's first tetralogy was begun by 1590 and concluded with *Richard III* probably late in 1591" (p. 61). Cf. Honigmann (n. 2 above).

23. Buckingham also recalls his oath to be true to Edward's "children and his wive's allies" (5.1.15).

24. *A Commentary on Shakespeare's "Richard III,"* trans. Jean Bonheim (London: Methuen, 1968), p. 69. Ironically, Clarence's description of trying to die—"but still the envious flood / Stopp'd in my soul, and would not let it forth" (37–38)—recalls the desperation of Richard's image of being "like one lost in a thorny wood," "Seeking a way, and straying from the way, / Not knowing how to find the open air, / But toiling desperately to find it out—" (*3 Henry VI,* 3.2.174; 176–78). What Richard seeks, of course, is "the English crown" (179).

25. See Clemen, *Commentary,* p. 215.

26. *Full Circle: Shakespeare and Moral Development* (New York: Barnes and Noble, 1972), pp. 118–19. See also p. 118: "When [Richard] is play-acting to deceive other characters, he plays at having a conscience. When he is play-acting in his soliloquies, he plays at not having a conscience. The first he finds easy; at the second he does not succeed, for he is always proving that he *ought* to be bad. . . . 'Ought' implies a conscience."

27. *The Meaning of Shakespeare,* 2 vols. (Chicago: University of Chicago Press, 1951), 1:39–40. Goddard's interpretation is cited by Larry S. Champion, *Shakespeare's Tragic Perspective* (Athens, Ga.: University of Georgia Press, 1976), p. 39, n. 25, as "more to the point" than Shaw's contention that "the ecstasy of the fight is worth a dozen kingdoms." Both interpretations seem off target, though on opposite sides of it. For further discussion of the line, and its possible sources, see Hammond, pp. 82–83, and his Appendix 3, p. 373.

28. Eugene M. Waith, in his recent edition of *Titus,* Oxford Shakespeare (New York: Oxford University Press, 1984), pp. 4–11, suggests a date of prior to 1592 for the composition of all but 3.1.

29. See Rudolph Stamm, "The Alphabet of Speechless Complaint: A Study of the Mangled Daughter in *Titus Andronicus,*" *English Studies* 55 (1974): 325–39.

30. See also the death of Mutius, who is killed by Titus (1.1.291). The nurse, according to her slayer, Aaron, manages only "Weeke, weeke!—so cries a pig prepared to the spit" (4.2.146).

31. According to Lawrence Danson, *Tragic Alphabet: Shakespeare's Drama of Language* (New Haven: Yale University Press, 1974), p. 12, "*Titus Andronicus* . . . is a play about silence, and about the inability to achieve adequate expression for overwhelming emotional needs."

32. Brian Gibbons, in his Arden edition of *Romeo and Juliet* (London and New York: Methuen, 1980), places it "between 1594 and 1596" (p. 31); Honigmann (see above, n. 2) in 1591.

33. As Roger Stilling observes, "[Romeo's] kiss takes the compression of love, death, and joy as far as it will go. It is a baroque metaphor made flesh" (*Love and Death in Renaissance Tragedy* [Baton Rouge: Louisiana State University Press, 1976], p. 74).

34. There are no death speeches in either *Henry V* or *Henry VIII* (the latter is ascribed, by Wells, *William Shakespeare,* p. 1343 [see above, n. 4], to Shakespeare and Fletcher).

35. See Honigmann (above, n. 2).

36. See Paul A. Jorgensen, "Vertical Patterns in *Richard II,*" *Shakespeare Association Bulletin* 23 (1948): 119–34; Arthur Suzman, "Imagery and Symbolism in *Richard II,*" *Shakespeare Quarterly* 7 (1956): 355–70.

37. Blunt, disguised as King Henry, is the only other character who dies onstage (*1 Henry IV,* 5.3); his death, at the hands of Douglas, is crowded into the climactic phase of the action: "*They fight. Douglas kills Blunt*" (13 s.d.)

38. See, however, Derek Cohen, "The Rite of Violence in *1 Henry IV,*" *Shakespeare Survey* 38 (1985): 77–84.

39. For incisive commentary on Henry and Hal in this scene, see Robert Ornstein, *A Kingdom for a Stage: The Achievement of Shakespeare's History Plays* (Cambridge, Mass.: Harvard University Press, 1972), pp. 164–67.

40. Suetonius, *The Historie of Twelve Caesars,* trans. Philemon Holland, in *Narrative and Dramatic Sources of Shakespeare,* ed. Geoffrey Bullough (New York: Columbia University Press, 1957–75), 5: 154. See also Caesar's account of his murder in the *Tragedy of Julius Caesar,* printed in the 1587 edition of *The Mirror for Magistrates* (Bullough, p. 173). Cf. *2 Henry VI,* 4.1.136–37 (already quoted in connection with the death of Suffolk).

41. See John A. Velz, "Cassius as a Great Observer," *Modern Language Review* 68 (1973): 256–59. Velz calls attention to the ironic dependency of Cassius, "the eyes of the conspiracy," on Brutus and (in this instance) on Pindarus: "Here at the end Cassius must once more trust the vision and interpretation of someone who is not a great observer, not even a competent one" (p. 259).

42. See G. Wilson Knight, *The Imperial Theme: Further Interpretations of Shakespeare's Tragedies Including the Roman Plays*, 3d ed. (London: Methuen, 1951), pp. 63–95 (esp. pp. 90–92).

43. "The Life of Marcus Brutus," *The Lives of the Noble Grecians and Romanes*, trans. Sir Thomas North, in *Sources*, ed. Bullough, 5:131.

44. *Hero and Saint: Shakespeare and the Graeco-Roman Heroic Tradition* (New York: Oxford University Press, 1973), p. 236.

45. "The Life of Marcus Brutus," in *Sources*, ed. Bullough, 5:105.

Chapter 8. Shakespeare (2)

1. In discussing *Hamlet*, I draw freely on some portions of my *"Hamlet* and the Satisfactions of Revenge," *Hamlet Studies* 3 (1981): 83–102.

2. Terence Hawkes, *That Shakespeherian Rag: Essays on a Critical Process* (London and New York: Methuen, 1986), pp. 73–74, finds much to commend in the "O, o, o, o" that follow Hamlet's last words in the Folio; they are, he declares (p. 73), "a perceptive gloss on the part [of Hamlet] by its first and rather astute critic, the actor Richard Burbage." In view of Shakespeare's emphasis on Hamlet's self-mastery during his final moments, one is skeptical about attributing these "O"s to Burbage; they seem the product of a sensibility akin to that of Rafe in *The Knight of the Burning Pestle* (see above, chap. 1, n. 4).

3. Hector's death, of course, would have been anticipated—but no more so than that of Troilus.

4. See S. L. Bethell, *Shakespeare and the Popular Dramatic Tradition* (Durham, N.C.: Duke University Press, 1944), p. 127. See also Alice Shalvi, " 'Honor' in *Troilus and Cressida*," *Studies in English Literature* 5 (1965): 292–93; and David J. Houser, "Armor and Motive in *Troilus and Cressida*," *Renaissance Drama*, n.s. 4 (1971): 133.

5. Shalvi, p. 292, remarks that "Hector falls victim to the savage attack of Achilles and his Myrmidons, just as Spenser's Red Cross Knight, unarmed by the wiles of Duessa, is overpowered by Orgoglio."

6. Printed within brackets in *Riverside*, which uses the First Folio as copytext.

7. At line 95 Othello raises the possibility that she lives only to dispel it: "I think she stirs again. No."

8. "Indian" (First Quarto) is used in *Riverside* instead of the Folio's "Judaean."

9. *T.S. Eliot: Selected Essays* (New York: Harcourt, Brace and World, 1950; reprint, 1960), p. 111.

10. "The Noble Moor," in *Shakespeare Criticism 1935–1960*, ed. Anne Ridler (London: Oxford University Press, 1963), p. 352.

11. *Shakespeare's Professional Skills* (Cambridge: Cambridge University Press, 1965), pp. xiv–xv. (The phrase, "terrible exposure of human weakness," appears on p. 110 of Eliot's essay.)

12. Gorgias, quoted in Bennet Simon, *Mind and Madness in Ancient Greece: The Classical Roots of Modern Psychiatry* (Ithaca: Cornell University Press, 1978), p. 148. (Simon's translation.)

13. Giorgio Melchiori, "The Rhetoric of Character Construction: *Othello*," *Shakespeare Survey* 34 (1981): 66; see also Gordon Braden, *Renaissance Tragedy and the Senecan Tradition: Anger's Privilege* (New Haven and London: Yale University Press, 1985), pp. 169–70; and Anthony Brennan, *Shakespeare's Dra-*

matic Structures (London, Boston, and Henley: Routledge and Kegan Paul, 1986), pp. 158–59.

14. Gardner, p. 366.

15. In discussing Cordelia and Lear I draw on my "The Death of Lear," *College English* 8 (1981): 63–70.

16. In the First Quarto, Lear's last words are "O, o, o, o." A better case could be made for a series of such outcries from a shattered Lear than from Hamlet. (See above, n. 2.)

17. *"King Lear" in Our Time* (Berkeley and Los Angeles: University of California Press, 1965), p. 84. Like most critics, Mack follows Bradley in believing that Lear dies in the illusion that Cordelia is alive (see p. 111). My own view is that "we can neither prove nor disprove Bradley's reading" ("The Death of Lear," p. 66): the lines seem fundamentally ambiguous.

18. It has been suggested by D. J. Palmer that Richard's death (*pace* the Folio's *"Enter Fighting, and Macbeth slaine"*) takes place offstage. See " 'A New Gorgon': Visual Effects in *Macbeth*," in *Focus on "Macbeth,"* ed. John Russell Brown (London: Routledge and Kegan Paul, 1982), p. 68.

19. *The Origins of Shakespeare* (Oxford: Oxford University Press, 1977), p. 220.

20. See H. N. Paul, *The Royal Play of "Macbeth"* (New York: Macmillan, 1950).

21. John Berryman, "He Resigns," *Delusions, Etc. of John Berryman* (New York: Farrar, Straus and Giroux, 1972), p. 40.

22. *Riverside* inserts this reading, from F3, for F1's "flatter'd."

23. See Janet Adelman, *The Common Liar: An Essay on "Antony and Cleopatra"* (New Haven: Yale University Press, 1973), pp. 68–69. For Adelman, however, Antony is consciously "reinterpreting" Virgil (p. 59); see also Barbara J. Bono, *Literary Transvaluation: From Virgilian Epic to Shakespearean Tragicomedy* ((Berkeley and Los Angeles: University of California Press, 1984), pp. 150, 187. Ronald R. Macdonald, "Playing Till Doomsday: Interpreting *Antony and Cleopatra,*" *English Literary Renaissance* 15 (1985): 98, suggests that Antony, living before Virgil, "cannot very well be misinterpreting" what had yet to be written, and is free to create his own version (This approach might yield interesting results if applied to Hamlet, who, living in pagan Denmark, does not always sound orthodox in his Christianity.)

24. *Virgil,* trans. H. Rushton Fairclough, Loeb Classical Library, rev. ed. (Cambridge: Harvard University Press, 1934; reprint, 1969), 1:539.

25. As Martha Tuck Rozett suggests, in "The Comic Structures of Tragic Endings: The Suicide Scenes in *Romeo and Juliet* and *Antony and Cleopatra,*" *Shakespeare Quarterly* 36 (1985): 164, "We can speculate that the untapped dramatic potential in the pattern of double suicides was one of the things that attracted [Shakespeare] to the story of Antony and Cleopatra, and that he was conscious of the structural echoes as he wrote the play."

26. See Walter C. Foreman, Jr., *The Music of the Close: The Final Scenes of Shakespeare's Tragedies* (Lexington: University of Kentucky Press, 1979), p. 40. Foreman remarks that Antony's "acceptance" implies "a recognition of [Cleopatra's] uniqueness, a uniqueness that includes the kind of petty thing she has just done. He loves her for that, too." One may agree that Antony is magnanimous without acceding to the description of what Cleopatra has done as "petty" or—what is even more astonishing—the idea that Antony loves her *for* doing it.

27. Ibid., pp. 57, 61.

28. For the most comprehensive discussion of this feature of the play, see Adelman, *The Common Liar.*

29. Foreman, p. 57.

30. See Richard S. Ide, *Possessed With Greatness: The Heroic Tragedies of Shakespeare and Chapman* (Chapel Hill: University of North Carolina Press, 1980), p. 124.

31. Adelman, p. 22.

32. Ed. William Frost, *Selected Works of John Dryden* (New York: Rinehart and Company, 1953).

33. T. S. Eliot discusses these two speeches in *John Dryden: The Poet, the Dramatist, the Critic* (New York: Terence and Elsa Holliday, 1932), pp. 30–31. "Ah, soldier!" is, for Eliot, an instance of "the 'poetically dramatic,' that which, when we read it, we recognize to have dramatic value, but which would not have dramatic value for us on the stage unless we had already the perception of it from reading" (p. 29). "I could not myself put into words the difference I feel between the passage if these two words . . . were omitted and with them. But I know there is a difference, and that only Shakespeare could have made it" (p. 31). It seems to me that the "difference" is not only less mysterious than Eliot suggests, but something one might experience whether or not he had read the play before seeing it. Hawkes, *That Shakespeherian Rag*, pp. 82–85 (see above, n. 2), notes that Eliot errs in supposing Charmian's two final words contain "nothing" which may be "express[ed] in action" (*John Dryden*, p. 31). Though Hawkes comments incisively on the close relationship of words to actions in *Antony and Cleopatra*, I remain unpersuaded that the gestural quality of "Ah, soldier!" is "orgasmic" (p. 84).

34. The quoted phrase is from Foreman (p. 61), who notes that "Shakespeare shows Cleopatra achieving by her triumph an art analogous to his own."

35. *Poetic Freedom and Poetic Truth: Chaucer, Shakespeare, Marlowe, Milton* (Oxford: Clarendon Press, 1976), p. 21.

36. See Adelman, pp. 102–6, and Sukanta Chauduri, *Infirm Glory: Shakespeare and the Renaissance Image of Man* (Oxford: Clarendon Press, 1981), pp. 191–92; also, more generally, Harriett Hawkins, *The Devil's Party: Critical Counter-Interpretations of Shakespearian Drama* (Oxford: Clarendon Press, 1985), chap. 1: "The Questions of Mimesis and Morality: Some 'Footnotes to Plato' " (pp. 14–60).

37. Of plays I have not discussed, only *The Two Noble Kinsmen* (with Fletcher, 1613) includes onstage death. That death—Arcite's (5.4.90–95)—has little dramatic interest.

Appendix. The Rhetoric of Death

1. *The Plays of George Chapman: The Tragedies* (1910; reprint, New York: Russell and Russell, 1961), vol. 2.

2. *A Select Collection of Old English Plays Originally Published by Robert Dodsley in the Year 1744*, ed. W. Carew Hazlitt, 4th ed. (1874–76; reprint, New York: Blom, 1964), 8:247. (When quoting from editions not providing line references I give volume and page rather than act and scene.)

3. *The Dramatic Works of Thomas Dekker*, ed. Fredson Bowers (Cambridge: Cambridge University Press, 1953–61), vol. 1.

4. Malone Society Reprints, 1914 (1915).

5. *The Dramatic Works of Thomas Heywood*, ed. R. H. Shepherd (1874; reprint New York: Russell and Russell, 1964), 3:200–201.

6. *The Riverside Shakespeare*, ed. G. Blakemore Evans (Boston: Houghton Mifflin, 1974).

7. Ed. Nicholas Brooke in Revels Plays (London: Methuen, 1964).

8. Ed. John Russell Brown in Revels Plays, 2d ed. (London: Methuen, 1966).

9. See Nicholas Brooke, *Horrid Laughter in Jacobean Tragedy* (London: Open Books, 1979), p. 44.

10. Ed. Anne Lancashire in Revels Plays (Manchester and Baltimore: Manchester University Press and Johns Hopkins University Press, 1978).

11. Ed. J. R. Mulryne in Revels Plays (Manchester: Manchester University Press, 1975).

12. Ed. Shepherd, 4:92.

13. Ed. Bowers, vol. 4.

14. *The Dramatic Works of Sir William D'Avenant,* ed. James Maidment and W. H. Logan (1872–74; reprint, New York: Russell and Russell, 1964), 1:87.

15. *The Dramatic Works and Poems of James Shirley,* ed. William Gifford and Alexander Dyce (1833; reprint, New York: Russell and Russell, 1966), 4:399.

16. Ed. Charles S. Forker (Bloomington: Indiana University Press, 1964).

17. *The Works of Thomas Nabbes,* ed. A. H. Bullen (1887; reprint, New York: Blom, 1964), 1:238.

18. *A Select Collection of Old English Plays,* 14:86.

19. *The Plays and Poems of Henry Glapthorne,* ed. R. H. Shepherd (London: J. Pearson, 1874), 1:54.

Works Cited

Adams, Robert P. "Critical Myths and Chapman's *Bussy D'Ambois.*" *Renaissance Drama* 9 (1966): 141–61.

Adelman, Janet. *The Common Liar: An Essay on "Antony and Cleopatra."* New Haven: Yale University Press, 1973.

Alphonsus, Emperor of Germany. [Robert Greene?] See Chapman, *The Plays of George Chapman: The Tragedies,* vol. 2.

Anderson, Donald K., Jr. *John Ford.* New York: Twayne, 1972.

Andrews, Michael Cameron. "The Death of Lear." *College English* 8 (1981): 63–70.

———. "Dramatic Variations on a Passage in Sidney's *Arcadia.*" *Sidney Newsletter* 6 (1985–86): 3–12.

———. "*Hamlet:* Revenge and the Critical Mirror." *English Literary Renaissance* 8 (1978): 9–23.

———. "*Hamlet* and the Satisfactions of Revenge." *Hamlet Studies* 3 (1981): 83–102.

Arden of Feversham. Edited by M. L. Wine. The Revels Plays. London: Methuen, 1973.

Astington, John H. "The Popularity of *Cupid's Revenge.*" *Studies in English Literature* 19 (1979): 215–27.

Ayres, Philip J. *Tourneur: "The Revenger's Tragedy."* London: Arnold, 1977.

Barnes, Barnabe. *The Divils Charter: A Tragœdy Conteining the Life and Death of Pope Alexander the sixt.* Ann Arbor, Mich.: University Microfilms, 1954.

Batchelor, J. B. "The Pattern of *Women Beware Women.*" *Yearbook of English Studies* 2 (1972): 76–78.

Beaumont, Francis. *The Knight of the Burning Pestle.* Edited by Sheldon P. Zitner. The Revels Plays. Manchester: Manchester University Press, 1984.

Beaumont, Francis, and John Fletcher. *The Dramatic Works in the Beaumont and Fletcher Canon.* General editor Fredson Bowers. 6 vols. to date. Cambridge: Cambridge University Press, 1966–.

———. *The Maid's Tragedy.* Edited by Howard B. Norland. Lincoln: University of Nebraska Press, 1968.

———. *The Works of Francis Beaumont and John Fletcher.* Edited by Francis Glover and A. R. Waller. 10 vols. 1905–12. Reprint. New York: Octagon Books, 1969.

Bergeron, David. "Art Within Art in *The Second Maiden's Tragedy.*" *Medieval and Renaissance Drama in England* 1 (1984): 173–86.

Bergson, Allen. "The Worldly Stoicism of George Chapman's *Bussy D'Ambois* and *The Tragedy of Chabot, Admiral of France."* *Philological Quarterly* 55 (1976): 43–64.

Berry, Ralph. *The Art of John Webster.* Oxford: Oxford University Press, 1972.

Berryman, John. *Delusions, Etc. of John Berryman.* New York: Farrar, Straus and Giroux, 1972.

Bethell, S. L. *Shakespeare and the Popular Dramatic Tradition.* Durham, N.C.: Duke University Press, 1944.

Bevington, David, ed. *Medieval Drama.* Boston: Houghton Mifflin, 1974.

Bliss, Lee. *The World's Perspective: John Webster and the Jacobean Drama.* New Brunswick, N.J.: Rutgers University Press, 1983.

Boas, Frederick S. *An Introduction to Stuart Drama.* Oxford: Oxford University Press, 1946.

Bono, Barbara J. *Literary Transvaluation: From Virgilian Epic to Shakespearean Tragicomedy.* Berkeley and Los Angeles: University of California Press, 1984.

Bowers, Fredson Thayer. *Elizabethan Revenge Tragedy 1587–1642.* Princeton: Princeton University Press, 1940.

Bradbrook, M. C. *John Webster: Citizen and Dramatist.* New York: Oxford University Press, 1980.

———. *Themes and Conventions of Elizabethan Tragedy.* 1935. Reprint. Cambridge: Cambridge University Press, 1964.

Braden, Gordon. *Renaissance Tragedy and the Senecan Tradition: Anger's Privilege.* New Haven and London: Yale University Press, 1985.

Brennan, Anthony. *Shakespeare's Dramatic Structures.* London, Boston, and Henley: Routledge and Kegan Paul, 1986.

Britton, Norman A. "Middleton's Styles: Adjectives and Authorship." In *Accompaninge the Players: Essays Celebrating Thomas Middleton 1580–1980,* edited by Kenneth Friedenreich. New York: AMS Press, 1983.

Brooke, Nicholas. *Horrid Laughter in Jacobean Tragedy.* London: Open Books, 1979.

———. "Marlowe the Dramatist." In *Elizabethan Theatre: Stratford-upon-Avon Studies* 9 (1966): 87–105.

Brower, Reuben A. *Hero and Saint: Shakespeare and the Graeco-Roman Heroic Tradition.* New York: Oxford University Press, 1973.

Bullen, A. H., ed. *A Collection of Old English Plays.* 4 vols. 1882–85. Reprint. New York: Blom, 1964.

Bullough, Geoffrey, ed. *Narrative and Dramatic Sources of Shakespeare.* 8 vols. London: Routledge and Kegan Paul; New York: Columbia University Press, 1957–75.

Buxton, John. *Elizabethan Taste.* London: Macmillan, 1963.

Caesar and Pompey, or Caesar's Revenge. See *The Tragedy of Caesar's Revenge.*

Cairncross, Andrew S., ed. *The Second Part of King Henry VI,* by William Shakespeare. The Arden Shakespeare. 3d ed. London: Methuen, 1957.

Chambers, E. K. *The Elizabethan Stage.* 4 vols. 1923. Reprint. Oxford: Clarendon Press, 1965.

Champion, Larry S. " 'Disaster With My So Many Joys': Structure and Perspective in Massinger and Dekker's *The Virgin Martyr."* *Medieval and Renaissance Drama in England* 1 (1984): 199–209.

———. *Shakespeare's Tragic Perspective*. Athens Ga.: University of Georgia Press, 1976.

———. *Tragic Patterns in Jacobean and Caroline Drama*. Knoxville: University of Tennessee Press, 1971.

Chapman, George. *Bussy D'Ambois*. Edited by Nicholas Brooke. The Revels Plays. London: Methuen, 1964.

———. *The Plays of George Chapman: The Tragedies*. Edited by Thomas Marc Parrott. 2 vols. 1910. Reprint. New York: Russell and Russell, 1961.

Chauduri, Sukanta. *Infirm Glory: Shakespeare and the Renaissance Image of Man*. Oxford: Oxford University Press, 1981.

Chettle, Henry. *Hoffman, or a Revenge for a Father. The Tragedy of Hoffman*. Malone Society Reprints, 1950 (1951).

Chettle, Henry, and Anthony Munday. *The Death of Robert, Earl of Huntington*. See Dodsley, ed., *A Select Collection of Old English Plays*, vol. 8.

Claudius Tiberius Nero. See *The Tragedy of Tiberius*.

Clemen, Wolfgang. *A Commentary on Shakespeare's "Richard III."* Translated by Jean Bonheim. London: Methuen, 1968.

———. *English Tragedy Before Shakespeare: The Development of Dramatic Speech*. Translated by T. S. Dorsch. London: Methuen, 1961.

———. "Some Aspects of Style in the *Henry VI* Plays." In *Shakespeare's Styles: Essays in Honour of Kenneth Muir*, edited by Philip Edwards, Inga-Stina Ewbank, and G. K. Hunter. Cambridge: Cambridge University Press, 1980.

Coghill, Nevill. *Shakespeare's Professional Skills*. Cambridge: Cambridge University Press, 1964.

Cohen, Derek. "The Rite of Violence in *1 Henry IV.*" *Shakespeare Survey* 38 (1985): 77–84.

Cole, Douglas. *Suffering and Evil in the Plays of Christopher Marlowe*. Princeton: Princeton University Press, 1962.

Danby, John F. *Poets on Fortune's Hill: Studies in Sidney, Shakespeare, Beaumont and Fletcher*. London: Faber and Faber, 1952.

Danson. Lawrence. *Tragic Alphabet: Shakespeare's Drama of Language*. New Haven: Yale University Press, 1974.

Davenant, William. *The Dramatic Works of Sir William D'Avenant*. Edited by James Maidment and William Logan. 5 vols. 1872–74. Reprint. New York: Russell and Russell, 1964.

Davril, Robert. *Le drame de John Ford*. Paris: Didier, 1954.

Dekker, Thomas. *The Dramatic Works of Thomas Dekker*. Edited by Fredson Bowers. 4 vols. Cambridge: Cambridge University Press, 1953–61.

Dodsley, Robert, ed. *A Select Collection of Old English Plays*. 4th ed. Revised by W. C. Hazlitt. 15 vols. 1874–76. Reprint. New York: Blom, 1964.

Dollimore, Jonathan. *Radical Tragedy: Religion, Ideology and Power in the Drama of Shakespeare and his Contemporaries*. Chicago and Brighton, Sussex: University of Chicago Press and Harvester Press, 1984.

Downer, Alan S. " 'The Life of Our Design': The Function of Imagery in the Poetic Drama." *Hudson Review* 2 (1949): 242–63. Reprinted in *Modern Shakespearean Criticism: Essays on Style, Dramaturgy and the Major Plays*, edited by Alvin B. Kernan. New York: Harcourt, Brace and World, 1970.

Dryden, John. *Selected Works of John Dryden*. Edited by William Frost. New York and Toronto: Rinehart, 1955.

Dunn, T. A. *Philip Massinger: The Man and the Playwright*. Edinburgh: Thomas Nelson, 1957.

Edwards, Philip. *Threshold of a Nation: A Study of English and Irish Drama*. Cambridge: Cambridge University Press, 1979.

Ekeblad, Inga-Stina. See Ewbank, Inga-Stina [Ekeblad].

Eliot, T. S. *T. S. Eliot: Selected Essays*. New York: Harcourt, Brace and World, 1950.

———. *John Dryden: The Poet, the Dramatist, the Critic*. New York: Terence and Elsa Holliday, 1932.

Ewbank, Inga-Stina [Ekeblad]. "The 'Impure Art' of John Webster." *Review of English Studies*, n.s. 9 (1958): 253–67. Reprinted in *Elizabethan Drama: Modern Essays in Criticism*, edited by Ralph J. Kaufmann. New York: Oxford University Press, 1961.

———. "Realism and Morality in *Women Beware Women*. *Essays and Studies* 22 (1969): 57–70.

Faulkner, William. *Faulkner in the University: Class Conferences at the University of Virginia 1957–1958*. Edited by Frederick L. Gwynn and Joseph L. Blotner. Charlottesville: University of Virginia Press, 1959.

Fielding, Henry. *The Works of Henry Fielding, Esq.* Edited by Leslie Stephen. 10 vols. London: Smith, Elder, 1882. Vol. 9.

Ford, John. *The Broken Heart*. Edited by T. J. B. Spencer. The Revels Plays. Manchester and Baltimore: Manchester University Press and Johns Hopkins University Press, 1980.

———. *John Fordes Dramatische Werke*. Edited by W. Bang. Materialen zur Kunde des älteren englischen Dramas, no. 23. 1908. Reprint. Vaduz: Kraus Reprint, 1963.

———. *'Tis Pity She's a Whore*. Edited by Derek Roper. The Revels Plays. London: Methuen, 1975.

Foreman, Walter C., Jr. *The Music at the Close: The Final Scenes of Shakespeare's Tragedies*. Lexington: University of Kentucky Press, 1979.

Forker, Charles S. *Skull Beneath the Skin: The Achievement of John Webster*. Carbondale and Edwardsville: University of Southern Illinois Press, 1986.

Forsythe, Robert Stanley. *The Relations of Shirley's Plays to the Elizabethan Drama*. 1914. Reprint. New York: Blom, 1965.

Freer, Coburn. *The Poetics of Jacobean Drama*. Baltimore: Johns Hopkins University Press, 1981.

Gardner, Helen. "The Noble Moor." In *Shakespeare Criticism 1935–1950*, edited by Anne Ridler. London: Oxford University Press, 1963.

Gibbons, Brian, ed. *Romeo and Juliet*, by William Shakespeare. The Arden Shakespeare. London and New York: Methuen, 1980.

Gill, Roma, ed. *Women Beware Women*, by Thomas Middleton. The New Mermaids. London: Benn, 1969.

Glapthorne, Henry. *The Plays and Poems of Henry Glapthorne*. Edited by R. H. Shepherd. 2 vols. London: J. Pearson, 1874.

Goddard, Harold C. *The Meaning of Shakespeare*. 2 vols. Chicago: University of Chicago Press, 1951.

Greenblatt, Stephen. *Renaissance Self-Fashioning: From More to Shakespeare.* Chicago and London: University of Chicago Press, 1980.

———. *Sir Walter Ralegh: The Renaissance Man and His Roles.* New Haven and London: Yale University Press, 1973.

Greenfield, Thelma N. "The Language of Process in *The Broken Heart.*" *PMLA* 87 (1972): 387–405.

Hallahan, Huston Diehl. "The Thematic Juxtaposition of the Representational and the Sensational in Middleton's *Women Beware Women.*" *Studies in Iconography* 2 (1976): 66–84.

Hammond, Antony, ed. *King Richard III,* by William Shakespeare. The Arden Shakespeare. London: Methuen, 1981.

Harbage, Alfred. *Annals of English Drama 975–1700.* Revised by S. Schoenbaum. Philadelphia: University of Pennsylvania Press, 1964.

Hattaway, Michael. "Marlowe and Brecht." In *Christopher Marlowe,* edited by Brian Morris. Mermaid Critical Commentaries. London: Benn, 1970.

Hawkes, Terence. *That Shakespeherian Rag: Essays on a Critical Process.* London and New York: Methuen, 1986.

Hawkins, Harriett. *The Devil's Party: Critical Counter-Interpretations of Shakespearian Drama.* Oxford: Clarendon Press, 1985.

———. *Poetic Freedom and Poetic Truth: Chaucer, Shakespeare, Marlowe, Milton.* Oxford: Clarendon Press, 1976.

Hensman, Bertha. *The Shares of Fletcher, Field, and Massinger in Twelve Plays of the Beaumont and Fletcher Canon.* 2 vols. Salzburg Studies in English Literature: Jacobean Drama Studies, no. 6. University of Salzburg, 1974.

Heywood, Thomas. *The Dramatic Works of Thomas Heywood.* Edited by R. H. Shepherd. 6 vols. 1874. Reprint. Russell and Russell: New York, 1964.

———. *A Woman Killed with Kindness.* Edited by R. W. Van Fossen. The Revels Plays. London: Methuen, 1961.

Hibbard, G. R. "Goodness and Greatness: An Essay on the Tragedies of Ben Jonson and George Chapman." *Renaissance and Modern Studies* 11 (1967): 5–54.

Hobson, Alan. *Full Circle: Shakespeare and Moral Development.* New York: Barnes and Noble, 1972.

Holmes, David M. *The Art of Thomas Middleton: A Critical Study.* Oxford: Clarendon Press, 1970.

Honigmann, E. A. J. *Shakespeare's Impact on His Contemporaries.* New York: Barnes and Noble, 1982.

Houser, David J. "Armor and Motive in *Troilus and Cressida.*" *Renaissance Drama,* n.s. 4 (1971): 121–34.

Hoy, Cyrus. *Introduction, Notes, and Commentaries to Texts in "The Dramatic Works of Thomas Dekker."* 4 vols. Cambridge: Cambridge University Press, 1980.

———. "The Shares of Fletcher and His Collaborators in the Beaumont and Fletcher Canon." *Studies in Bibliography* 8 (1956): 129–46; 9 (1957): 142–62; 11 (1958): 85–106; 12 (1959): 91–116; 13 (1960): 77–108; 14 (1961): 45–67; 15 (1962): 71–90.

Huebert, Ronald. " 'An Artificial Way to Grieve': The Forsaken Woman in Beaumont and Fletcher, Massinger and Ford." *ELH* 44 (1977): 601–21.

————. *John Ford, English Baroque Dramatist.* Montreal and London: McGill-Queen's University Press, 1977.

Ide, Richard S. *Possessed With Greatness: The Heroic Tragedies of Shakespeare and Chapman.* Chapel Hill: University of North Carolina Press, 1980.

Ionesco, Eugène. *Notes and Counter Notes.* Translated by Donald Watson. New York: Grove Press, 1964.

Jackson, MacD. P. *Studies in Attribution: Middleton and Shakespeare.* Salzburg Studies in English Literature: Jacobean Drama Studies, no. 79. University of Salzburg, 1979.

————. "Three Old Ballads and the Date of *Doctor Faustus.*" *Journal of the Australasian Universities Language and Literature Association* 36 (1971): 187–200.

Johnson, Samuel. "Preface to Shakespeare." In *Criticism: The Major Texts,* edited by Walter Jackson Bate. Enl. ed. New York: Harcourt Brace Jovanovich, 1975.

Jones, Emrys. *The Origins of Shakespeare.* Oxford: Oxford University Press, 1977.

Jonson, Benjamin. *Sejanus.* Edited by Jonas A. Barish. New Haven: Yale University Press, 1965.

————. *Volpone.* Edited by Alvin Kernan. New Haven: Yale University Press, 1962.

Jorgenson, Paul A. "Vertical Patterns in *Richard III.*" *Shakespeare Association Bulletin* 23 (1948): 119–34.

Kaufmann, Ralph J. "Ford's Tragic Perspective." *Texas Studies in Literature and Language* 1 (1960): 522–37. Reprinted in *Elizabethan Drama: Modern Essays in Criticism,* edited by Kaufmann. New York: Oxford University Press, 1961.

Kay, Carol McGinnis. "Deception Through Words in *The Spanish Tragedy.*" *Studies in Philology* 74 (1976): 20–48.

Kehler, Dorothea. "Middleton and Rowley's *The Changeling,* V, iii, 175–77." *Explicator* 26 (1968): Item 41.

Kirsch, Arthur C. *Jacobean Dramatic Perspectives.* Charlottesville: University of Virginia Press, 1972.

Kistler, Suzanne F. " 'Strange and Far Removed Shores': A Reconsideration of *The Revenge of Bussy D'Ambois.*" *Studies in Philology* 77 (1980): 128–44.

Knight, G. Wilson. *The Imperial Theme: Further Interpretations of Shakespeare's Tragedies Including the Roman Plays.* 3d ed. London: Methuen, 1951.

Kyd, Thomas. *The Spanish Tragedy.* Edited by Philip Edwards. The Revels Plays. London: Methuen, 1959.

————. *The Works of Thomas Kyd.* Edited by Frederick S. Boas. 1901. Reprint. Oxford: Clarendon Press, 1954.

Lake, David J. *The Canon of Thomas Middleton's Plays: Internal Evidence for the Major Problems of Authorship.* Cambridge: Cambridge University Press, 1975.

Leech, Clifford. *The John Fletcher Plays.* London: Chatto and Windus, 1962.

————. *John Ford and the Drama of His Time.* London: Chatto and Windus, 1957.

Leggatt, Alexander. *"Arden of Feversham."* *Shakespeare Survey* 36 (1983): 121–33.

————. "Tone and Structure in Chapman's *Byron.*" *Studies in English Literature* 24 (1984): 307–26.

———. "The Tragedy of Clermont D'Ambois." *Modern Language Review* 77 (1982): 524–36.

Lever, J. W. *The Tragedy of State*. London: Methuen, 1971.

Levin, Harry. "Marlowe Today." *Tulane Drama Review* 8 (1964): 22–31.

Locrine. In *The Shakespeare Apocrypha: Being a Collection of Fourteen Plays Which Have Been Ascribed to Shakespeare*, ed. C. F. Tucker Brooke. 1901. Reprint. Oxford: Clarendon Press, 1954.

Lucow, Ben. *James Shirley*. Boston: Twayne, 1981.

Lumiansky, R. M. and David Mills, eds. *The Chester Mystery Cycle*. Oxford: Oxford University Press, 1984.

Lust's Dominion, or The Lascivious Queen. See Dekker, *The Dramatic Works of Thomas Dekker*, vol. 4.

McAlindon, T. *English Renaissance Tragedy*. Vancouver: University of British Columbia Press, 1986.

McDonald, Charles O[sborne]. "The Design of John Ford's *The Broken Heart:* A Study in the Development of Caroline Sensibility." *Studies in Philology* 59 (1962): 141–62.

———. *The Rhetoric of Tragedy: Form in Stuart Drama*. Amherst: University of Massachusetts Press, 1966.

Macdonald, Ronald R. "Playing Till Doomsday: Interpreting *Antony and Cleopatra*." *English Literary Renaissance* 15 (1985): 78–99.

McGrath, Juliet. "James Shirley's Use of *Language*." *Studies in English Literature* 6 (1966): 323–39.

Mack, Maynard. *"King Lear" in Our Time*. Berkeley and Los Angeles: University of California Press, 1965.

MacLure, Millar. *George Chapman: A Critical Study*. Toronto: University of Toronto Press, 1966.

McMillan, Scott. "The Figure of Silence in *The Spanish Tragedy*." *ELH* 39 (1972): 27–48.

Manley, Frank. "The Death of Hernando in Shirley's *The Cardinal*." *Notes and Queries* 12 (1965): 342–43.

Marlowe, Christopher. *The Complete Plays of Christopher Marlowe*. Edited by Irving Ribner. New York: Odyssey Press, 1963.

Marston, John. *Antonio's Revenge*. Edited by Reavley Gair. The Revels Plays. Manchester: Manchester University Press, 1978.

———. *The Plays of John Marston*. Edited by H. Harvey Wood. 3 vols. Edinburgh: University of Edinburgh Press, 1934–39.

Marston, John, and William Barkstead. *The Insatiate Countess*. Edited by Giorgio Melchiori. The Revels Plays. Manchester: Manchester University Press, 1984.

Massinger, Philip. *The Plays and Poems of Philip Massinger*. Edited by Philip Edwards and Colin Gibson. 5 vols. Oxford: Clarendon Press, 1976.

Mehl, Dieter. *The Elizabethan Dumb Show: The History of a Dramatic Convention*. Cambridge, Mass.: Harvard University Press, 1966.

Melbourne, Jane. "The Inverted World of *Bussy D'Ambois*." *Studies in English Literature* 25 (1985): 381–95.

Melchiori, Giorgio. "The Rhetoric of Character Construction: *Othello*." *Shakespeare Survey* 34 (1981): 61–72.

Middleton, Thomas. *Women Beware Women*. Edited by J. R. Mulryne. The Revels Plays. London: Methuen, 1975.

———. *The Works of Thomas Middleton*. Edited by A. H. Bullen. 8 vols. Boston: Houghton Mifflin, 1885–86.

Middleton, Thomas, and William Rowley. *The Changeling*. Edited by N. W. Bawcutt. The Revels Plays. London: Methuen, 1958.

Mincoff, Marco. "Shakespeare, Fletcher and Baroque Tragedy." *Shakespeare Survey* 20 (1967): 1–15.

Montaigne, Michel de. *Montaigne: Essays*. Translated by John Florio. 3 vols. Everyman's Library. London: Dent; New York: Dutton, 1965.

Muir, Edwin. " 'Royal Man': Notes on the Tragedies of George Chapman." In *Shakespeare's Contemporaries: Modern Studies in English Renaissance Drama,* edited by Max Bluestone and Norman Rabkin. Englewood Cliffs N.J.: Prentice-Hall, 1961.

Mulryne, J. R. "*The White Devil* and *The Duchess of Malfi*." *Jacobean Theatre: Stratford-upon-Avon Studies* 1 (1960): 201–25. Reprint. New York: Capricorn Books, 1967.

Murray, Peter B. *A Study of Cyril Tourneur*. Philadelphia: University of Pennsylvania Press, 1964.

Nabbes, Thomas. *The Works of Thomas Nabbes*. Edited by A. H. Bullen. 2 vols. 1887. Reprint. New York: Blom, 1964.

Nashe, Thomas. *The Works of Thomas Nashe*. Edited by Ronald B. McKerrow. Revised by F. P. Wilson. 5 vols. Oxford: Clarendon Press, 1958.

Neale, J. E. *Queen Elizabeth I: A Biography*. 1934. Reprint. Garden City, N.Y.: Doubleday, 1957.

Novy, Marianne L. *Love's Argument: Gender Relations in Shakespeare*. Chapel Hill: University of North Carolina Press, 1984.

Oliver, H. J., ed. *"Dido Queen of Carthage" and "The Massacre at Paris,"* by Christopher Marlowe. The Revels Plays. London: Methuen, 1986.

Orbison, Tucker. *The Tragic Vision of John Ford*. Salzburg Studies in English Literature: Jacobean Drama Studies, no. 21. University of Salzburg, 1974.

Ornstein, Robert. "Bourgeois Morality and Dramatic Convention in *A Woman Killed With Kindness*." In *English Renaissance Drama: Essays in Honor of Madeleine Doran and Mark Eccles,* edited by Standish Henning, Robert Kimbrough, and Richard Knowles. Carbondale: Southern Illinois University Press, 1976.

———. *A Kingdom for a Stage: The Achievement of Shakespeare's History Plays*. Cambridge, Mass.: Harvard University Press, 1972.

———. *The Moral Vision of Jacobean Tragedy*. Madison and Milwaukee: University of Wisconsin Press, 1965.

Palmer, D. J. " 'A New Gorgon': Visual Effects in *Macbeth*." In *Focus on "Macbeth,"* edited by John Russell Brown. London: Routledge and Kegan Paul, 1982.

Parker, R. B. "Middleton's Experiments With Comedy and Judgement." *Jacobean Theatre: Stratford-upon-Avon Studies* 1 (1960): 179–99. Reprint. New York: Capricorn Books, 1967.

Paul, H. N. *The Royal Play of "Macbeth."* New York: Macmillan, 1950.

Peele, George. *The Life and Works of George Peele*. General editor Charles Tyler Prouty. 3 vols. New Haven: Yale University Press, 1952–70.

———. *The Old Wives Tale*. Edited by Patricia Binnie. The Revels Plays. Baltimore: Johns Hopkins University Press, 1980.

Plutarch. See Bullough, ed., *Narrative and Dramatic Sources of Shakespeare*, vol. 5.

Potter, Lois. "Realism Versus Nightmare: Problems of Staging *The Duchess of Malfi*." In *The Triple Bond: Plays, Mainly Shakespearean, in Performance*, edited by Joseph G. Price. University Park and London: Pennsylvania State University Press, 1975.

Preston, Thomas. *Cambyses*. In *Tudor Plays: An Anthology of Early English Drama*, ed. Edmund Creeth. Garden City, N.Y.: Doubleday, 1966.

Price, Hereward T. " 'Like Himself.' " *Review of English Studies* 16 (1940): 178–81.

The Revenger's Tragedy. [Thomas Middleton?] Edited by R. A. Foakes. The Revels Plays. London: Methuen, 1966.

Ribner, Irving. *Jacobean Tragedy: The Quest for Moral Order*. London: Methuen, 1962.

Riggs, David. *Shakespeare's Heroical Histories: "Henry VI" and Its Literary Tradition*. Cambridge, Mass.: Harvard University Press, 1971.

Rozett, Martha Tuck. "The Comic Structures of Tragic Endings: The Suicide Scenes in *Romeo and Juliet* and *Antony and Cleopatra*." *Shakespeare Quarterly* 36 (1985): 152–64.

Salgādo, Gāmini, ed. *Eye-Witnesses of Shakespeare: First Hand Accounts of Performances 1597–1890*. New York: Barnes and Noble, 1975.

Sanders, Wilbur. *The Dramatist and the Received Idea: Studies in the Plays of Marlowe and Shakespeare*. Cambridge: Cambridge University Press, 1968.

Sargeaunt, M. Joan. *John Ford*. 1935. Reprint. New York: Russell and Russell, 1966.

Saunders, Claire. " 'Dead in His Bed': Shakespeare's Staging of the Death of the Duke of Gloucester in *2 Henry VI*." *Review of English Studies*, n.s. 35 (1984): 19–34.

Schoenbaum, Samuel. *Middleton's Tragedies: A Critical Study*. New York: Columbia University Press, 1955.

Schwartz, Elias. "Chapman's Renaissance Man: Byron Reconsidered." *Journal of English and Germanic Philology* 58 (1959): 613–26.

The Second Maiden's Tragedy. [Thomas Middleton?] Edited by Anne Lancashire. The Revels Plays. Baltimore: Johns Hopkins University Press, 1978.

Seneca, Lucius Annaeus. *Seneca His Tenne Tragedies Translated into English*. Edited by Thomas Newton. 1581. Reprint. With an introduction by T. S. Eliot. 2 vols. London: Constable; New York: Knopf, 1927.

Shakespeare, William. *The Riverside Shakespeare*. Edited by G. Blakemore Evans. Boston: Houghton Mifflin, 1974.

Shalvi, Alice. " 'Honor' in *Troilus and Cressida*." *Studies in English Literature* 5 (1965): 283–302.

Shirley, James. *The Cardinal*. Edited by Charles S. Forker. Bloomington: Indiana University Press, 1964.

———. *The Dramatic Works and Poems of James Shirley*. Edited by William Gifford and Alexander Dyce. 6 vols. 1833. Reprint. New York: Blom, 1965.

———. *The Traitor*. Edited by John Stewart Carter. Lincoln: University of Nebraska Press, 1965.

Shullenberger, William. " 'This For the Most Wrong'd of Women': A Reappraisal of *The Maid's Tragedy.*" *Renaissance Drama,* n.s. 13 (1982): 131–56.

Simon, Bennett. *Mind and Madness in Ancient Greece: The Classical Roots of Modern Psychiatry.* Ithaca, N.Y.: Cornell University Press, 1978.

Slater, Anne Pasternak. "Hypallage, Barley-Break, and *The Changeling.*" *Review of English Studies* n.s. 34 (1983): 429–40.

Soliman and Perseda. [Thomas Kyd?] See Kyd, *The Works of Thomas Kyd.*

Spencer, Theodore. *Death and Elizabethan Tragedy: A Study of Convention and Opinion in the Elizabethan Drama.* Cambridge, Mass.: Harvard University Press, 1940.

Stamm, Rudolph. "The Alphabet of Speechless Complaint: A Study of the Mangled Daughter in *Titus Andronicus.*" *English Studies* 55 (1974): 325–39.

Steane, J. B. *Marlowe: A Critical Study.* Cambridge: Cambridge University Press, 1963.

Stilling, Roger. *Love and Death in Renaissance Tragedy.* Baton Rouge: Louisiana University Press, 1976.

Suetonius. See Bullough, ed., *Narrative and Dramatic Sources of Shakespeare,* vol. 5.

Suzman, Arthur. "Imagery and Symbolism in *Richard II.*" *Shakespeare Quarterly* 7(1956): 335–70.

Thompson, Peter. "Webster and the Actor." In *John Webster,* edited by Brian Morris. Mermaid Critical Commentaries. London: Benn, 1970.

Thorssen, M. J. "Massinger's Use of *Othello* in *The Duke of Milan.*" *Studies in English Literature* 19 (1979): 313–26.

Tricomi, Albert B. "The Problem of Authorship in the Revised *Bussy D'Ambois.*" *English Language Notes* 17 (1979): 22–29.

———. "The Revised Version of Chapman's *Bussy D'Ambois*: A Shift in Point of View." *Studies in Philology* 70 (1973): 286–305.

Tourneur, Cyril. *The Atheist's Tragedy, or The Honest Man's Revenge.* Edited by Irving Ribner. The Revels Plays. London: Methuen, 1964.

The Tragedy of Caesar's Revenge. Malone Society Reprints, 1911 (1912).

The Tragedy of Tiberius. Malone Society Reprints, 1914 (1915).

Ure, Peter. "Chapman's Tragedies." In *Jacobean Theatre: Stratford-upon-Avon Studies* 1 (1960): 227–47. Reprint. New York: Capricorn Books, 1967.

Velz, John. "Cassius as a Great Observer." *Modern Language Review* 68 (1973): 256–59.

Virgil (Publius Vergilius Maro). *Aeneid.* In *Virgil.* Translated by H. Rushton Fairclough. Loeb Classical Library. Rev. ed. 2 vols. Cambridge, Mass.: Harvard University Press, 1934.

Waith, Eugene M. *The Herculean Hero in Marlowe, Chapman, Shakespeare and Dryden.* New York: Columbia University Press, 1962.

———. *Ideas of Greatness: Heroic Drama in England.* New York: Barnes and Noble, 1971.

———. *The Pattern of Tragicomedy in Beaumont and Fletcher.* New Haven: Yale University Press, 1952.

———, ed. *Titus Andronicus,* by William Shakespeare. New York: Oxford University Press, 1984.

Walker, Keith, ed. *Doctor Faustus,* by Christopher Marlowe. Edinburgh: Oliver and Boyd, 1973.

Webster, John. *The Duchess of Malfi.* Edited by John Russell Brown. The Revels Plays. London: Methuen, 1964.

———. *The White Devil.* Edited by John Russell Brown. The Revels Plays. 2d ed. London: Methuen, 1968.

Wells, Stanley, and Gary Taylor, eds. *William Shakespeare: The Complete Works.* The Oxford Shakespeare. Oxford: Clarendon Press, 1986.

Wharton, T. A. "Old Marston or New Marston?" *Essays in Criticism* 25 (1975): 357–69.

Wilson, F. P. *Marlowe and the Early Shakespeare.* Oxford: Clarendon Press, 1953.

Zimansky, Curt. "*Doctor Faustus:* The Date Again." *Philological Quarterly* 41 (1962): 181–87.

Index

Collaborative plays are listed under each of the authors. Anonymous plays, and those of uncertain authorship, are listed by titles.